Seeds of Salton

BARBARA MARSHAK

Barbara Marshak
Ephesians 3:20

BLUE
PRAIRIE
PRESS

Cover design: David Majchrzak
Cover photos: Barbara Marshak
Edited by: C. S. Lakin
Permission for DANCE, THE; Words and Music by TONY ARATA ©
1989 MORGANACTIVE SONGS, INC. and EMI APRIL MUSIC
INC. All rights administered by MORGAN MUSIC GROUP INC. All
Rights for the World Outside of North America Administered by WB
MUSIC CORP. All Rights Reserved.

Billy Graham quote: Timeless Truths
  May 12, 1977, South Bend, Indiana
  http://www.youtube.com/watch?v=yEf0zAtWS50
Permissions for "Forgiveness" – Matthew West
Permissions for "Amazing Grace" – John Newton (1725-1807)
Permissions for "Have You Ever Seen the Rain?" – John Fogerty
The Christian Life Bible – The New King James Version © 1985
  By Porter L. Barrington, Thomas Nelson Publishers

Printed in the United States of America
First Printing 2013

ISBN-10: 0615885365
ISBN-13: 978-0615885360

Request for information should be addressed to:
Blue Prairie Press
12138 Ray Smith Drive
Hill City, SD 57745

BLUE
PRAIRIE
PRESS

Seeds of Salton

*"I want to finally set it free
So show me how to see what Your mercy sees
Help me now to give what You gave to me
Forgiveness, Forgiveness"*

From the song "Forgiveness" by Matthew West

Dear Reader,

The story you are about to read is true; the names of the characters and some establishments have been changed for obvious reasons. The locations are accurate and the events are very real. On a mission trip in 2006 I was asked to share my testimony. In my early 40s, I opened up my personal pains for the first time to a small group from our church. Soon after Barbara approached me about turning my testimony—my life story—into a book.

I struggled with the thought of putting so many deeply personal events and emotions into print for others to read. After months of long, heart wrenching, soul searching I agreed to the project. I had no idea how intense the process would be; how reliving the events—buried for decades—would bring up such deep emotion and vivid memories of events long past. I commend Barbara for taking my rambling stories and explanations of events and putting them on paper. She was very patient and is an extremely gifted writer.

I wanted to make one thing clear from the start—I did not want *Seeds of Salton* to bring any attention to myself, rather I want the story to show how God has had an intimate role in my life, even when I was rebellious, self-centered, and had rejected him. More than anything I want this book to demonstrate to others how very real God is and how He has a deep and abiding love for all His children. *Seeds of Salton* should not be viewed as simply a story about my life, but how my life was continually guided and protected, until I found the greatest gift of all.

My hope is that this story will touch you; that it will give you the courage to look back and offer this same gift to those who have caused hurts in your own life. It's a gift that will give you far more than what you give…a gift that will set you free; a gift that will give you peace.

The gift is *forgiveness*.

To Him be the Glory,
Bernie Mischel

"The greatest word in all the world is forgiveness."

Billy Graham
Timeless Truths
South Bend, Indiana
May 12, 1977

**FROM THE LAST WILL & TESTAMENT
OF PIERRE WIBAUX:**

*"Life with some object in sight,
some purpose to fulfill is good to live,
but it is not a joke, it is a very serious matter.
As an atom in the universe I have played my part
and would not care to live my life over again,
however, had I an opportunity to do so,
I would try to do better and accomplish greater things…"*

*"I will give you a new heart and put a new spirit
within you; I will take the heart of stone out of
your flesh and give you a heart of flesh.*

Ezekiel 36:26

PART I

CHAPTER ONE

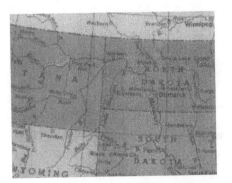

Eastern Montana, 1974

    Sixteen-year-old Grady Kramer gripped the passenger
door handle of the '67 GMC as it barreled north on the section
road, the rugged Montana landscape passing by in a blackened
blur. He wanted to yank the door open and jump out, but he
figured at this speed the crushed lava scoria that covered the
gravel road would tear him to smithereens.

    "She's a looker, Grady," his dad said between drags on
his Winston, one hand guiding the steering wheel. "And she's up

for anything I want to try." His dark eyes danced as he exhaled with a deep raunchy laugh. "Ya hear what I'm saying?"

Grady grunted a weak "yeah" and nodded to appease his dad. He forced a smile, as though this disgusting news impressed him—that Frank Engel Kramer, husband and father of four, was some kind of ladies' man, right up there with the likes of Burt Reynolds or Robert Redford out in Hollywood. Truth be told, his father resembled the rugged Burt Reynolds in *Deliverance*, a muscular outdoorsman with a dazzling smile, jet black hair, and dark eyes—not an ounce of fat on his thirty-eight-year-old frame.

The mere thought of his dad with another woman twisted Grady's stomach into knots, like the large den of rattlesnakes he stumbled on out near the rough breaks behind Malone's wheat field. Much to his mother's dismay, Grady's fascination for snakes had turned into a hobby. But nothing prepared him for the type of venom spewing from his father's mouth. Each word, each vile utterance, sent a surge of poison through Grady's mind as his father rattled off detailed descriptions of each sex act. "And if you so much as blab a word of this to your ma, I'll have your hide, boy. You hear me? I'll have it good."

Grady swallowed hard. How could he even face his mother when they got home? How could he look her in the eye, knowing what he knew now? His gut burned with anger but he didn't dare let it show. He knew firsthand the two distinct versions of his father. Friends and neighbors saw the fun-loving Frank Kramer who thrived on attention and loved showing off. But Grady and the younger kids were privy to a darker side, a raw and angry man who always hovered near a dangerous, vindictive edge.

Grady's eyes settled on the outline of the rugged buttes starting to take shape as a hint of light softened the lacquered blackness of the early morning sky. Hunting was by far one of Grady's greatest passions, especially big game hunting in the fall. Whitetail. Mule deer. Antelope. He loved the outdoors more than anything.

"Hey, what about you?" his dad asked in a low voice. "Did you get any last night?" He reached across the cab and slapped Grady's shoulder.

"Daaad! Knock it off." He squirmed on the bench seat, an uneasiness pressing through him like a cold winter wind out of the Rockies.

"Well, did ya?" he said. "C'mon, tell your ol' man." His dad sucked in a long breath on his cigarette and exhaled a blue ring between him and the steering wheel. His profile radiated in a sultry glow from the dashboard lighting.

"Forget it."

"Lucky for me this little lady lives over in Beach." His dad cocked a black eyebrow and continued. "Couple blocks behind Roy's Repairs. Close enough, but not too close."

Grady used every ounce of raw strength to hold back his exploding emotions. He knew exactly what his dad meant. Beach was seven miles east of Wibaux, less than a mile inside the North Dakota state line. His mom worked in Wibaux and rarely drove to Beach unless Dad or he and the younger kids were with her. How could he do this to his own wife? Carol Teresa Kramer was a beautiful, caring mother who did everything in her power to keep a decent home, raise her kids, and proclaim her devotion to God and family on bended knees at mass each week.

Grady had a girl he liked over in Beach too: Naomi Laureen Braden, the prettiest cheerleader on the sidelines for the Beach Buccaneers. He and Naomi could sit for hours in the front seat of his '62 Bel Air out on Beaver Creek Road, holding hands, talking, sneaking kisses. Sixteen or not, he couldn't imagine doing such things with Naomi as his father had just described. Yes, he had urges and strong physical feelings for her, but he would never disrespect her in such a way. *Never.*

"It's just you and me here. C'mon, tell me." Frank leaned forward, his face turned toward Grady, waiting. "What'd you get last night?"

"Dad, me and Naomi went to a bonfire in Lorentz's pasture. There was a whole bunch of kids from Beach and Wibaux hanging out."

"Boy, that ain't gonna get you nothing," he said with a sneer. "Take a lesson from your old man."

Grady cringed. "I don't need any lessons," he said through clenched teeth.

"Listen, if you won't take my word for it, I picked up a new magazine at that one truck stop outside of Miles City. You think you got enough sense in that brain of yours to follow a picture?"

"Not interested." Grady turned toward the window, the toxic mixture of hate and anger swelling inside him again. His own reflection stared back at him—squared face with a pointed chin; rounded nose; dark, deep set eyes. Other than the long scar, a younger version of his father. The resemblance repulsed him every time someone made a comment.

"Whoa," his dad said, braking. He leaned forward, looking for the half-section post marking and stopped at the fence line. "This the right one?"

"Yup." Grady hopped out to open the pasture gate, thankful for the diversion.

"You better make damn sure you close the gate right or Dale won't let us hunt back here again," Frank said as soon as Grady climbed back in. "He's got a big herd of Angus in the northwest section."

"I remember." He glanced up at the stars, flickers of tiny diamonds positioned against a rich and velvety tapestry. Desperate to get his dad's mind off sex, he blurted, "How much sausage are we smoking this year?"

Frank slapped the steering wheel and licked his lips. "Mmmm! Can't ya just taste it? Depends on what we come home with. Whitetail, muley, prairie goat. A muley will give us more meat to mix up. That ol' steer we just butchered had some good meat on him, didn't he?"

Grady nodded, his stomach relaxing slightly. "I can't wait for some of them steaks." He patted his abdomen, toned and rigid from another summer baling hay and digging postholes on Malone's ranch.

"The butcher hog was pretty decent too. Should make for a good batch of summer and breakfast sausage."

"Are Grandpa and Grandma Hoffman coming down again?"

"They'd better; we need the help. Did I tell you? Dale Radermacher liked my sausage so much, he asked for some more of it this year. Said it was the best he ever tasted. Pretty fair trade for hunting on his land, don't ya think?"

"Sure is."

"Even told the guy who writes in the Glendive paper about it."

"Really?"

"I hear it all the time down at the Silver Dollar, 'Frank, you make the best darn sausage 'round these parts. When you gonna pass s'more of that around?' "

Grady learned long ago to recognize when his dad needed his ego stroked. "That's good, Dad," he said, "real good."

Another mile in, Frank turned east onto the next half-section road, downshifting as the pickup bounced along the narrower gravel lane. Daylight emerged in less than grand fashion as low-lying clouds nearly touched the ridge on the eastern horizon. In November one could expect anything from a warm rain to a full-blown blizzard that might threaten the lives of man and beast alike.

The worn brakes squeaked as his dad stopped the truck at the top of a draw, a natural gully formed by the runoff of summer rains and melting spring snows. "Just in time," he said, glancing at the sky. "I'll drop you here and meet you in the southeast section." Frank shifted into neutral and pulled another Winston out of his pack, the engine idling.

Grady got out and grabbed his rifle from the gun rack in the back window. His dad had taken him to the army surplus in Glendive last summer and he picked out a World War II 7.57 mm Mauser with the tightest barrel he could find, a pretty good bargain for twenty-one bucks. Course, it wasn't really meant for hunting, but it was all he could afford. He cleaned it up, sanded the wood down, and put on a fresh coat of stain that brought out the pretty grain of the beech wood. It had a nice leather sling, and he'd be the first to admit it looked pretty darn sharp.

"Gimme a sec to load." Grady stood next to the open door and flipped up the top of his ammo box on the seat. He'd learned how to make his own bullets using the brass from store-bought shells. Not only were his bullets smaller and faster, but he could make a round for a nickel a piece. One by one, he loaded five rounds into the magazine. He closed the bolt on his rifle, flipped up the safety, and slipped five more rounds into his pocket.

Frank nodded toward Grady's right hand. "I saw that." He leaned against the steering wheel, the sleeves of his quilt-lined coveralls stained with grease.

"Just in case."

"If you need more'n five bullets boy, you shouldn't be hunting." His head fell back and he laughed hard.

Grady shrugged off his father's comment and laid his rifle on the bench seat. He pulled on a blaze orange sweatshirt over his Carhartt overalls. "It'll be a while before I get back to the truck; this is a long draw," he said, pointing toward a pillow of fog that rested along a deep crevice to the south about a quarter mile. He tugged an orange stocking cap over his long dark hair that touched his shoulders.

"Hmm, maybe not. I got a good feeling," Frank said, nodding toward the barrel of his Springfield .30-06 rifle in the upper rack. He cracked a smile and pushed back his cap. A few lines creased his forehead, visible indicators of his daily drinking habit. "I'll park the truck on that ridge where we looked last week."

Grady knew from their years of hunting the deer would be coming back from the fields at dawn toward their bedding spots, where they stayed throughout the daylight hours. They'd enjoyed some good outings since they moved to Wibaux, although Grady's style was a little different than his father's. Frank—an excellent shot—always aimed for the heart and could hit any size animal dead center at three hundred yards out. Grady preferred to aim for the head and had practiced long hours target shooting behind the machine shed to perfect his shot.

"Hey," Frank said, taking a long drag, "if we get a couple right off, I'll have time to run over to Beach and go at it with her one more time." He puckered his lips and gave a crude laugh.

Grady picked up his Mauser and gripped it tightly, the comment gnawing at him. His eyes narrowed and he glared at his father. "That a fact?" He tried to hide the edge in his voice, but it cut its way through like a blade saw.

"What's eating you?" he asked, his jaw thrust outward. A rough layer of morning whiskers covered his chin.

Grady bit his lip. "Nothing." He kicked a dried clump of rusty brown Montana mud from the wheel well and slammed the door.

Frank turned the truck around and rolled down his window. "Let's get rollin'." His eyes narrowed as he scanned the morning haze and he pointed to the contour where the land changed in elevation. "I'll be waiting just across on the hill facing west. If you flush anything out I'll get a decent shot, no matter which side they head up."

"See you on the other side," Grady said, watching the rectangular red taillights disappear over the ridge. He crawled through the barbed-wire fence, the double-strand stretched tight between a long row of crooked cedar posts and headed toward the trees and buffaloberry brush that grew close to the low spots with water. He walked the top edge of the rough gully, stepping carefully on the uneven ground, his muzzle in ready position, itching to shoot the first thing that moved.

After a quarter mile Grady stopped, listening. A flock of geese in V-formation passed overhead, squawking noisily, heading south in search of warmer weather. In each direction the dingy brown terrain spread for miles until it met up with the gray, gloomy skies overhead. Pockets of sagebrush sprung up randomly, hiding grouse or rabbits, their feathers and coats blending chameleon-like with the background as all of nature prepared for the winter about to descend. Trees were scarce on the open range and on most days the wind blew without interference. By mid-November the tall prairie grasses were headed out and gone to seed, some crushed and flattened by the animals that roamed the vast open territory, much of it looking the same since the days before there were fences, and Indians were the ones out in hunting parties.

The frost-coated air cleared Grady's mind as he eyed the iron-hard land, trying to erase the images of his dad with another woman. The hate swelled inside him, but he knew better than to lose it in front of his ol' man. Too many times he'd suffered the consequences of his father's explosive temper. All four kids—himself, Melinda, Kurt, and Dean—were subject at any given moment to his favorite instrument of pain: the jar of wheat seeds.

His dad kept a Mason jar of hard red spring wheat on the shelf next to the milk separator in the porch, and even bragged that the spring wheat was fatter than the winter wheat and would cause more pain. The jar stayed there year-round, poured out in little piles at least once a week. "Go get the jar; get the wheat seeds right now," he'd say. "Roll up your pants." Bare kneed, they were punished for some trivial infraction, like answering in the wrong tone or leaving a gate unlatched. And God forbid if one of them eased off their knees during the half-hour ritual— he'd add more time *and* a whipping.

Most often he used the razor strap, an old-fashioned double strap with one piece made of thick canvas and one of darkened leather—three inches wide and two feet in length, hooked at the top with a buckle. The strap hung on a hook by the back door; both instruments of discipline always in plain sight. Other times he grabbed whatever was within reach—the belt around his waist, an electric cord, a fan belt.

More than anything Grady hated watching his younger sister and brothers take their turns with the strap; he'd rather take it himself. It killed him to see his father use every ounce of his adult strength to whip Melinda, Kurt, and sometimes Dean, although being the youngest he missed the worst of it. The whole scenario was degrading and humiliating, forced to pull down their pants in front of each other. Melinda especially, the only girl. She was thin—pure skin on bone—and it sickened him to watch the big red welts rise up on her milky white flesh. Kurt's thighs and buttocks were a little meatier and each strike sent ripples across his backside in waves. Bare skin lost every time. *Whap! Whap! Whap! Whap!* Grady tensed; the distinct sound still vivid in his memory.

Movement under a clump of blue grama grass near a rock pile caught Grady's eye. A white-tailed jackrabbit darted out from underneath a buffaloberry shrub. He recognized it by its long ears and hind legs, the fur already a pale gray in preparation for winter, the tail snowy white. It scampered across an open area, then stopped, nibbling on a patch of creeping juniper. He might 'a' took a shot at it when he was a kid, but now he was willing to wait for big game.

Grady wiped the stock with his sleeve, shining the rich beech wood. He looked up as a red-tailed hawk swooped down and snatched the young rabbit in its sharp talons. The hawk carried it to a bare branch on a dead elm about twenty yards away, ready to tear into its prey. "The laws of nature," Grady said in a whisper, watching the scene unfold in living color. "The hunter and the hunted."

Grady followed the wide curve of the draw, the ground tilting downward to a rocky, brush-filled bottom. In the distance a light dusting of snow capped the knobs and buttes that stuck up against the otherwise bleak backdrop. A circle of birds congregated over a rough patch of buffalo sod grass, probably one of the "towns" where the prairie dogs burrowed tunnels in the ground. Black dots strategically covered the farthest hillside looking like toys—Dale's herd of Angus.

No sign of a whitetail or muley so far. He breathed in the moist, cold air and let it fill his lungs, eyes scanning an S-curve in the Missouri Breaks, the not-so-badlands of Montana. The land was rougher here than a few miles south where it flattened out and ranchers could plant more fields, but not as bad as the official Badlands in North Dakota, thirty miles to the east. The deep ravines and coulees of the Missouri Breaks made it easy to lose cattle if ranchers weren't careful. Some years they got caught by an early snowstorm and had a devil of a time rounding up their big herds. Most ranches in these parts were measured by sections, 640 acres to a section, each one divided by a gravel road, a red ribbon of scoria gravel that ran north-south, east-west, straight as an arrow, up and down the never-ending slopes. One time, just for the heck of it, Grady had driven all the way to Glendive on section roads, all twenty-seven miles, and he'd had a hoot, raising red dust behind his Bel Air the whole way.

Normally, he loved this time outdoors, but this morning he was distracted, upset, sickened by his father's new secret. He wanted to tell his ol' man exactly what he thought, but who was he kidding? No one with half a brain would tell Frank Kramer something he didn't want to hear, not with his quick temper, and especially not when the man was carrying a loaded gun.

When Grady was younger he didn't understand why his mom never dared come between his dad and the whippings. Not ever. Could he really blame her? A grizzly bear wouldn't cross paths with his ol' man when he was bent on setting his kids straight. Growing up, Grady believed his dad was just downright mean for doling out all the beatings and whippings, but what he'd heard this morning topped it all.

He reached the end of the draw, surprised he hadn't flushed anything out. He neared the pickup and waved an arm to signal he was back. A few seconds later his dad's orange cap crested the hill, indicating he'd seen Grady's signal and was on his way to meet him at the truck.

Kill him and get it over with.

The thought struck Grady so hard and fast it sucked away his breath.

Kill him. He deserves to die.

Grady's heartbeat quickened as he watched his dad come into full view, about a hundred yards to the east on a nice gentle slope. The thought took hold, gaining justification with each pulse of blood and adrenaline that rushed through his veins. It was perfect, a dead-bang shot. He could make it look like one of those tragic accidents that happen every November during deer hunting season. Grady envisioned the headline: *Sixteen-year-old Wibaux boy accidentally kills father while hunting.*

Another rush of hate washed over Grady as he contemplated his shot, the cold air biting his cheeks. Yes, he could take a head shot and drop him before he even knew what

Seeds of Salton

happened. The man was using up good oxygen and didn't deserve to live.

He lifted his rifle, pulled the bolt back, and ran a shell into the chamber, the sound echoing eerily in his right ear, as if to remind Grady the Mauser was built to kill men, not animals. With newfound boldness, he rested one hand underneath the forestock and positioned the other around the grip, resting his arm on the hood of the truck to guarantee a steady shot. In precision-like movements Grady pushed the safety in and eased his index finger around the cold metal of the trigger.

His emotions roiled inside and he fought to keep his hands steady. He released a breath slowly, calculating his dad's every move, eyeing him through the iron sights at the end of his muzzle. His father walked with the Springfield pointed up, looking for tracks in the ground. Grady took a deep breath and held it, just as his dad had taught him, the butt tight against his shoulder. He wasn't about to back down now, not after this day.

Do it Grady. Do it right now.

A surge of satisfaction took hold in knowing his dad had no clue that his own role had suddenly changed. The great and mighty hunter was now the hunted. Maybe this was the answer he'd been looking for all along. No more walking on eggshells day and night.

A raw wind rustled a Russian olive tree nearby. All Grady had to do was squeeze the trigger. Payback for all those times he'd been forced to kneel on those damn seeds. Payback for the whippings. Payback for listening to Mindy cry and hide in her room.

No. Wait. He didn't want to shoot him in the head. He wanted his dad to see it coming, to know his own son pulled the trigger.

Grady lowered the muzzle ever so slightly and took a bead on his dad's shirt button showing through the opening of his overalls. This way he would see the flash, hear the report from the rifle. There would be enough time for him to know his own son had taken his life and wonder why.

Grady kept his dad's chest in his sights and drew slight tension on the trigger. Nervous sweat trickled into his eyes. He blinked and focused again, the rifle poised with deadly accuracy. He watched his dad descend the slanted hillside, on alert for signs of deer. He was headed right toward him, taking long strides across the pasture like a proud banty rooster. Grady had a wide open, clear shot.

Now, Grady! Do it! If he moved his finger a hair more it would be over.

Do it, Grady, you can do it. He deserves to die. He deserves to rot in hell with all the other child beaters and adulterers!

Grady held the rifle steady, fingering the sensitive trigger. *You got him, you got him. Now!*

Somewhere in the deep recesses of his mind, a voice told him it was wrong.

Grady's knees buckled out from under him. He released his finger and lowered the rifle. He couldn't do it. As much as he wanted to, he couldn't go through with it.

Hands shaking, Grady's breaths came in deep heaves. He leaned against the truck for support. Despite the chill in the air, he was sweating under his outer layers. The thought tore at him, how close he had come to killing his own father, retching through him like a jagged bolt of lightning. He spit at the ground and stared into the vast, brutal terrain that stretched out before him.

Like some sorry animal caught in a trap, he was destined to live under his father's sordid rules. The realization hit him swift and hard, like an angry rodeo bull knocking him into the ground. He wiped his eyes, his heart pounding in erratic, hopeless beats as he watched his father close in. Strong and surefooted with each step, rifle in hand, Frank Kramer carried the appearance that he was rougher and tougher than Montana itself.

CHAPTER TWO

"Get up boys!" Carol's voice carried up the staircase. "Time for chores!"

Grady rolled over and eyed the small clock face on his nightstand. The pale greenish hands glowed straight up and down like a section road, as if to proudly declare the time: six a.m. sharp. Couldn't his mom oversleep just once, like until five after?

It was nice and toasty under the covers, Grandma Hoffman's wool quilt was so thick and heavy it pressed him into the mattress, insulating him from winter's frozen depths lurking beyond the farmhouse walls. He crawled out of bed and reached for his barn clothes. At least it was Friday and the end of another school week.

"C'mon, Kurt," he said, flipping on the light switch. The cold floorboards creaked under his bare feet, and he hurried to find his socks. Frost lined the darkened windows, as it did most winter mornings.

Kurt squeezed his eyelids shut and faked a loud snore.

"Get up and get dressed."

His younger brother didn't budge.

"I know you're awake, dummy."

Kurt threw back the crazy quilt, his sandy brown hair sticking up like a bale of straw that busted out of its twine. "Fooled ya!" he said with a high-pitched squeal. He sat up, the wool quilt scrunched up in a kaleidoscope of colors, his gray-blue eyes as bright as their grandma's porcelain.

"Not hardly, ya dork." Grady zipped up his jeans and pulled on an old sweatshirt. "Hey, little buddy," he said, rubbing Dean's shoulders. "Time to get up." He threw Dean's overalls onto his bed. The three boys shared the larger bedroom upstairs. Grady had the single bed, and Kurt and Dean shared a double bed.

"Brrr," muttered Dean, rubbing his eyes. The two-story farmhouse had a coal furnace with a single floor register in the dining room on the main floor. The only heat to reach the upstairs had to drift up through the stairway or the smaller registers in the walls.

"It'll be toasty in the kitchen," Grady said. "C'mon, can't you smell it?"

Grady took the stairs down two at a time. The popping sound of bacon sizzling drew him to the stove like a magnet. "Morning, Mom," he said, warming his hands against the side.

"Morning, Grady," Carol answered, already dressed in her light blue uniform. The white blouse and blue skirt signified her job as a clerk and fry cook at Beckel's Drugstore between the corner of Main and First Streets in Wibaux. "Are the boys up?"

"Yup, they'll be down in a sec'."

"Time to get crackin'," she said, pouring a bowlful of whipped eggs into a hot skillet. The egg and milk mixture bubbled along the sides as Carol scraped her fork around the edges of the pan. "It's cold out there, Grady. Make sure you boys dress warm when you head out. It snowed some last night—a few inches I'd say. The thermometer said eighteen and I don't think it's lying."

Grady listened as his mother rattled off a full weather report like she did every morning. He could read the thermometer himself, but he enjoyed her version of what to expect when he ventured outside.

"I went out and brushed off the steps for you," she said, stirring the scrambled eggs with a wooden spoon.

"I coulda done that."

"Oh, well," she said, eyeing Grady with a grin, "it's already done. It don't hurt me none, either."

Grady stood next to the cast iron range—a permanent fixture in the kitchen—while keeping a watchful eye on the bacon. The massive appliance radiated warmth whenever his mom had wood burning in the firebox. Lined with nickel trim, the stove had six burners and a hinged side for extra pots. A water tank hung on the other side, providing instant hot water whenever the stove was in use.

"Smells mighty good, Mom," Grady said. He picked up a fork and flipped the pieces as hot grease popped out of the pan. The flat-out best reason to get up on a cold winter morning was the mixed aroma of wood burning and bacon frying!

"That's some of your dad's famous bacon, ya know," she said with a smile, rinsing her hands at the sink. A faded apron clung to his mom's too-thin frame. The cistern outside provided running water; every few weeks his dad had to haul water in a five-hundred-gallon tank from town, which brought the cistern up past half full. The family learned how to conserve the precious resource. Baths were once a week, dishes were "dip-rinsed," and his mom made sure no one left the faucet running for no good reason.

Melinda came down the stairs in a baby blue smock blouse and corduroy slacks, already dressed for school, since she didn't have to help with the outside chores. Being the only sister, she was kept busy inside the house.

"My punch card is empty, Mom. Can I come down to Beckel's for lunch?" Melinda said, putting out the plates and silverware.

Carol leaned her back against the counter. "I think the school menu said pizza for today."

"Really?" Melinda said. "Then I'll eat at school. Can I have thirty-five cents?" She put a pitcher of milk on the gray Formica table.

"Of course you can," Carol said, wiping her hands on the apron. "We can't have you going without lunch now." She reached into a Folgers coffee can sitting on the window ledge, coins rattling in the bottom, and pulled out a roll of one-dollar bills. "Why don't you just pay for today and then I'll give you money for a new punch card on Monday."

"How about you, Grady?" she asked, handing a quarter and a dime to Melinda. A few wrinkles lined her green eyes, but to Grady she was still one of the prettiest moms around.

"I'm good; I've got three or four punches left."

"Well, that means I won't need to put forty burgers on the grill at lunch. I never get the full crowd of you kids coming down when the cafeteria serves pizza. But Jiminy Cricket, when they serve up their famous meatloaf, then we get the whole bunch of ya!" She laughed and stuffed the bills back in the can. "Grady, have Dean pull the eggs this morning so I can take them to Steuben's before I start my shift. My coffee can's getting low." Steuben's Supervalu depended on local farmers to supply much of the fresh dairy and produce and it generated a little extra income for Carol's tight budget.

Kurt and Dean pushed through the stairway door simultaneously and took their places at the table. "Gimme the milk," Kurt said to Melinda. His light brown hair and pale blue eyes stood out from the rest of the family, who all had darker features.

Carol frowned. "Boy-howdy, young man," she said in a stern voice, "you use your manners."

"It's too early," Kurt said, making a face at his sister.

Melinda used both hands to pick up the heavy glass pitcher and pass it to her brother. "Here."

Frank came out of the bathroom wearing his dark blue uniform, the State of Montana patch fixed prominently on the right shoulder. "Did I hear you sass your mother?" He directed his eyes squarely on Kurt while he strapped on his work belt. He reached above the fridge and slipped a Smith and Wesson .38 special into the holster.

Kurt's expression turned serious and he straightened in his chair. "No, sir."

"Better not have," he said with a harsh tone. Frank took his place at the head of the table. "I swear young man, if you had a half a brain, you'd be dangerous." He turned to Carol. "What are you waiting for?"

Carol sprinted into action. "Got it right here." She grabbed a hot pad, frayed and covered in burn marks. "Here's your eggs and bacon." Frank's eggs were over easy, fixed the same way every morning. She twirled back to the stove and grabbed the coffee pot and filled his cup. He took a gulp of the dark, steaming liquid, black and thick enough to float a bullet. Carol put a plate stacked with toast and a large bowl of scrambled eggs for the kids on the table. Then she loaded a plate with crispy bacon slices; the thick-cut bacon still had the rind on, the boys' favorite.

Finally, she sat down opposite Frank, head bowed, hands folded in front of her. Frank cocked his head and eyed his eggs before closing his eyes. "Bless us, O Lord," he began, and Carol and the kids joined him, "and these, thy gifts that we are about to receive from your bounty. Through Christ our Lord, amen," they recited in unison, followed by the sign of the cross.

The clanks and clinks of silverware and dishes in motion filled the kitchen. "*Pass* the bacon," Kurt said, kicking Grady under the table. Grady eyed Kurt with a quick nod of understanding.

"Don't take all day, Mindy." Kurt folded his hands and rested them on the table, twirling his thumbs.

"Hold on," Melinda said, picking through the pieces. "I like the ones not so crispy."

"I'm starving over here," Kurt said, snapping his fingers.

"Here," she said, handing Kurt the plate.

Kurt stuffed a large piece in his mouth and put three on his plate.

Melinda shook her head. "You're so gross."

"Don't talk like that at the table," Frank said sternly.

"There's more on the stove, Kurt," Carol said, motioning with her fork.

"Listen up. I'm not on the scale tomorrow, so we're doing sausage." Frank paused and made eye contact with each one at the table. "That means you kids are staying home to help. Grady, you get the basement set up tonight, tables, sausage maker. I want it ready to go first thing Saturday morning." He pointed a finger at Melinda and Grady. "No running into town tonight, no friends. None of that until we're done. Got it?"

"Yes, sir," Grady said, downing a spoonful of eggs.

Melinda nodded in response while swallowing a drink of milk.

Frank took a gulp of coffee and turned to Carol. "Are the tubs of meat out of the freezer?"

"Oh, yes," Carol said. "I had Kurt take them all out. They should be thawed out just right by the time we get started."

"The meat can't be half froze." Frank turned his head to the side. "Make sure he got them all—beef, pork, venison."

Carol nodded at Frank. "Yes, I went down and checked."

Frank scoffed. "Well, check again. I need all of it for my recipes."

"As soon as I finish up with breakfast." She turned to Dean and brushed a few stray hairs out of his eyes. "Guess what, Buddy? Grandma and Grandpa should be here by the time you get home from school."

"Goodie!" Dean's brown eyes came to life and he put his fork down. "I like Grampa's funny stories."

"We all do," Carol said with a soft laugh. "He's got some good ones." She turned to Frank, catching his expression. "What is it? Do you want more bacon or toast?" she asked, her own plate still empty.

Frank nodded. "Two pieces of toast."

Carol hopped up from her chair and put two pieces of bread into the toaster.

"I think I'm full," Dean said, his voice sounding sleepy. He rubbed his eyes with a pudgy fist and yawned, displaying a mouthful of half-chewed breakfast.

"I think you're hardly awake's more like it," Carol said, watching the toaster.

"You eat every last bite," Frank said, pointing a fork at Dean. "We don't waste food in this house." Being careful not to catch his father's eye, Kurt mouthed the words along with him, while Melinda held back a giggle. Frank took another gulp of coffee and held up his empty cup. Carol grabbed the coffee pot and filled it again. Some days Grady wasn't sure if his mom ever sat down during a meal.

Grady cleaned his plate a second time, irritated how his dad demanded his mom's constant attention. Carol scooped a small spoonful of eggs onto a plate with a single piece of bacon and sat down, after she'd buttered his toast. Grady strode to the hooks by the back door and grabbed his lined Carhartt jacket.

"Ready, boys?" he asked, pulling on his boots, stocking cap, and gloves.

"Almost." Kurt grabbed one more piece of bacon and slipped out of his chair.

Melinda began scraping leftovers into an old enamel dishpan marked with so many rust spots it looked as if it had a rare tropical disease, like from the strange rice paddies and jungles in Vietnam they heard so much about on the nightly news. "Kurt, give this to Razor when you go out," Melinda said. She set the dog dish by the door and scooped hot water from the tank into the good dishpan, ready to start the dishes, humming softly as she worked.

Frank stood and dumped the last bit of coffee into the single porcelain sink. He grabbed his coat off the hook next to Grady. "You be home on time," he said before slipping his winter coat on over his uniform.

Grady nodded as Frank brushed past him and out the door. "Mindy," Grady called from the porch, "you need a ride home from school?"

"No, I'll take the bus."

"Can I sit with you?" Dean asked.

"She'll be sitting with bug-eye Billy Malone," Kurt said.

"I will not," Melinda answered, making a face at Kurt.

"I gotta use the bathroom," Kurt said in a loud voice.

"Don't take all day," Grady said. There was no use waiting. He opened the back door and a rush of cold, bitter wind whipped around his neck and down the back of his jacket. Grady yanked up his collar as their German shepherd bounded up the steps, mouth open, tail wagging. "Hey, Razor. Were you waiting for me, boy?" He stroked his stiff fur for a short moment, watching his dad's LeSabre disappear down the driveway.

He wondered what story his dad would come home with tonight. Wearing a badge and carrying a loaded pistol were a real power trip for him. More times than he could count, his dad had gotten into scrapes with truckers who didn't appreciate his my-way-or-the-highway attitude. One night he was so bound and determined to get a driver to open the seal on his load that he nearly severed his own fingers trying to rip the metal bands open with his bare hands. His mom got the call and had to rush him to the hospital in Beach. Most days though, he'd go straight to the Silver Dollar after his shift and tell the regulars how he'd set this driver or that trucker straight.

When Grady was a kid they'd lived in the Rocky Mountains near Missoula, where he could go fishing all the time. But his dad quit his job driving logging trucks and they moved to Wibaux, a tiny dot of a town on the eastern border, where he worked at the weigh station on Interstate-94, the most northern east-west U.S. route, at the Montana state line. Funny thing was Naomi's dad worked the North Dakota weigh station in Beach across the border. The two fathers might hold the same job, but they were as different as night and day

His mom's morning forecast was right on—winter had hit the Northern Plains in full force overnight. Temps dropped below freezing and a couple inches of fresh snow covered the ground. "Don't worry, Raz, your breakfast is coming." Grady pulled down his ear flaps and headed through the early morning blackness toward the barn. The bittersweet mix of hay, baled and stacked in the hay loft, two brood hogs, a half-dozen barn cats, and last night's accumulation of cow shit greeted him in wafts as soon as he stepped inside. He flipped on the light switch and walked down the alley to the back door. "Come, boss!" he hollered. "C'mmm, boss!"

The two dairy cows fenced behind the barn turned their heads and meandered toward the open door. They walked down the alleyway to their stanchions and turned in like trained circus animals, the same song and dance every morning and evening. He slid the door shut behind them and tossed his jacket onto a straw bale. Manure was starting to accumulate in the gutter, but he could save that chore for the afternoon.

Grady scooped a shovelful of range cake to each cow. Clara, a Brown Swiss, was gentle and easy to milk. Tillie, on other hand, was a temperamental Jersey-Holstein cross and always kicked when being milked. He grabbed the hobble and hooked it onto Tillie's two hind legs to avoid ending up black-and-blue.

Grady pushed through the swinging door into the milk house and grabbed a clean five-gallon galvanized milk pail, the door squeaking like a litter of newborn piglets. He caught the swing on the open as he cut back and sidestepped through an empty stanchion.

The quietness was interrupted by Dean and Kurt coming through the barn door. "Knock it off, ya dummy," Kurt said, and then shoved his younger brother.

"You're a big fat bully!" shouted Dean.

"Hey, hey, what's going on?" Grady asked as he plopped his stool between Clara and Tillie.

"He shut the door on me," Kurt said.

"On accident," Dean said.

"Kurt, leave him alone. Go feed the hogs and check their water. Dean, you can feed the chickens and pull the eggs for Mom, okay?"

"Dee-ny is a wee-nie," Kurt said in a sing-song, and stuck out his tongue. He stomped toward the side door to the hog pen. "Dee-ny is a wee-nie . . ." echoed through the barn wall.

"You're a dumb——," Dean started to shout, blinking back tears.

"Ignore him," Grady said to his youngest brother, cutting him off. "Go get the eggs and bring them up to the house for Mom."

Dean wiped his snotty nose with his sleeve. "I don't like him today," he announced, reaching up for the basket hanging on a nail. He pushed through the swinging door, his favorite shortcut to the chicken coup.

Kurt filled a five-gallon bucket of feed at the feed chute for the two Hampshire brood sows; the rest of the hogs had all been sold or butchered for the year. "Breakfast is served, girls," he called, leaning over the gate. "Come and get it, right from the Dairy Delight."

"Move over, Clara," Grady said with a pat on her backside. He used a rag and warm water to clean Tillie's teats. "Take it easy now," he said, keeping a close watch on her hind legs. "Atta, girl. Nice and easy does it." With both hands he started squeezing, first the left front teat, then the back rear, alternating in a smooth rhythm. *Swish, swoosh, swish, swoosh.* He loved the soothing sound of the milk squirting into the pail. *Swish, swoosh, swish, swoosh.*

Meow! Meow! Meow! Like clockwork, the barn cats came from all corners and closed in, requesting their morning treat. The gray cat rolled up at Grady's feet like a furry football with legs, licking drops of milk off his boots. Grady angled a teat at the black-and-white cat and gave her a squirt, the rest meowing and mingling on the alleyway, demanding their turn.

"That's enough," Grady said to the noisy felines. "I gotta get the pail filled too." He resumed milking, and when the warm, foamy milk nearly reached the top, Grady carried it to the milk house and came back with an empty one for Clara. He averaged six gallons from the morning milking.

"Let's go, girl," he said, switching to Tillie. "We've got business to take care of. Give me all you got, atta girl." Grady thought the cows enjoyed his morning small talk, convinced the more he chatted, the more milk they gave. Naomi had giggled when he shared this little tidbit with her, but later she said she believed him. After all, she was a town kid and knew nothing about the habits of dairy cows.

Grady pulled down a hay bale and divided it between Clara and Tillie. "Kurt!" he called, pulling on his jacket. "You ready? Let's head outside."

"Can I drive?" Kurt said, slumped on the loose hay. "I'm thirteen now, c'mon, Grady. Let me drive."

"Yeah, right, and listen to you grind the gears like last time." Grady started up the Jimmy and drove behind the machine shed to the large haystack. Kurt hopped out and pulled down twenty-five bales, stacking them in the back end. Grady drove a half mile to the quarter-section pasture on the north side of the house, where the beef cattle were fenced during the winter months. Roughly a hundred head of Angus huddled together in a big black mass against the strong northwest wind. As soon as they heard the pickup, they began trailing behind the truck toward the bunks. Grady drove at a snail's pace while Kurt climbed in the back to cut the twine and toss the hay into the feed bunks.

Dieter Haase owned all but a half dozen of the herd, as well as the entire farm. Frank made a deal with Dieter to lower their rent by taking care of the cattle year-round. In the winter the herd was fenced near the farm in order to get their feed and water, but from March through October they roamed the large open range west of the farm and ate grass. The native prairie grass ripened early and cured while standing, a distinction that had drawn cattlemen to the range a century earlier, ideal for raising stock. A small, spring-fed creek ran through the section and provided water until it dried up, usually in mid-August. Semi-retired, Dieter lived in town and owned a small gas station, but drove out occasionally to check on things or collect the rent.

It was a nice spread of land five miles west of Wibaux, right off the frontage road that paralleled the interstate, the tower for his dad's weigh station within easy view. The white farmhouse had a welcoming front porch with thick pillars. Besides the big red barn there was a machine shop, three round metal granaries, and a chicken coup. A corral and loading chute were positioned next to the barn for the roundups every May. Despite having to do chores every morning and evening, Grady liked living on the farm. He found a sense of fulfillment in working with the land and animals, even if it didn't belong to them.

Kurt threw out the last bale and closed the gate behind the truck. Grady and Kurt rode back to the farmhouse in silence as an orange glow began to emerge on the eastern horizon. Like a thousands days before and a thousand days yet to come, it was God's grand invitation to watch his fashioning of another day in spectacular rivers of color that filled the Montana sky, a sight that had left Grady in breathless awe more than once.

CHAPTER THREE

Leave it to Dan Iverson to brighten up another boring day in school. This time he taped a Playboy pin-up in the chalkboard-sized United States map in Mr. Crandall's fourth-hour Geography class while the teacher was out of the room. Halfway through class, Mr. Crandall pulled down the map to point to the San Andreas fault line and to his shock, a bare-breasted blonde babe covered the western portion of California. Grady wasn't sure if Mr. Crandall's jaw or his pointer stick hit the floor first as the room erupted in laughter.

Mr. Crandall stammered for the class to be quiet, fumbling to pull the cord. The map spun up at lightning speed, flapping against the chalkboard just as Mr. Kettle, Wibaux High's all-knowing, all-seeing principal walked by and heard the ruckus. The room instantly quieted and brown-noser Larry Knutson was only too happy to give up the guilty party. "Dan Iverson did it, Mr. Kettle," he said in a whiny, goody-two-shoes voice. "I saw him by the map before class started." Mr. Kettle gave Dan a look that meant business and promptly ordered him to the office.

Poor Mr. Crandall rarely had control of his classroom and the fourth-hour eleventh- and twelfth-graders took advantage of it on a daily basis. Grady kinda felt sorry for the guy some days. He wore stretched-out pilly sweaters and hiked his plaid pants up too high. He figured it was the first time Mr. Crandall had ever laid eyes on such a voluptuous image.

Grady scooped up his algebra book at the sound of the final bell that announced the end of another school day—even better, another week. He stopped at his locker and tossed the book inside.

"Grady! Tom!" Wes Scheinberg called from a dozen lockers away. A thick mop of light brown curls crowned his head but it was the dimple in his left cheek that generated the most attention from the girls. "C'mon over to my house. Let's play cards or somethin'."

"Sure man, I'm game," Tom said. A guard on the Wibaux football team, Tom Lorentz was solid and broad shouldered, and grew stubble on his chin in an effort to solidify his athletic image.

"Can't," Grady said. "I gotta get home."

"Tomorrow then?"

"Nah, I'll be up to my elbows in sausage all weekend."

"Too bad for you, Kramer," Shiny said, shaking his head.

Jake Wensman hurried past with his royal blue and gold Longhorn letter jacket hung over one shoulder, his shaggy hair angled just below the ear.

"Hey, Wens, you want in a card game?" Shiny asked.

"Nah, I gotta work." Jake's folks owned the Gambles Hardware in town, and unless it was football or track season he spent most afternoons behind the front counter.

"What about you, Dan?" Shiny said in a desperate plea.

"Can't," Dan said, sober-faced. His plaid flannel shirt was untucked, sleeves rolled to his biceps. "I got a date with ol' man Kettlehead."

Grady shut his locker, the metal clanking loudly. "You got detention?"

Dan shook his head, his long bangs falling across his forehead. "Not exactly. Made it sound like we'll be joined at the hip." He pushed his bangs to the side, twisting his face into a contorted expression.

Grady gave him a friendly shove. "You really did it this time, man."

Dan took out a toothpick and tucked it in the corner of his mouth. "Did you see that look on Crandall's face? He went white as sheet, I swear," he said with a crooked grin as laughter erupted among the boys.

"I think he was in shock," Tom said.

"Imagine what he'll be dreaming about tonight," Dan said, and they roared again. "Oh, man . . . it was worth it!" He turned and shuffled toward the office.

"Uh-oh, I'm late for my shift," Jake said, turning toward the doors. "Let's party or somethin' Saturday night."

Kevin Thompson strode up to Grady, Tom, and Shiny. "Guys, we're makin' a beer run down to Colorado tonight," he said in a low voice. "Be back tomorrow." Kevin was a senior and the only kid in Wibaux High School with a full mustache and long, thick sideburns. He looked darn near ten years older than all the other boys and had the aura of the "Stranger" in *High Plains Drifter.* "Who wants in?"

"Coors?" said Shiny. "Hell yeah!"

"Keep it down, dumb ass." Kevin rapped his knuckles on Shiny's forehead.

"How much room you got?" asked Tom, rubbing his whiskers.

"We're taking my dad's Impala," Kevin said. "It's brand spankin' new, 454 big block, with leather. A *smooooth* ride, boys. She can *flyyyyyy.*" He arched his eyebrows and made a quick glance down the hall. "She's got a trunk big enough for a coffin, I kid you not. We can load up twenty, maybe twenty-five cases, no problem." When the minimum legal drinking age was lowered to eighteen, access to beer and booze greatly improved for the high school population. Several senior boys—Dan, Tom, Willie, and Kevin—had already celebrated their defining birthdays, stamped and certified Legal Adults.

"How many are in so far?" Shiny asked.

"I've got enough for fifteen cases," Kevin said in the tone of an operative undercover.

"How soon you takin' off?" Grady asked.

"As soon as I can find who's in for about five more cases. No use to drive dang near six hundred miles one way if we ain't got enough people in."

"Hey, man, count me in," Tom said, taking out his wallet. He handed a ten-dollar bill to Kevin. "I'll take a case."

"Shiny, let's you and me split a case," Grady said, digging in his jeans. "You got five bucks?"

"Yeah, man." Shiny reached in his front pocket and pulled out a small wad of dollar bills. One by one he unfolded them and turned them over to Kevin.

"I say hurry up and get going, man." Tom gave Kevin a push backward toward the front doors. "You're wasting time."

Kevin cracked a smile and raised his arm in a formal salute while clicking the heels of his boots. "See you boys on the flip side."

"Who's going with?" Grady asked.

"Me and the Snyder boys," he called. Stepping backward, Kevin didn't see Mr. Kettle coming out of the science lab. "We're trying to beat our old record."

"What record is that, Kevin?" Mr. Kettle asked, his head tilted in earnest interest.

Kevin's eyebrows arched as though his secret detail had been exposed. He calmly turned on his heels and tipped his cap. "Gettin' to St. Peter's for mass, Mr. Kettle," he said and strode to the double doors. He exited the building, his lanky frame disappearing into the late afternoon rays like the hero in the final scene. The only thing missing was the musical score.

A typical Friday afternoon, the mud-covered pickups and cars couldn't get out of the parking lot fast enough. Grady took the shortcut through the railroad underpass, painted in the blue and gold Longhorn colors, slowing for the flashing amber sign at the main intersection. If he turned left, he'd head for the westbound frontage road, but if he turned right and drove to the east end of town, he could hop on the freeway entrance ramp. West meant home. East meant Beach . . . and Naomi. In a flash of spontaneity, he cranked the wheel right.

His dad's speech at breakfast meant there'd be no time for a date with Naomi all weekend, but if he got over to Beach quick enough he could catch her coming out of school and explain the reason. Of course, he could call her, but then he'd miss the chance to see her pretty smile. He pressed a little harder on the gas pedal and passed a dually pickup pulling a horse trailer as if it were standing still. According to the State of Montana, the interstate speed limit was defined as "reasonable and prudent," which in this case meant roughly 87 miles an hour.

The school day in Beach ended twelve minutes later than Wibaux, which worked well for him. Grady took the single exit for Beach and drove two short blocks to the high school with three minutes to spare. He parked the Beast on the edge of the lot—his pet name for the '62 Bel Air. Grady fished a rag from the glove box and wiped the dust off the dash. Even though it was a losing battle on gravel roads, he did his best to keep it looking sharp. Some of the town kids with newer cars called it a beater, but it was *his*. Besides, he'd saved it from a sorry life of ice fishing.

Two months earlier the car had belonged to Kevin Thompson, and Grady's dad had talked Kevin into selling it to him for seventy-five bucks. Grady came home on a Saturday afternoon in September and saw the car parked in the yard. He walked inside expecting to see Kevin and found only his dad. "Where's Kevin?" he asked, wondering why he'd be over when Grady wasn't home.

Frank was still in his blue uniform and already had a cold bottle of Old Milwaukee in his hand. "He ain't here."

"His car's parked by the machine shed." Grady waved a hand toward the kitchen window, confused.

"It ain't his car no more; it's mine," Frank said matter-of-factly.

"What'd you buy another car for?"

"Do you know how many damn trucks I had lined up by eleven o'clock this morning. Man, what a bunch of cranky ol' codgers, jackin' their jaw about losing time on the road. Like I wanna listen to that all the livelong day. I told one of 'em to get the hell outta there before I shoved it where the sun don't shine." He took a long swallow of beer. "Man, I needed that!" He washed his hands at the sink, looking out the kitchen window.

"Dad . . . the car?"

"That's my new ice fishin' car. Don't she look good?"

"What?"

Frank dried his hands on a flour-sack dishtowel, a flowery *Monday* embroidered in yellows and pinks. "I'm gonna cut holes in the floorboards in the back, then I can drive right out onto the ice and sit in the back and fish through the holes." His face lit up at the prospect of his grand idea. "Like a mobile ice house."

Grady stood in the middle of the kitchen, hands on his hips. "Dad, you can't cut holes in that car, it's in too good of

45

condition! Besides, I need a car," he said, tapping his chest. "I'll buy it from you."

Frank shook his head. "Negatory. Go get your own car, 'cause this is my ice fishing car." He pulled out another bottle from the fridge and retreated to the recliner.

Grady followed on his heels. "How much did you pay for it?"

"Seventy-five bucks," Frank said, tipping his chair back.

"Dad, you can't cut that car apart!" Grady's voice carried a sense of desperation. "It runs good. I've been in it a dozen times with Kevin this summer. You can't be serious about cutting holes in the floor."

"Yeah? Well I'm tellin' you, I'm dead serious."

"You can't flat-out ruin a good car. It's in perfect condition," he said, raising his voice. "It's got plenty of room inside, three-on-the-tree with overdrive, it'll get good mileage. I can drive me and Melinda to school and we won't have to spend an hour on that stupid bus."

Unmoved by Grady's pleas, Frank cocked his hands behind his head. "Turn on the TV for me."

"C'mon, Dad, sell it to me. I'll buy it from you, same as what you paid for it. You know I need a car real bad."

For four solid days Grady hounded his dad until he finally relented and Grady turned over the wad of cash. He spent the next week giving it a much-needed overhaul, inside and out. The outside paint had oxidized from too much sun, so Grady buffed it down and applied a thick coat of Turtle wax. Jake Wensman knew a lot about cars and showed him how to rebuild the carburetor and change the fluids. Jake helped him take the engine apart, hone the cylinders, replace the rings and bearings, and do a complete valve job on the head. It was a solid car; the front dash was all steel and he couldn't have been prouder.

The sun, already low in the sky, warmed the interior and Grady rolled down the driver's window. He adjusted the ignition back one notch and turned the knob to KFYR, a 50,000-watt clear-channel AM rock'n'roll station out of Bismarck he could pick up without static. Grady turned up the volume for a favorite Credence Clearwater song:

I want to know, have you ever seen the rain?
I want to know, have you ever seen the rain?
Comin' down on a sunny day?

Students began to spill through the front entry and Naomi exited the double set of glass doors with her two best friends at her side. All three girls wore bell-bottom jeans, nylon jackets, and had long hair parted down the middle. They looked like a singing trio, walking in unison. Naomi was by far the prettiest, and at times Grady wondered how he was so lucky to get a girl like her. She wasn't even bothered by the long scar that ran down the center of his face. When he had told her the story of how he got it, she gently traced it with her finger and then kissed him on the bridge of his nose where it showed the most.

A part of Grady wanted so badly to share with her what had happened out deer hunting, but he didn't dare. How could he tell her that he'd almost killed his own father? What would that make him? A *murderer*, almost. The thought sickened him. No, he could *never* tell a soul. One more secret to bury deep within.

Naomi spotted Grady's car and he watched as she said good-bye to her friends and hurried over. "What are you doing here?" she asked through the open window. Her blue eyes lit up like sapphires in sunlight and a soft grin formed at the corners of her mouth.

"Oh, we gotta make sausage this weekend. Grandma and Grandpa are at the house already. I'll be in trouble if I don't get home right away, but I wanted to let you know why I couldn't see you."

"You gonna do that all weekend?" she asked, wrinkling her perfect nose. Her cheeks were flushed a pale shade of pink from the cool air.

"Haven't you ever made sausage before?"

"Are you kidding? Dad goes to Kal's Meats and buys it by the case." Naomi came from a family of ten siblings where everything was purchased in bulk. "I'm glad you stopped. Marsha and Dan want to run over to Glendive tonight to see *Towering Inferno*. It's only two bucks a person and Marsha is dying to see it." The cool breeze caught Naomi's hair and it fell back in a feathery motion across her shoulders.

Naomi's sister Marsha dated Dan Iverson and the two couples often went out as a foursome. "You sure about Dan?"

"I think so, why?"

"He's in detention and he might not get out till graduation." Grady laughed and relayed the story from fourth hour.

"He's always pulling something crazy."

"I can't go tonight anyway, I've got strict orders. Maybe tomorrow night if we finish up. I could pick you up after church."

Naomi wrinkled her flawless face. "I have a babysitting job tomorrow night. I can only go out tonight."

His eyes met hers, mesmerized by their deep blueness. "If I could, I would. Trust me."

Naomi leaned in, resting her arms on the window, and caressed Grady's forearm. "It's okay, I understand."

A warm, tingling sensation crept from the back of his ears, swirled around, and hit him in the chest with a thunderous jolt. He knew she meant it, and that was all he needed for now. Just being around Naomi made him feel like a lovesick puppy. In truth, it went much deeper. From the moment he'd first spotted her at the sock-hop, he *knew* she was special. The Wibaux Dancehall had been packed with kids from Beach and Wibaux.

She had on the best looking pair of Rocky Mountain jeans he'd ever seen and a pale pink turtleneck, but it was her smile that caught his attention. He saw Melinda talking to her across the dance floor and he about knocked his sister down in a mad dash to inquire about her.

Melinda made a quick introduction and explained that Naomi was a cheerleader for Beach. The two girls saw each other whenever the Beach Buccaneers played the Wibaux Longhorns in football or basketball. Grady didn't waste a minute and asked Naomi to dance. They danced to every song until the dancehall closed at eleven o'clock. Between songs he had held her hand, amazed how perfectly it fit his. When all was wrong at home, he could replay those first moments with Naomi over in his mind, convinced there were good things in life yet to come.

Grady raced the Beast back to Montana via the interstate, the concrete lifeline that connected the little towns in the sparsely populated region. "Better get on home," he whispered under his breath, "and get your mind off Miss Naomi Braden."

CHAPTER FOUR

Grady exited at Wibaux, pronounced *Wee-bo* and named for the French cattle baron Pierre Wibaux who founded the tiny town in the 1880s, population 598. An oversized International Harvester combine took up most of the gravel frontage road, lumbering along at a snail's pace. "Get over, red rover," Grady muttered. He swerved to the left and sped around it. The tin shack and tower at the weigh station where his dad worked poked high above the prairie grass to his left. On his right the wheat stubble was chopped at about ten inches in order to provide a little grain for the pheasants and prairie chickens and to catch the snow to help bring much needed moisture come spring.

A giant cloud of dust trailed the Beast as he rounded a curve, fishtailing through a muddy dip in the road, the farm in his sights. The truth was, he looked forward to the family's annual tradition. Times making sausages held some of his best memories. He loved it when the whole family worked together, side by side. His dad was usually in a good mood, and for a brief period they were like a normal family, cutting up, making jokes.

This was his dad's time to shine as a "wurstmacher," showcasing his German heritage and flavorful meats, everything from headcheese and liverwurst to breakfast links and kielbasa sausage. The butchering started with an Angus steer. It was Grady's job to lead the unlucky beast to the end of the alley in the barn and turn him sideways. His dad stood twenty feet or so down the alley with his loaded .22 rifle. As soon as Grady was a safe distance back, his dad fired one shot and the huge animal hit the pavement with a thud. His dad never failed to kill an animal with a single bullet.

Butchering a steer was a several-day process. They had to gut it and hang the large animal with hooks and pulleys. Grady and Kurt then took tubs of bloody guts out to a ravine about a mile north of the barn to use as bait in their traps. So far they'd caught four coyotes and two fox. And thanks to the pretty ladies in the big cities who wanted to wear fur coats, they could get thirty-five to forty-five dollars per hide in Glendive.

The steer hung in the barn until the meat cooled and aged, usually seven to ten days. Then his dad took the meat saw and split the cow right down the spine and cut it into quarters. The boys carried the quarters into the basement where it was divided into individual cuts, wrapped in white paper, and taped with masking tape. His mom used a black crayon to mark each package. *Porterhouse steak. Rump roast. Rib eye. Chuck Roast. Shoulder Roast. Spare ribs. Soup bones. T-bone. Hamburger. Tenderloin. Butterfly steak.*

Next, they repeated the same scenario with one of the Hampshire hogs. Butchering a pig was slightly different because the massive animal had to be dipped in boiling water in order to scrape the course hair from the hide. The hanging market weight of a hog often reached three hundred pounds. They used a propane burner to heat the water in a large copper tub and strung a rope through a pulley to lower it into the scalding water. Pigs were quartered different than cows in order to save the belly in two big slabs for bacon and salt pork.

Scraps of meat not good enough for packaging were deboned and saved for making sausage. The poured concrete floor and block walls in the basement made it easy to wash the bloody mess down the floor drain at the end of the day. Frank didn't believe in waste. He threw in the snout, cheeks, ears, jowl—everything. If Grady heard it once, he heard it a thousand times: *We use everything but the squeal.* At the end of the day only the bones were left—cleaned smooth, like a ham bone a dog had spent a long afternoon with under the porch.

Butchering was timed to coincide with hunting season. The cool temperatures in mid to late November were a hunter's best friend. After the first outing when Grady's hate nearly got the best of him, their subsequent outings proved more bountiful. Grady and his dad had netted three muleys—two does and a buck—and a doe antelope. The same butchering process took place for each animal they brought home. His mom washed down the long tables in the basement and arranged them in assembly-line order. Everyone in the family had a job to do, even young Dean, who mostly ran up and down the stairs for odds and ends, aprons, butcher paper, paper towels, and helped stack the wrapped meat in the freezers.

Frank's butcher knives were handmade by his older brother Ed, crafted from an industrial band saw. His dad bragged that Uncle Ed's knives were the sharpest, longest-lasting around, and he was right. Last week the whole family had been in the basement deboning pieces of the antelope. His dad liked to work at a fast pace, and his mom—ever mindful of the kids—saw Kurt with a hind quarter. "Kurt, watch it! Don't cut toward yourself," she said. "That knife is sharp."

"Yeah," Grady said, elbowing his brother. "Never cut toward yourself; always cut toward other people." There was a pause and they all burst out laughing, even his dad.

"Normal" was possible—just rare.

Frank had bought an old grocery store freezer at an auction and hauled it home on Dieter's flatbed trailer. The oversized chest freezer took up the width of one whole wall with four two-by-two-inch top-lifting compartment lids. Scuffed and dented in one corner, it wasn't much to look at but it served the family well. Two smaller chest freezers served as backups, and in a good year they filled all three. Carol packed the freezers in order: beef, pork, venison, and antelope. Things were tough in some respects, but the Kramer dinner table was rich in hearty, plentiful meals.

The Beast rumbled across the cattle guard and up the long driveway. He parked next to Grandpa Hoffman's Ford Galaxie 500, the North Dakota plates barely visible under a thick layer of dust. He grabbed his cap from the dash and slipped it on to hold back his long hair. Razor lay up against the door of the smokehouse, his tail swishing the snow and gravel into cinnamon sugar.

Grady approached the wood shack and heard muffled voices from inside. He tapped on the door. "Dad?" Frank kept a close watch on the thermostat and Grady knew better than to open the door unless he okay'd it.

"Grady? C'mon in."

"Move over, Raz." Grady shoved Razor aside with his boot and stepped inside. Sweet smoky smells filled his nostrils, triggering a growl deep inside his stomach. "Mmm, smells good, Dad." Grady's eyes adjusted to the darkness, the small interior giving the aura of a secret culinary society. Frank's denim shirtsleeves were rolled up to the elbow as he poured a little water in the tray. Grady grinned as soon as he saw the shorter man standing next to him. "Hey, Grandpa. How ya doing?"

"Finer'n frogs' hair," Clarence Hoffman said. He grasped Grady's hand and gave it a solid shake. Dressed in faded overalls and a flannel shirt, Clarence gave a smile that spread through his cheeks, browned and creased from decades of trying to best Mother Nature and make a living as a farmer in the Knife River valley of North Dakota. At sixteen, Grady already stood a few inches taller than his maternal grandfather. "Boy, I swear you get another foot taller every time I see you." He gave his grandson a pat on the shoulder.

"Aw, Grampa, you say that every time you come."

"That's 'cuz you keep growing, shootin' up like one of them danged weeds I keep fightin' with. Taller'n the corn on a good year, aren't ya?" Clarence glanced up at the rows of meats. "Boy, your dad has some good stuff here."

The bacon and hams were strung on broom handles near the top of the smokehouse. The handles were suspended from the roof on hooks, parallel to the ceiling, running end-to-end. Frank wrapped his hands around a large ham, checking the temperature, juices dripping from the moist cut. He adjusted the burner on the smoker a little lower. "There . . . that's better," he said, wiping his hands on his dark blue work pants.

"What kind of chips you using?" Grady asked.

"I got apple and hickory in this tray, and maple over here." He reached into a brown paper bag and sprinkled a few more maple chips in the tray. Soaking the chips in water released the flavor. "These'll be done by tomorrow," Frank said, checking another ham. "They're on their fourth day."

"Lookin' good, Frank," Clarence said. "Real good."

"It's making me hungry," Grady admitted with a pat to his stomach.

"Me too. My stomach's beginning to think my throat's been cut," Clarence said with a hearty laugh. "Let's go see what your ma's got cooking."

"Sure, Grampa."

"I bet it's something mighty tasty," Clarence said, opening the door.

Sunlight flooded the doorway as the three men stepped out of the smokehouse. Razor promptly jumped to his feet and trotted ahead of them toward the house. Frank caught Grady's shoulder with a firm grip. "Hold up there. You got chores, Grady."

"I know," Grady said, nodding.

"Get the manure hauled out tonight."

"There's not much; it won't take me long."

"I want the hogs switched to the other half of the pen, fresh straw, the works." Frank planted his feet in front of Grady in a confrontational posture.

"What? Tonight?" Grady stood eye-to-eye with his dad in a mirrored stance, hands on his hips. He waved a hand toward the house. "Grandma and Grandpa are here."

"Looks like your dinner will be late tonight." Frank leaned into Grady's face and squinted. "How much gas you use up today?" he asked, raising his voice. "Huh? Driving all over the place for no good reason, wasting gas. Shoulda come straight home like I said."

Grady glared at his father. "I pay for my gas. Besides, I only pay twenty-eight cents bulk and everyone else pays thirty-two cents in town."

Frank shook his head in a look of disgust. "Why don't you use that head for something besides holding up that hat?" He brushed past Grady and grabbed Clarence by the shoulder. "Whadaya say we go get a deck of cards and open a cold one."

He watched his dad steer Grandpa Hoffman across the gravel farm yard, the dog trailing at their feet. Razor stopped, tilting his head at Grady as though urging him to join the older men. Grady stood alone, the sun slipping behind a line of dark ominous clouds moving in from Canada.

"Damn you, anyway," Grady said between clenched teeth as they disappeared into the house. This was his dad's way of getting to him, now that Grady nearly matched him in size. He flat-out told Grady one day, "I can't give you a whipping anymore, but I'll still find ways to punish you." He'd take the coil wire out of the Beast or hide the keys.

Across the freeway a coal train rumbled on the railroad tracks that lined the south side of the interstate. Every once in a while a train loaded full with coal would pick up too much speed coming down Beaver Hill, a five-mile-long incline, and lose control on the descent eastbound into Wibaux, whistle blaring as a warning. Nothing could stop it. Empty trains heading west to the coal mines had to pull onto a siding, a set of tracks two or three miles long adjacent to the main tracks, to let the full train pass. In some ways Grady felt like his dad was the runaway train, bent on running him into the ground at all costs, no matter who or what was in the way, bearing down until the man destroyed every ounce of him, leaving him as flat and worthless as the pennies he and his friends used to line up on the rails as kids.

Grady flung the barn door open with so much force it hit the wall and rattled shut in front of him. He pushed it open a second time and spied a feed bucket within reach. In a flash of rage he threw it down the length of the alley, the bucket crash-landing in the center before spinning into the gutter. "Stupid piece of crap," he muttered.

He leaned against a stanchion frame and lit up a heater, kicking at a pile of loose hay, calling his dad every name in the book. By the time he took the last drag of his cigarette, he'd run out of things to call him and crushed the butt with his heel. Grady pulled down three straw bales in the back of the barn and tossed them into the empty pen. He grabbed the pitchfork out of the corner, nearly hidden by the stacked bales. He spread the straw around the pen until the tong caught on something. Grady pushed the straw back and uncovered a hammer.

"Stupid Kurt," he said, grumbling. "Never puttin' stuff back and then we all pay for it." He picked it up, gripping the rough handle. Images of his dad cozied up in the kitchen, drinking a beer, winking and putting on a show for Grandma and Grandpa flashed through his mind.

Grady turned on his heels and with every ounce of his 145 pounds slammed it into the post. *Wham!* The force reverberated in his hand, stinging his fingers and wrist, jolting clear up to his shoulder. *Wham! Wham! Wham! Wham!* He pounded it again and again until his hand cramped and the hammer dropped to the floor with a *clunk*. He winced, pain shooting up his arm to his shoulder. Sweat dripped from his forehead and he leaned against the splintered post, out of breath. No matter how hard he tried, he couldn't kill the ache inside.

CHAPTER FIVE

Grady and Kurt finished their Saturday morning chores and came in the house just in time for breakfast. His mother's large cast-iron frying pans covered three burners on the big stove and within mere minutes the family devoured heaps of chopped potatoes, onions, green peppers, scrambled eggs, and salt pork. Clarence rubbed his stomach and pushed back his chair, twirling a toothpick in his mouth. "Mmm, mmm! Mighty good eattin', Carol. Grady, think we got time for a quick game?" he asked, reaching for the deck of cards.

"Oh no you don't," advised his wife of forty-seven years. Vernice Hoffman shook her head with a look that meant business and snatched the worn cards right out of his hands. A heavyset woman with grayish blue eyes, rosy cheeks, and tight gray curls, she had loose, soft skin that smelled of talcum powder.

"I can't git away wit nuttin' no more," he said in a low growl and winked at Grady. Clarence stood with his coffee cup and Carol promptly filled it.

"I'll help Melinda clean up the kitchen while the rest of you get started," Vernice said.

"You sure, Mom?" Carol asked, already scraping the scraps into Razor's dish.

"Yeah! Shoo, go on," Vernice said, taking the dishes from Carol's hands. "I can do this much, for goodness' sake."

"Okay, then. Kurt, grab the box of casings." Carol pointed to a cardboard box in the porch.

Frank stood at the basement doorway, rolling up his sleeves. "Let's get rolling."

"You finished with your plate, Grady?" asked Vernice.

"Maybe one more piece of this and I will be," Grady said, reaching for the salt pork. "Thanks, Grandma."

"My oh my, I can't get over how much you look like Frank when he was younger," Vernice said, glancing at Grady and Frank. "A stranger would know you're father and son, that's for sure."

Frank turned at the mention of his name. "Handsome devil, isn't he?" he cracked, and then winked at Vernice before he descended down the steps.

Grady's back stiffened and the tiny hairs on the back of his neck stood up straight. *I may look like him physically but I am nothing like him! He's the last person on this earth that I want to be like!* The thoughts screamed through him but he held them inside, like always. He faked a wide grin and brushed his hair back. Long hair was in style, but for him it was one more attempt to expunge any similarity to his father. He gave Vernice a kiss on her cheek. "Thanks for breakfast, Grandma."

"Shoot, your ma done all the work."

Carol clapped her slender hands. "Okay, let's get at it. Jeepers, creepers, time's a wasting." She smiled and her eyes sparkled an exquisite shade of green.

Frank, Clarence, Carol, Grady, Kurt, and Dean gathered in the basement around the collection of casings, aprons, seasonings, attachments, and a new spool of string. Frank clamped the Chop-Rite sausage stuffer onto a two-by-ten and arranged the tables.

"Kurt, Grady, get the bins out," Frank said in a voice that left no question as to who was in charge. "Clarence, set the spices right here." He pointed to a small wooden table. "I like 'em within easy reach."

"Sure thing," Clarence said. One by one he moved the small containers from a frayed cardboard box onto the table that wobbled each time he added a jar or can.

"We're gonna start with breakfast sausage," Frank announced.

"Sounds good to me," Carol said. "Don't it, boys?"

Frank stood in front of the metal washtub, rubbing his hands in anticipation. "Kurt, put the pork right here, and then the beef," he continued. "Bring one bin of venison too."

Kurt picked up a bin full of meat scraps already ground and carried it to his dad. "Don't add too much venison this year," Carol said, making a face at the boys.

"Oooh, woman, don't you mess with my recipes," Frank said in a teasing manner.

Kurt lifted a full tub of beef onto the table beside the pork. Grady slid the bin of venison next to it.

"Mine was heavier." Kurt flexed his right arm.

"Have at 'er, big shot," Grady said. Kurt promptly retrieved the next bin.

Frank picked up a small jar with a dark gold label, his right index finger missing the first digit. He'd lost it six years earlier when he used his finger to press the meat into the two-inch auger instead of using a wooden dowel, one of the hazards of making sausage. "Look here at this Bavarian Mustard from Lowensenf," Frank said to Clarence. "This is good stuff. I couldn't find it last year, but ol' Rueben Swanson over in Glendive called me up the other day. He knew I was looking all over creation for it." Over the years Frank had acquired a large collection of spices and seeds. Small tins and mini jars filled with sage, fennel seeds, allspice, paprika, cloves, mace, bay leaf, juniper berries, pimento, garlic, thyme, parsley, laurel, and caraway were all needed, depending on each recipe.

"Yeah, that's good stuff. You're gonna have another good batch here, Frank."

Frank scooped handfuls of pork, beef, and venison into the thirty-gallon galvanized washtub until it was nearly full—roughly seventy-five pounds of beef, twenty-five pounds of pork, and fifteen pounds of venison. He mixed and worked it by hand, squeezing the greasy mishmash of raw meat between his fingers. Next he added selected spices and seeds into the mixture until it was nice and uniform. Frank's dark eyes widened and he nodded. "This is it. Let's go! Grady, make sure you've got the plastic casing; the natural casings will bust too easily for this."

"Got it." Grady reached forward with the casing, hands in ready position. "Let it roll, Dad."

"Which nipple did you put on?"

Grady looked at the front end. The no. 35 sausage stuffer had a cast-iron cylinder with a spigot underneath that could use either brass or stainless-steel nipples. On one side was a big crank and an acme-threaded rod onto a cast-iron plunger. "The one-inch for breakfast sausage, right Dad?"

"You got it."

Kurt scooped the meat by handfuls and packed it down with his fist, working up a sweat as he pressed the meat into the stuffer.

"Pack it tight, Kurt," Frank said. "We can't have no air in there. It'll rot the meat. C'mon, work it down."

Frank swung the lid closed, spun the rod and brought the plunger on top of the meat as Grady grabbed the handle and turned it. "C'mon, Grady! Crank, crank!" he said. He held a casing onto the nipple until it reached the end. Frank controlled the pressure. The harder he squeezed, the harder it was for Grady to crank.

"Oh, my, here it comes," Carol said, guiding the cased meat onto a tray. "Very nice, very nice." She held the long unending tube of breakfast sausage with her hands and at regular intervals twisted the casing to make a link.

Other than a short break at noon for dinner, the process continued all day. Dean and Melinda carried trays of breakfast sausage, kielbasa, bratwurst, and summer sausage out to the smokehouse for Clarence to hang until the tubs were all empty.

"You got some mighty fine meats there, Frank," Clarence said.

Frank beamed—his dark eyes shining—and wiped his brow. "I'll hand out some to the neighbors for Christmas."

"I'm hungr-eeee," Kurt said. He slumped to the floor, arms folded across his bony chest.

"Grandma's got a big roast all ready for supper," Carol said, washing out the sausage stuffer.

"Grady, Kurt," Frank said, nodding toward the stairway. "Get yourselves on out to the barn for chores before we eat. We can still make it to seven o'clock mass. Melinda, Dean, help your mother get this cleaned up."

Grady and Kurt finished the chores in near record time. It was easy to see where their mom inherited her cooking skills from. Vernice served the family a delicious tender roast, mashed potatoes, thick gravy, dinner rolls, topped off with her famous sour cream chocolate cake.

"We gotta hurry up and get changed for mass," Grady said, patting Dean on the backside.

Dean sat on the edge of the bed, trying to match the button with the right buttonhole. "Grady, why does Mom call these Sunday clothes when it's Saturday?"

"Good question," Grady said. "I guess 'cause we used to go to mass on Sunday."

"How come we don't anymore?" Dean asked.

"Boys!" Carol called up the stairs. "Your father's almost ready."

"Comin', Ma!" Kurt shouted, tripping over Dean's dress shoes.

"How come, Grady?" Dean asked again.

"I don't know, little buddy."

Kurt promptly kicked one of Dean's shiny brown Woolworth specials under the dresser and dashed into the hall. After having lost too many tussles with Grady, Kurt opted to pick on the youngest Kramer brother instead. He poked his head around the door jamb. "Better hurry up, Deanny Weanie, or you'll get a whipping!" His laugh bounced off the narrow hall walls.

"Kurt, grow up!" Grady shouted in vain to the sound of Kurt's dress shoes clomping down on each wooden step.

Dean sat on the edge of the bed, pants unzipped, shirt unbuttoned.

"Here's your shoe," Grady said, pulling it out from underneath the dresser. "No pouting now, okay, buddy?"

Dean nodded, bottom lip protruding as Grady buttoned his shirt. "Zip your pants now." Grady and Dean descended the staircase into the kitchen.

"Grady, git the cards," Clarence said, motioning with an arthritic finger. "C'mon, sit down. We got time for a quick game of gin." He pulled out a chair for Grady and tapped the Formica tabletop. "Deal 'em up. *Vas ist los?* One, two, tree." His yellowed teeth, stained from years of drinking coffee, showed as he counted out each card against the smooth surface.

"Melinda, grab the empty roaster for me," Carol instructed, pointing to the table. "That doesn't need to be on the table." Her crisp white blouse was tucked neatly in a navy blue skirt, accenting her narrow waistline. She had a navy scarf tied around her neck, the short ends poised off to one side. Grady thought she looked radiant, her dark brown hair curled and styled in a nice bob above the shoulder.

Melinda twirled on her toes, her dress flowing in a smooth motion, and handed the large enamel pan to her mother.

"Carol, did you make this?" Vernice asked, feeling the fabric of Melinda's lavender dress.

"Oh, yes," Carol answered with a bit of pride in her voice. "That one and a couple more upstairs."

Vernice adjusted her glasses, using the lower bifocals to study the seams just below the bust line. "Is it supposed to sit this high?"

"It's the empire waist, Grandma," Melinda said with a smile, showing off the paisley print. "Do you like it?"

"As a matter of fact, I do. Maybe your Grandma should wear one like this?"

Melinda giggled. "Sure, why not?"

Vernice laughed. "Oh, goodness, can you imagine that?"

"That's the latest fashion, you know," Carol advised. "Shirley Malone, my neighbor, found the pattern over at Bostwick's in Jamestown, so I borrowed it and made three dresses for Melinda. One has short sleeves and one has a different collar."

"You're a much better seamstress than I ever was. I'd have guessed this came right from J. C. Penney's," Vernice said with amazement in her voice. In contrast she wore an old-fashioned shirtdress, two broaches pinned on her collar. The cotton print hugged her well-rounded curves, the narrow belt nearly invisible under her full, heavy chest that met up with her bulging waistline.

"Grandma, look at me," Dean said, tugging on his white dress shirt, eyes begging to be noticed. His dark brown hair was combed neatly and parted in the middle. Concentrating on Melinda's invisible back zipper, Vernice failed to notice her youngest grandchild. "Grandma," Dean said again. His pudgy fingers held his shirt out in front. "Grandma . . ."

Vernice turned around in an exaggerated pivot. "Ooooh, look at you, Dean Allen," she said, enunciating each syllable. A visible layer of rouge and powder covered her wrinkled cheeks, but couldn't hide the sparkle in her eye. "Don't you look handsome! You're all growed up. Look at these dress pants, fancy leather shoes, starched shirt. My oh my. You ain't my baby anymore!" She squeezed his cheeks and Dean grinned from ear to ear, absorbing every ounce of his grandmother's love.

"He is too a baby," Kurt mumbled with a mischievous grin.

"Ignore him, Grandma," Melinda said, giving Kurt a quick shove. "Kurt wishes he was still the baby of the family so he could get all the attention."

"I'll have you know this grandma can have two babies," Vernice said, giving Kurt a tight squeeze. He giggled and promptly squirmed free, peering over Grady's shoulder. "Grandpa, Grady's got two aces."

Grady made a fist and reached for Kurt, who sprinted out of reach.

"Young man, you never tell what cards a man is holding in his hands," Clarence said in a playful growl. "You do that again and I'll put a knot on your head big enough for a calf to suck on."

"You'd have to catch me first!" Kurt announced, racing around the table until he knocked over an empty chair.

"Kurt Jacob, pick that up right now," Carol said, shutting off the kitchen lights.

"Mom, did you get my sweater?" asked Melinda.

"I saw it on the davenport," Vernice said.

Frank came in from the living room, a pack of Winstons showing through the front shirt pocket, his short black hair slicked back. "Let's go. Melinda, Kurt, get your coats on."

"Sixty points, Grady," Clarence said, turning up his cards. "Whatcha got?"

"Not enough, Grandpa," Grady said, sliding his cards across the smooth tabletop. "You got me again."

"Won't be the last time neither, Son." Clarence stood and roared in laughter. His worn gray trousers hung low on his narrow hips, held up by bold red suspenders.

"Good heavens, Grady, I forgot my head covering," Carol said in a panic, touching her hair. "I can't go to mass without it. Will you run up and get it for me? It's on the ironing board. I starched it when I pressed your shirts this morning." When the Vatican published the new Order of the Mass in 1970, Carol no longer wore a full veil to church but didn't feel right going without the smaller head covering. Vernice, on the other hand, declared she couldn't accept the modern interpretation and proudly wore her black veil made of Rebecca and Venice lace to mass every week.

"C'mon young'uns, let's head outside," Clarence suggested. "We'll get the car warmed up."

Grady raced up the stairs to an oversized closet at the end of the hall that Carol used as a sewing room. The Singer sewing machine was buried under scraps of fabric, partially sewn blouses, and Dean's jeans with holes in the knees, waiting to be mended. Harvest gold sunflowers climbed up the walls and slanted ceiling in a bold wallpaper that she'd found at Wensman's Gambles, this room the one place in the house where his mother's personality came to life. The tiny room radiated of her, the long hours she painstakingly pieced together dresses for Melinda, plus ones for herself.

Grady picked up the round doily-thing and hurried back down the steps. "Here you go," he said, handing the lace cloth to his mother.

His mom reached up and tenderly pushed back a wayward piece of his dark hair that had fallen across his forehead. A somber look crossed her face and she gently traced the scar that ran from his forehead to the tip of his nose. "I'll never forget how close we came to losing you that day." Her pale green eyes shimmered and Grady noticed a hint of tears. "Sometimes I look at you, Grady, and I see such a fine young man. I want you to know I'm proud of who you are." Her voice was soft and loving, and he had to lean in to catch her words.

The timing of the poignant moment caught him off guard, knowing his dad was waiting in the car. "Mom…"

"I know sometimes, well, your father, he can be a hard man to live with." She pulled her hand back and paused, covering her mouth. The simple gold band on her ring finger caught Grady's eye. "You're a good son, Graden Kramer," she said with a soft smile. "Don't you ever forget that." She turned, straightened her back, and walked toward the door.

A cold wind swept into the Buick LeSabre as the doors opened and the last two family members piled into the oversized sedan. "Dean, make room for your mother," Frank said. "Sit on Melinda's lap."

"Come here," Melinda said, patting her legs.

"What took so long?" Frank asked, making eye contact with Grady in the rearview mirror.

"That's okay; we'll be fine," Clarence said, patting his own lap. "Maybe Grandma should sit on my lap."

Vernice gasped while Melinda and Kurt giggled. "Don't be talkin' like that on the way to mass," she scolded. "In front of the kids?"

* * *

The Kramer family dutifully filed into the tenth pew on the right side of the new St. Peter's Catholic Church. The kids all attended catechism in the old St. Peter's Catholic Church on the block behind. Covered in dark lava scoria walls, it was nicknamed the Rock Church, built by Pierre Wibaux way back in 1895, the complete opposite of the buttery beige bricks on the modern version of St. Peter's.

Ding! Dong! Ding! Dong! The church bells echoed loudly in the front tower and the Order of Mass officially commenced. Father Shannon stood on the altar platform in an ankle-length black robe. "In the name of the Father, and of the Son, and of the Holy Spirit," he proclaimed in a loud voice.

"Amen," the congregation responded in unison, followed by the sign of the cross.

Father Shannon read aloud from the Old Testament in a voice so shaky Grady wondered if the old priest had been around since Moses came down from the mountain. "The word of the Lord," he said, and the congregation responded, "Thanks be to God." After a long pause, Father Shannon began the second reading, calling out the words of Scripture in a formal narrative and ending with "The word of the Lord," followed by the same mundane response, "Thanks be to God."

It was the same every week. Grady figured he could do it in his sleep. Sit, kneel, stand. Kneel again. Recite the proper response on cue. Not much different than his morning routines with Clara and Tillie, pretty much the same song and dance and about the same enthusiasm.

His eyes went down the row in front of him, familiar faces like Mrs. Pinnard, the retired school librarian who wore her hair in a bun so tight that if it ever unwound Grady was sure it could pull-start an auger engine. Old Mr. Kropp was over ninety and still drove to town every morning for coffee at the Palace Cafe. Tom and Theresa Schmitz and their seven kids, whose names all started with *T*, took up the whole fifth pew on the left side.

In Grady's humble opinion no one looked a bit interested in the "Holy Sacrifice of the Mass." Shells of bodies in robotic motions, detached from any external signs of joy or emotion.

Eyes lowered, expressions blank, yawns spreading down the second row. Where was God in all of this?

Grady spotted Jake Wensman sound asleep in the back pew, head cocked to the side, mouth wide open. Grady watched as Mr. Wensman put an arm around his son's shoulders and nudged him awake. If that had been Grady, he'd have gotten a sharp knuckle against his temple.

Grady had been twelve or thirteen before he realized other kids didn't get whipped as punishment. He about choked in disbelief the first time Jake told him he'd gotten a time-out.

"A time-out?" he asked. "What's that?"

"I have to go sit in my room," Jake explained.

"Yeah, but what was your punishment?"

"That was my punishment."

Grady shook his head, trying to understand. "You just go sit somewhere?"

"Yeah."

"You didn't get the belt or anything?"

The expression on Jake's face revealed his innocence. "No."

The discovery had hung in Grady's mind for weeks. He thought all kids got the belt or razor strap. All those times he'd gotten worked over—once a week, sometimes more—and Jake had only to sit in his room. Something about that didn't seem right.

The beatings had started as far back as he could remember, back when he was three or four, when they'd lived on the original Kramer farm site near Richardton, North Dakota, about twenty-five miles east of Dickinson. He never liked going back there to visit his uncle. Something about the old house, the worn linoleum floor, the limestone chicken coop, the damp storm cellar that always smelled like musty potatoes, all reminded him of a whipping, a beating, kneeling on wheat seeds or sometimes gravel, if they were outside.

And near as he could figure, his dad had never gotten whipped as a kid. This was something Frank Kramer devised on his own, an attempt to develop life skills in his kids, fundamental principles for his picture-perfect Catholic family to take forward in life. Trouble was, last time Grady'd seen the old place, the stones under the house were crumbling, leaving wide gaps along the foundation on both sides. It wouldn't be long before the whole thing would collapse into the earthen cellar beneath it. Some days, when his dad was on a drunken roll, his mom crying and upset, the kids scared what might happen next, he felt as though his family was on the edge of an abyss, about to plunge into a deep, dark pit and be lost forever.

At the close of mass, Grady knelt on the hard wooden rail and bowed his head along with everyone else. He folded his hands, closed his eyes, and came to a decision. *If my heavenly Father is anything like my earthly father, I'm in no hurry to get to heaven.*

CHAPTER SIX

Grady wasn't about to sit home on a Saturday night and watch his ol' man tie one on the minute they got home from mass. As soon as Frank poured himself a glass of whiskey, Grady gave his mom and grandma a kiss on the cheek and made his escape to Jeff Willis's place. He stood on the front porch, his navy parka unzipped. "Word is out," Grady said in a low voice. "The boys are back from Colorady!"

"Now you're talking!" Willie said, eyebrows raised. His blond hair reached his shoulders, parted in the middle from a small cowlick. He tucked his green plaid shirt into his Wranglers and motioned for Grady to come inside. "C'mon in a sec, I gotta grab my wallet." He was tall and broad, the Longhorn's best running back and captain of the football team. The senior class had thirty-six students to Grady's junior class of only twenty-nine. Many of his good friends were seniors, including Willie—Wibaux's newly crowned Homecoming King.

"Evening, Grady," Elaine Willis said from a comfortable perch on the living room davenport. She smiled at Grady, her honey brown hair wound tightly around rows of pink curlers.

Grady tipped his head. "Evening, Mrs. Willis."

"By the way," she said, pointing her crochet hook at Grady, "I heard what your dad did for Mrs. Steffens, fixing her car last week. Poor thing, she's been so worried about it with winter coming up. And he didn't charge her a thing. That was so nice of him to do that for her; you be sure to tell him we appreciate how much he does for her."

"I'll do that," Grady said with a nod.

"I've heard he helps out a few of the other widows around here."

Grady hesitated. After the last twenty-four hours it was hard for him to digest any compliments about his ol' man. "Yeah, I guess he does."

"Well, that's mighty good of him. I know Mrs. Steffens thinks the world of him." Her fingers continued to work the crochet hook up and down the V-pattern of the afghan. Skeins of yarn in variegated yellows, oranges, and browns covered the sofa cushions like autumn's prairie flowers. "What are you boys up to tonight?" she asked. Grainy color images of Buck Owens and Roy Clark a pickin' and a grinnin' in Kornfield Kounty flashed on the RCA console television in the corner.

"Oh, not much, Mrs. Willis. Probably ride around town, maybe stop for a shake or something."

She pulled the string of yarn and the skein tumbled onto the floor. "Have a good time and stay out of trouble, you hear?"

"We will," Grady said.

Willie rushed in and spun Grady around, pushing him toward the porch. "Bye, Mom!"

"See ya, Mrs. Willis," Grady said. As soon as they were out the door he added, "If I hear one more verse of 'Rocky Top' I'm gonna puke."

"Why do you think my dad's out in the shed. Let's go!"

Grady climbed behind the wheel of the Beast and promptly punched the button for KFYR. The last half of Three Dog Night's "Mama Told Me Not To Come" came on and he cranked up the volume. "I gotta get that country crap out of my head," Grady said in a loud voice, the music blasting through the front and back speakers. They picked up Wes Scheinberg in town and cruised the loop down First Avenue and Main Street three times before they spotted Dan Iverson's '67 Barracuda.

"There he is." Shiny and his curls hung over the seat back. "Pull a U-ey. Quick!"

"Geez, criminy, shout in my ear why don't ya!" Grady cranked the wheel, hand over hand, until the tires turned tight enough to make a 180-degree turn in front of the Methodist Church. "Maybe he's seen Kevin already."

Grady pressed the gas pedal, the tires squealing as he straightened the wheel. "Did he see us?"

"Yeah, he's pulling over," Willie said.

Grady pulled up next to Dan's forest green Plymouth 'Cuda and turned down the volume. "Hey, you seen K. T. and the Snyder boys yet?"

Tom Lorentz leaned forward in the passenger seat, riding shotgun with Dan. "Nothing like a cold-tasting Coors when you're lookin' down the barrel of a Saturday night!"

"Now you're talking!" Willie said.

"They're waiting for us down by the Conoco," Dan said.

"Time to get this show on the road," Grady said, revving the engine.

"Change of plans. North slab tonight. More privacy," Dan said. "Wouldn't want to give up a full case of Coors to the cops."

"You got that right!"

Dan pulled out and the tires on the Barracuda screeched for a quarter of a block. Grady kept the Beast right on his tail, both cars heading north of town. Beaver Creek started between

Wibaux and Baker in Montana and meandered north to the Little Missouri National Grassland and then further north to the Theodore Roosevelt National Park in North Dakota. When the snows melted each spring, the creek exploded into a raging river of currents that washed out the gravel road. To prevent that, the county had installed large concrete culverts where it crossed the winding creek, one six miles north of town and the other one three miles south of Wibaux. The rest of the year the culverts were nothing more than two concrete slabs away from the prying eyes of the law, an impromptu party place when winter's snow piled too deep to have keggers in the field.

Grady thought it was actually pretty along the slabs, especially in the summer and fall. Beaver Creek rushed northward, the cragged and crooked buttes in the backdrop, yellow warblers, meadowlarks, and robins serenading in song. A century earlier Pierre Wibaux had selected the Beaver Valley as the site for his ranch. The topography—deep draws and coulees, spring-fed holes with water, thickets of buffaloberry and chokecherry bushes, the sharp buttes, knolls capped with a thin layer of shaly sandstone—was ideal for the new range-stock industry in the northwest. Pierre Wibaux wasn't the only great man with the same forethought when he stuck his stake in 1883—twenty miles east a young man named Teddy Roosevelt ran the Maltese Cross and Elkhorn Ranches. The cattle kings had the indomitable spirit needed to tame the iron-hard land, performing the laborious duties of a cowboy, "sleeping and eating under the canopy of heaven."

Grady parked the Bel Air along the edge of the gravel road behind the Barracuda. Kevin stopped the Impala on the opposite side and popped the trunk. A dozen boxes with the famous red Coors label stared back at the boys. In a brown leather jacket and new blue jeans, Kevin waved a hand at his bounty. "Oh, man," Willie said, as though he'd been smitten by a love bug. "Just look at 'em."

The Coors Brewery in Golden, Colorado, was the hottest brewery in the country these days. Their distinctive tasting beer—brewed with the purest Rocky Mountain water—and limited distribution fueled cross-country road trips from people hooked on the beer's mystique, a pale lager nicknamed the banquet beer.

"Pass 'em out; let's get on with it," Tom said, taking a case from Kevin.

"Shiny, here's yours and Grady's," Kevin said.

Shiny pushed up the sleeves on his hooded sweatshirt and carried the Coors box to Grady's trunk while Kevin passed out the cases according to order.

"Hey, Shiny, throw me one," Grady said, raising his hands.

Shiny whipped a can toward him and Grady ducked to avoid getting hit in the face. "Damn!" he yelled.

"Sorry, man."

"Watch out, Shiny," Dan said, "or Grady'll have another scar on his pretty face."

"Shut up." Grady picked up the can and held it at arm's length, tapping the top before he popped it open.

"Guys, look at this!" Shiny said. "It's got the new push-button top. Far out!"

"Watch now," Jimmy said, demonstrating. "This tab is for venting and then you drink out of the bigger one." He took a big chug and wiped his mouth on the sleeve of his sheepskin-lined denim jacket. "We tested a few on the way home."

Grady copied Jimmy's demonstration and took a swig. "It *does* taste fresher, doesn't it?"

"Damn right it does," Kevin said. "These yellow bellies are the best. Worth every mile, I might add."

"Man, how long did it take to get down there?" Shiny asked.

"Seemed like forever going through Wyoming and back," Kenny said. "That's one boring drive." He had on a red baseball-style jacket with a Skelly's Truck Stop patch on the front—the gas station where both he and Jimmy worked.

"How would you know?" Jimmy said, knocking the stocking cap off Kenny's head. "You were sleepin' the whole damn way!"

"That's 'cause you made me sit in the back the whole damn way!" He picked his cap out of the gravel and brushed it off.

"Loser!" Jimmy said with a laugh.

"We timed it goin' down," Kevin said as the others gathered around him. "Took us flat-out six hours and twenty-seven minutes going down. Hit the first bar across the Colorado state line, didn't we, boys?" He tipped his beer at Jimmy and Kenny. "They're used to people coming from out of state and loading up. He was more'n happy to sell us twenty cases. Ain't it good to be eighteen!"

"Man, I'll go next time," Shiny said.

"Hey, Grady," Kevin said. "Pull the ol' Beast up here; we need some music." Grady moved the Bel Air forward a few yards to the slab. "Man, that's still a sharp car!" he said, a grin spread from ear to ear.

"Bet you wished you hadn't sold it!" Willie said.

"It didn't look that good when I had it," Kevin said, rubbing a hand on the side panel. "That ol' Grady's got the touch."

"She's lookin' good, ain't she?" Grady said with pride. He turned the parking lights on and slid onto the hood, swinging his legs over the side, his navy parka open.

Dan picked up a small rock and jiggled it in his hand. "Bet ya I can hit that boulder on the side, right there," he said, pointing at a dark gray shape with water rushing around it on both sides. "Who wants to bet? First try."

"No way!" Kevin ran down the slope and stood next to Dan, beer in hand.

"Watch." Dan unsnapped his jean jacket and arched his arm.

"How we gonna know if you hit it or not," Jimmy said. "It's too dark." He joined the others, swinging his cap in one hand.

"Dipshit, you'll hear it hit the rock or the water."

All eight boys lined up along the edge of the slab, rocks in hand, making one foolish bet after another.

"Hey, Iverson, how was detention yesterday?" Tom asked.

"Yeah," Grady said, chiming in. "I bet Mr. Kettle was pretty worked up."

"Naw," he said with a moan. "His bark is worse than his bite. I'm expecting an invitation for Thanksgiving dinner with the Kettle clan any day."

"In your dreams, Iverson," Tom said, and Dan roared in laughter.

"Headlights!" Shiny pointed up the road about a mile. "Think it's the cops?"

"Naw," Dan said, unconcerned.

"How do you know?" Shiny retreated halfway back to Grady's car.

"Well, for one thing, *dumb ass,*" Dan said, "he'd be coming from the other direction."

"Hey, remember last winter when Iverson stole the cop car and left it on the south slab?" Willie said.

"You're always in some kind of trouble, ain't ya?" Grady said to Dan.

"Yeah, but that time I didn't get caught." His eyes held a prankish sparkle in the reflection of the moonlight.

"Right on!" Grady said, giving him a high five.

"Make sure the beer is out of view!" shouted Jimmy. "Just in case. Sometimes ol' Mr. Roggenkamp gets worked up about kids hanging out here."

"Just look cool and they'll leave us alone," Kevin said, his frame silhouetted against the amber lighting.

"Yeah," Willie said in agreement. "If it looks like nothin's going on, we're good to go."

The boys watched as the pair of headlights approached. Grady recognized the sound of the rocker arm clicking. Cougars were known to leak exhaust off the manifold on the number six cylinder on the 351 Cleveland engine—one of the things he'd learned from Jake Wensman this fall. "No worries!" he called. "It's Jake."

"Open the trunk then," Tom said, tossing an empty can through the open window of the Beast into the front seat. "I need another one."

Shiny responded with a prolonged, six-second belch. He patted his stomach and burped again. "Aaah, that feels better."

Jake Wensman eased the '72 Cougar onto the slab and rolled down his window. "What's a guy gotta do to get a yellow belly around here?"

"Park it and pop your trunk," Kevin said, pulling out another box. "I'll give you a whole damn case."

"So, what happened with the cop car again?" Shiny asked.

"Man, haven't you heard this story?" said Willie. "Dan, tell him how you outsmarted ol' Pistol Pete!"

"Hold on, I gotta take a leak," Kenny yelled. He unzipped his jeans and turned toward the brush.

"What's up, guys?" Jake asked as he popped open a Coors.

"Dan's gonna tell his cop car story," Willie said. "You're just in time."

Dan whipped his head to the side and his long bangs fell back. He leaned against the Beast as the others gathered around. "You know ol' Pistol Pete has a reputation where he don't go looking for trouble. The old man wants to put his time in and go home without working up a sweat."

"I swear he's so old he's probably got moss growin' on him!" Kenny said, tucking himself in and zipping up.

Dan looked around at the circle of guys. "We've all seen him leave the cop car running in front of city hall in the winter. Course, he does that so he can sit in the lobby of the library where it's nice and warm, watching through that big glass window and still keep an eye on it. Well, one night last winter I swear it was damn near twenty below. I'd gotten a ride into town and spent a few hours in the Silver Dollar."

"Leave it to Wibaux to have a bar right next to city hall," Kevin said, shaking his head.

"Anyway, my ride took off and I came out of the bar real late and didn't have a way to get home." A low laugh started at the back of Dan's throat.

"You didn't!" Shiny said.

"How come you're the only idiot who doesn't know this story?" Jake asked, giving Shiny a shove.

"It seemed the perfect solution to my problem. I mean, I needed a ride home and there sits the cop car, idling, all nice and warm. Just like ol' Pistol Pete had left it for me. I glanced through the windows at city hall and couldn't see hide nor hair of him, so I slid real easy-like into the front seat. Course, I made this decision courtesy of a few too many brews," he said with a laugh, "and gave myself a ride home, thanks to our own Wibaux P.D."

"What'd you do with the squad?" Shiny asked.

"Parked it on the south slab."

"Oh, man!" Tom said, admiration oozed from his voice.

"It had just snowed, but luckily I had enough sense to think about my tracks, so I walked up the road to the next quarter section and cut through the field. They never did find out who did it," Dan said with a sense of well-deserved pride.

"Course, Pistol Pete comes out and the cop car's gone," Willie said, picking up the story for Dan, "so he had to call Bunny to help bail him out."

"Oooh, I bet the sheriff wasn't too happy about that!"

"We heard the two of them drove all over the county half the night looking for the squad car. Finally found it on the slab," Dan said.

"Course, we all knew who'd taken it, but no one told," Willie added. "Cops never did figure it out."

"I swear," Kevin said, taking a long drag on his Marlboro, "ol' Pistol Pete couldn't find his way out of a paper bag without somebody showin' him the way." Smoke curled out of the corners of his mouth and trailed up his sideburns on either side. He sat stoically on the hood of the Beast, flicking ashes into the blackness that surrounded them.

Grady lit up his own heater, grinning. He'd heard Dan's story a half-dozen times and it made him laugh every time. He sucked in a long breath on the filtered end and exhaled into the night air. A full moon inched its way above the creek and coulees in a slow, gradual climb, turning the sky a myriad of dark blue velour. Moonlight hid heaven's stars, casting wayward shadows of willow scrub across the gravel road. The boys' laughter mingled with the rhythmic rushing water, echoing along the bends of the riverbank. Grady flicked his ashes, feeling more at ease on the slab than he ever did at home.

CHAPTER SEVEN

Grady picked up Naomi after school and drove back to Wibaux to meet up with Dan and Marsha. They cruised up and down Main Street Wibaux, out past the city park with the twice-life-size statue of Pierre Wibaux. Legend had it Wibaux renamed the town back in 1895 when he ordered his cowboys to surround the town and not let anyone enter or leave until they signed a petition changing it from Mingusville to Wibaux.

Grady drove past the school yard with the swings where he and Naomi often sat and talked, through the railroad underpass, and back past Helvick's Grocery and the Wibaux Dancehall where he and Naomi had met.

"We can try down by the grain elevator, in case they went in the Davis Addition."

"May as well," Naomi said, and then added with a giggle, "I like riding around together."

"Me too." They sat side by side, her slender body molded perfectly against his. He drove down First Avenue to the Wibaux

Co-op Elevator and turned around in the large gravel lot, the office building dwarfed by the twin wooden cribbed grain elevators that stood on either side.

He waited for a cattle truck to turn in at the stockyards across the road. During the late 1800s, Wibaux was a major shipping point for ranchers that needed to get their sheep and cattle to the stockyards in Chicago. Sets of corrals and barns were still positioned next to the railroad, now used on a smaller scale.

They passed by the old Drake Livery Stable, the front covered in two-by-three-foot boards that displayed each rancher's cattle brand, insignias that carried deep meaning to the families in Wibaux County. The blackened symbols burned into the wood were visual tributes to the generations of ranchers that worked the open range through the good years and bad.

"Maybe they ran over to Glendive. Marsha saw a pair of bell-bottom jeans at Bostwick's that she's been dying to buy," Naomi said. "And lucky her, she got paid ten dollars for babysitting at Tabery's last night. *Ten* dollars! It's not fair she always gets what she wants."

"Well, forget them. Let's go have a shake at Beckel's. I think Mom's still working."

"Good idea." Naomi grinned and squeezed his arm. "I'm up for that."

Grady parked in front of the Stockman Bar with its famous longhorn STOCKMAN BAR sign that stuck out perpendicular to the two-story brick building and walked a half block to the drugstore. A metal bell attached to the door handle jingled as they walked through the double entry into Beckel's Drugstore, catching the attention of Donna Sorenson at the front register.

"Afternoon, Grady!" Her full-throated voice bellowed up to the embossed tin ceiling panels. She emptied a box of

Christmas candy into a display case, her navy wool skirt exposing legs that were as wide and stiff as fence posts.

"Hey, Donna. Is Mom still here?"

"Yup, she's back there," she said, pointing to the lunch counter. "Hi, Naomi."

"Hi, Mrs. Sorenson."

"Say, you be sure to tell your mom our church is having our annual *lefse* sale again. Last year we made twenty-five hundred pieces and sold every last one of 'em."

Wow," Naomi said, tucking her hands in her jacket pockets. "That's a lot of *lefse*."

"I don't get why people are so crazy about smashed up potatoes that are flattened and fried," Grady said.

"It's not just the *lefse*," Donna said, shaking her finger at Grady, "it's all about the butter and cinnamon sugar or ligonberry that you spread on top." She smacked her lips and gave a hearty laugh. "Grady, you bringing Naomi to the big doin's at the Shamrock on New Year's?"

"Wouldn't miss it," Grady said.

"They're having a live band this year," Donna said. "I bet the whole town will show up."

"Probably everyone from Beach will too," Naomi said.

Grady and Naomi meandered down the souvenir aisle. The old wooden floor creaked beneath their feet, echoing the rustic charm in the century-old drugstore. "Look, Grady," Naomi said. "Who would honestly buy this?" She pointed to a plastic Santa and sleigh with *Wibaux, Montana*, painted on the side.

"Hey, Mom," Grady said as they neared the dining counter. "Can me and Naomi get a chocolate shake?"

Carol turned her head as she poured a decanter full of water into the coffeemaker. "Naomi and I," she said, correcting him.

"Yeah, that," Grady said with a grin.

"Hey, Naomi," Carol said with a smile. She dried her hands on a ruffled apron. "My, it's good to see you again. How's your Mom doing?"

"She's doing really good, Mrs. Kramer."

"Did I hear she had gallbladder surgery?"

"She thought she might have to, but it turned out it she didn't need it." Naomi unzipped her jacket. "She's back to her old self."

"One shake and two straws, same as usual?"

Naomi nodded. "Yup." Grady sat down on a red vinyl stool next to Naomi and propped his feet on the ledge.

"My treat today," Carol said. "I'm so glad you kids stopped by." She turned around and grabbed a stainless steel container to make the ice cream treat. "You just missed Melinda and a couple of her friends." She wiped her hands on a white towel before connecting the cup to the sleeve.

"Oh, shoot," Naomi said. "I haven't seen her since football ended."

"Basketball starts up pretty soon, I suppose," Carol said, flipping the switch. The *whrrr* of the machine hummed in the background.

Grady recognized Henry Johnston, the retired mailman, take a stool down at the end. He waved a hand to catch Carol's attention. "Got some fresh coffee in that pot, Carol?" he asked. The bill on his John Deere cap couldn't hide the black crow wings in a feathered row above his eyes.

"You know I do, Henry." Carol smiled and picked up the pot. "Here you go," she said, pouring the hot coffee. "You want a menu today?"

"Piece of that blueberry pie is what I want," he said, pointing to the dessert case.

"Coming right up," she said.

Carol set the tall frosty glass with two straws sticking out of the blended ice cream in front of Grady and Naomi. "Now, which one of your sisters is dating Jimmy Snyder?"

"It *was* Marsha, but she's dating Dan Iverson now," Naomi said.

"Speaking of the Snyder boys, did you hear what Jimmy and his brothers did?" Grady asked, holding back a laugh.

"What?" Naomi asked in a curious tone.

"Wait one second." Carol opened the glass dessert case and cut a generous piece of pie—the rich blueberry filling oozing out on both sides—and handed it to Henry. "Okay," she said, folding her arms.

"You know Jimmy's sister Francine got married last Saturday, right?"

"Yeah."

"Jimmy and his three younger brothers were all in the wedding party and they'd rented tuxes, right?" Grady burst into laughter again. "Sunday morning all four of them did their chores with their tuxes on. Can you believe that?"

"Oh, lordy, them boys!" Carol said, clapping her hands. "And Jimmy, he's a shyster, that one!"

Naomi giggled. "That's too funny."

"Mr. Snyder claimed the cows gave an extra milk can full that morning," Grady said. "Said they got their money's worth out of them."

"Where'd they get the tuxes?" Carol asked, still laughing.

"You know Francine, she's spoiled rotten, being the only girl. She made them go all the way to Bismarck for everything, Glendive and Dickinson weren't good enough."

"Land sakes, can't you just picture them in the barn dressed up like that? Oh, my!" Carol leaned against the counter and drew a long breath, a tissue tucked under her watchband. "Uffda, it's been busy today. But that's good, keeps me on my toes."

Naomi sucked on her straw. "Mmm, Mrs. Kramer, this is nummy. Thank you so much."

"My pleasure, Naomi. You and Grady can stop and get one every day, if you want."

"Thank you; that's sweet of you."

"Maybe more selfish than sweet. Otherwise I hardly see the boy!" Carol looked up as Mr. Beckel came out of the tiny office carved out of a storage room along the back wall. "Did you remember to order that fixture we need for the baked goods?" Carol asked Mr. Beckel. "We gotta keep our mornin' bunch happy; they don't want their caramel rolls getting dried out."

"Oh, that's right," he said, putting a finger to his temple. "What would I do without you, Carol? Thanks for reminding me. My goodness, is that Grady under all that hair?"

"Hard to see his face some mornings, let me tell you," Carol said, studying Grady. "This is his girlfriend, Naomi Braden."

"You must be from Beach?" Mr. Beckel asked.

"Yup." Naomi nodded.

"Did you play football this year, Grady?"

"No . . ."

"Sure looks like you could. You got some good-sized shoulders on you, Son," he said, grabbing hold of Grady's bicep.

Grady laughed. "Aw, that's just from baling hay and digging postholes for Malones."

"Maybe you oughta think about it for next year." He tipped his head. "Please excuse me, I have to pick up the missus at the church. The Methodists are having their annual bazaar . . ." He snuck a quick look to the front and lowered his voice. "And they can't be outdone by the Lutherans and their *lefse*, you know. There's one lesson I learned a long time ago—don't keep the missus waiting!" He made a worried face and waved good-bye. "See you, kids."

"Don't let him fool you," Carol said in a hushed voice. "He dotes on her hand and foot. That woman's got it better than Betty Ford herself, living in that big ol' fancy White House!"

The bell *jingled* as Mr. Beckel went out the front doors and two bowlegged leathered ranchers strode through the center aisle and took a seat at the counter.

"Whoops, excuse me, kids." She grabbed the coffeepot and put on her best smile.

Grady sipped the last of the shake. He twirled to the right and his knee bumped Naomi's leg. Their eyes locked and Naomi smiled. He studied her eyes, remembering the first time he had seen her at the sock hop. He had felt it right away: a heart connection. It was the only way he knew to describe it. She was standing next to another girl from Beach that night who was outwardly more beautiful, yet she had nowhere near the radiance of Naomi. The other girl had a superficial beauty: shallow, phony. Naomi was the real deal; he could see it in her eyes—a warmth, genuine sincerity. Just like now—and he loved spending time with her. When Naomi smiled it was as though she held a deep secret, and Grady wanted to know every single thought inside her pretty head.

"You okay?" she whispered.

He nodded. "Perfect."

Grady glanced at his mom, serving up two plates of hot meatloaf sandwiches for the ranchers. Naomi reached over and squeezed his hand out of view from the adults. Her skin felt silky soft, and he gently wrapped his fingers around hers, intertwining them together. If he could, he would freeze this moment in time.

CHAPTER EIGHT

With one flip of the calendar, November disappeared into the pages of history and December took over with the force of Old Man Winter. Temperatures dropped and snow fell from the sky in feet rather than inches. Locals did what they could to adjust and settled in for another long winter. The fall harvest work was done; hunting season was over, animals butchered and in the freezer.

There was far less work to do outdoors, which Grady didn't mind, but it also meant his dad had more time to drink and carouse. Grady still had his part-time job at the Conoco in town, which gave him enough money for gas and taking Naomi to the Bijou Theatre in Beach once in a while. Grady, Melinda, Kurt, and Dean had signed up with the youth group from St. Peter's to help package food boxes and socks and mittens for Christmas gifts for poor kids, the *really* poor ones. Grady didn't consider too many folks around Wibaux as rich, but there were a few people who had next to nothing, including some from the

Northern Cheyenne Indian reservation out by Lame Deer. The entire youth group spent Sunday afternoon packing boxes at the church in Glendive with plans to stop at the indoor minigolf afterward.

Grady didn't feel like sticking around for minigolf and asked Mrs. Malone to give Mindy, Kurt, and Dean a ride home. He stomped his boots to get the snow off, and before he could hang his coat on the hook, his dad's voice boomed from the living room.

"Grady! Kurt!" Frank hollered. "Get in here!"

Grady's guard went up the instant he heard his father's tone. "What's up, Dad?" he asked, walking into the living room.

"Couple a Dieter's cows got out. You and Kurt better get out there and get 'em in before Dieter comes out to get the rent." Empty beer bottles stacked by the recliner solidified the image forming before Grady's eyes. His blue work shirt was untucked, the top few buttons undone. No doubt he'd gone right from the scales to the bar and came home primed.

"Kurt's not home."

"Where the hell is he? I told your mother I'd sic you kids on them cows as soon as you got home." He didn't wait for an answer. "Carol!" he yelled and then said to Grady, "Why ain't he with you?"

Carol came out of their bedroom; her slender fingers gripped a pillowcase and her eyes held a worried look. "What's the matter? Are you home early?"

"All the others stayed to play minigolf and eat dinner. I didn't feel like sticking around."

"Who the hell said they could do that?" Frank stood up and staggered a step, grabbing the back of the chair. He thrust an empty bottle at Carol. "Huh?"

"I told you this morning the kids would be gone all afternoon. Remember?" She folded and refolded the pillowcase in her hands. "Besides, it's not very often they get to play minigolf. It's their reward for volunteering with the youth group," she explained in short breaths. Grady watched her self-worth evaporate with each word.

"Well, ain't that just great." Frank's face had that look of drunken meanness that went hand in hand with his ornery moods. "Now what, huh?"

"I can go without Kurt." Grady wished now he'd stayed in Glendive. "I'll bet they're in the big draw just north of Malone's water tank, trying to get out of the wind."

"What are you—sixteen or six?" He motioned Grady toward the back door and his voice took on a raw edge. "You need two people in case you get stuck. Don't you even know that much? If they did go north, we're gonna be in some deep snow. Get out there and chain up the pickup. Put three on."

Grady knew that meant he wanted a tire chain on each rear wheel and only one on the front wheels to control steering on the side hills. The thought of heading out with his dad when he was like this stiffened his body into concrete.

"You gonna take all night, dumb ass? Them chains ain't gonna get on by themselves!"

Bristling with anger, Grady forced his legs to move. His mom followed him to the back porch to layer up in boots and coveralls. "Listen now, you be careful out there," she said, handing him his gloves after he laced his boots. "Don't go slipping off the road; some of those draws are pretty steep."

"It's okay, Mom."

Frank came up behind Carol and pointed a finger in her face. "If Dieter shows up to get his money, you tell him to come and see me. You're not to talk to him, do you understand? I don't want him in this house if I'm not here." His voice escalated and his face turned a darker shade of red with each word. "You're probably sleepin' with him anyway, aren't you?"

Carol gasped. "Frank! No!" She shook her head defiantly, dropping the pillowcase. "Why would you say that? When I took my wedding vows I meant every word and I've kept them. And I will . . . till death do us part."

Frank folded his arms across his chest, glaring at Carol. "I bet you're sleeping with him. That's why he's willing to get the rent late." His tone turned nasty and he continued, "Aren't you! You're sleepin' with him behind my back!"

"That's a bunch of crap, Frank Kramer, and you know it!"

"Sure, that's what you're telling me," he said, nodding. His face held a dark, sinister look that Grady knew all too well. "I know better. I seen him looking at you . . . and you looked right back!"

"Stop it!" she cried, pressed up against the kitchen counter. "I won't hear of it!"

"Dad!" Grady shouted. "Let's go before it gets dark."

Frank stumbled around the table and pushed a chair out of his way. "You're not gonna find the damn cattle standin' in here!" he shouted at Grady, nodding toward the door. "Get on with it!" He reached for his insulated coveralls, leaning into the wall for support.

Grady retrieved the chains from the machine shed and put them on the tires in five minutes flat. He tossed two scoop shovels in the back end of the Jimmy in case they needed to dig out of a snowdrift. Frank climbed behind the wheel and Grady took the passenger seat; both doors slammed shut in unison. "We'll have to go around to the north side of Malone's pasture and come in from the back," he said, turning down the driveway.

Recent blasts of snow had turned the range into a dirty white windswept landscape the locals called *snirt*: snow mixed with dirt. The days were at their shortest, pitch dark by four-thirty in the afternoon. Drifts formed in ribbonlike rows of smooth geometric patterns, curled and turned like ocean waves frozen in time. Brown tips of prairie grass stuck through in spots, daring to defy December's forceful winds.

"I saw 'em standing in that low spot next to Malone's fence this morning," Frank said. "We can start back there."

Grady exhaled a long breath. His dad had known all day the cows were out but he waited for him and Kurt to get home. The lazy drunken bum! He remembered a couple of times last summer Dieter hired Frank to fix fence, only to stop out and find out he'd made Grady and Kurt do all the work. Grady overheard Dieter and Frank have it out in the barn afterward. Dieter told his dad it wasn't right how hard he worked his boys, and his dad told Dieter it was none of his blankety-blank business.

Frank drove to the next quarter section road and turned east, the same windswept view over each rise. "Grady, I didn't tell you . . ." A deep laugh escaped his throat and his mood suddenly changed.

Grady bit his lip. "What?"

"I had time to run over to Beach yesterday after my shift," he said with a snicker. "She doesn't start work until four o'clock. When she knows I'm coming she'll lounge around with this li'l see-through black—"

"Dad!" Grady leaned forward, pointing out the side window into the barren landscape. "I think I saw 'em."

Frank hit the brakes and the truck fishtailed to a cockeyed stop. "Where?"

"Guess not," he said, leaning back again. "Must a been a muley."

Irritated, Frank punched the clutch and shifted into first gear, the chains fighting to find traction. He followed the fence line another half mile, loose snow blowing across the narrow road, forced now to go much slower. "Keep your eyes peeled." He reached inside his coveralls and pulled out a paper bag, glass clinking. "Want a beer? I got two of 'em."

"Naw," Grady answered, staring out the frost-coated window. Sometimes after baling hay in the dead heat of summer, Frank would bring Grady with him to the Silver Dollar to throw down a few cold ones. The first time Old Jack the bartender knew Grady was only fifteen, but he figured if Grady was with his dad, there wasn't much he could do about it. Course, his dad said if Bunny, Wibaux's county sheriff, came in, he was to slide his bottle down to him and Bunny would look the other way. Cold beer tasted pretty good on a bristling hot summer day or when hanging with the boys, but not here, not now.

Frank guzzled a good third of the bottle and let out a long sigh. "Well, they ain't back here," he said, wiping his chin. "May as well turn this thing around."

"Wait," Grady said, sitting up straight. "Look over there."

"Where?"

"Right there," he said, pointing to the hoofprints in the ditch on his side.

"Yup, I see 'em." Frank shifted into second gear and busted the squared front end of the Jimmy through a deep snowdrift. The prevailing winter wind was out of the northwest, so the deepest snow collected in drifts on the north sides of the draws. "I can't take the truck any farther or we'll get stuck," he said, slipping the knob into neutral. He cut the engine, looking out the windshield. "Better walk down through there and get 'em back this way. Then we'll push 'em home with the truck."

Grady zipped up the top of his coveralls and pulled on a stocking cap. The strong northwest winds nearly knocked him to the ground the minute he opened the door. No wonder the steers wandered way back here to get out of the wind. Maybe they weren't as dumb as he thought.

"This way," Frank called, pulling down the flaps of his wool cap.

In the late afternoon shadows, the long draw looked as if a giant claw had come down and gouged the earth in a strange crooked row. A thin layer of snow whipped across the frozen buttes like a swift river. The biting snow and wind stung Grady's cheeks as he trudged alongside his father. With one step, his boot

93

stayed on top of the snow's crust, the next one his weight pushed his leg right through the drift, a constant seesaw effect that made it difficult to walk.

From the top of the ridge he could see a fair distance, and their yard light caught his eye. He saw headlights on the frontage road and his gut churned. He hoped it wasn't Dieter coming out to get the rent. If his dad found out Dieter had stopped while they were out there, who knew what would happen. His dad might go off on Dieter again and they'd be kicked out of their house. Or maybe he'd go off on his mom. Once, Grady heard him accuse her of sleeping with Mr. Beckel, saying that was why she got treated special at the drugstore. He couldn't figure out what made him accuse her of doing the very thing he was doing behind her back. It made no sense; she would *never* cheat on him.

The blowing snow hid the topography and it was difficult to gauge the distance in the bursts of whiteouts. Twilight turned the sky and ground a bluish gray of ghostly silhouettes. He could almost hear his mother's words echo in the howling wind.

I made a vow, till death do us part . . .

I made a vow . . .

Grady figured the cattle should be right below them in the draw. They walked around a patch of brush and within a few yards the hoofprints narrowed into a single lane going into the draw. Grady fell back, forced now to track behind his father's long steps. His right boot fell directly in his father's footprint and he shuddered.

He would *never* follow in his father's footsteps. *Never.* Grady moved off the natural path to the icy slanted sides of the draw in order to avoid his father's boot prints. And then it hit him, like a frigid blast of ice and snow. What if that voice had been wrong? What if he should have squeezed the trigger?

PART II

CHAPTER NINE

Billings, Montana, 1976

Mr. Steinar strolled the aisles of the classroom, clipboard and pen in hand. "Okay, gentlemen, here are your work orders for today. Bill and Jim, you've got a '71 Ford Galaxie that needs an alignment. Jake and Grady, you boys will be on the Plymouth Duster; it needs a brake job, front and back. Steve and Drew, you get the Chevy pickup . . ." He rattled off the entire list of scheduled repairs.

The school offered townsfolk from Billings an economical way to get their cars fixed. Customers only had to pay for parts, and the labor was provided courtesy of the students.

"C'mon, Grady," Jake said, hopping up from his desk. "Shop time!"

Grady shut his notebook and followed Jake into the shop. So far, the auto mechanics course at Eastern Montana Vocational Center had been a perfect fit. He liked it because they studied each topic in class in the morning and then went right out and worked on it, hands-on. Even better, his high school buddy Jake Wensman had signed up for the same course and they were shop partners. When Grady had arrived in late August, he thought he knew a ton about fixing cars after all the work he'd done on the Beast, but he soon discovered there was a lot more he didn't know and he was eager to learn.

His ol' man had given him a whopping forty-two dollars at his graduation ceremony back in May as an official send-off. "Let me know how it works out," were his parting words. Not surprising, his mom had been the one to loan him the $285 for the auto mechanics tuition. Grady had saved up enough money working on Malone's ranch and the Conoco to cover his books and dorm expenses. The technical school had an agreement with Eastern Montana College that allowed their students to room in the college dorms. Wes Scheinburg had signed up for the refrigeration and air conditioning course and was Grady's roommate. The three Wibaux grads from the Class of '76—Grady, Jake, and Shiny—had been in Billings just shy of four weeks.

Grady and Jake pulled out their entry-level toolboxes: six drawers and a top lid in Sears's famous battleship gray. Grady's was still pretty empty, but each week a rep from Mac Tools stopped by with a line of products for the eager new students. Grady and Jake decided it made the most sense to each buy different tools and trade back and forth. Last week Grady bought a set of end wrenches with a box end and open end and Jake bought a twelve-volt test light.

Grady and Jake wheeled their toolboxes to their lab station and eyed the stop-sign red Plymouth Duster. "Nice car, huh?" said Jake, eyebrows raised.

"Not bad." Grady wiped his hands on his blue pleated Dickies work pants. In one sense the uniform was kinda dorky, but when he put it on in the morning he felt official, the real deal.

"You wanna do the front first?" Jake asked.

"Yeah, let's start on the disc brakes," Grady said, lifting the hood. "Throw me a three-eighths-inch Allen wrench, will ya?"

"Here it comes," he said, tossing it over.

Grady grabbed the long tool and tucked it in his back pocket. "Throw me a beater too."

Jake grabbed the three-pound hammer from his toolbox and lobbed it over to Grady. The shop was noisy, but in a good way. Constant shouting between teams, wrenches clanging on the concrete floor, air ratchets going off, *aat-aaat-aat, aat-aat-aaat*.

Grady and Jake took the calipers off the front disc brakes first, pulled the rotor off, and put it on the work bench to measure with a micrometer. From there they could determine how much meat was left on the brakes. "Check the specs," Grady said. "I'm not sure how far we can turn the rotor down on this one."

Jake flipped the pages of their guidebook until he found the right one. "I dunno. Looks pretty thin to me. You better scrap it out."

"Tell Mr. Steinar. He'll have to call the owner before we can make a parts run for a new rotor."

When class ended at four o'clock, Grady and Jake had completed a full brake job on the Duster, back and front, with new wheel bearings, shocks, and ball joints. Grady stood at the large industrial sink and pumped two squirts of Gojo hand cleaner soap into his hands. Between shop at school and working part-time at K-Mart's garage, black grease clung in the tiniest of creases of his fingers no matter how hard he scrubbed.

Living in Billings was a world away from tiny Wibaux—and Grady loved it. There was so much to do he couldn't get bored if he tried. Most bars had live bands every weekend, and if he didn't like the music in one place, he could shoot pool or go to the next one. He could walk into a store and buy something off the shelf rather than ordering it from a catalog and waiting for it to come in the mail like they did in Wibaux.

Parties, too, were in a whole different league. Every time he turned around there was a stash of mind-altering substances like pot, speed, crank, or crystal meth ready at the asking. Grady tried pot a few times, but he'd made up his mind that he wasn't about to mess things up by doing any hard stuff.

Life in a dorm was nothing like he'd anticipated. The room was small and cramped compared to the old farmhouse. Shiny proved to be a messy roommate, leaving fast-food wrappers and dirty clothes everywhere. On top of that, he stuffed his mouth with snacks half the night and snored louder than their old Hampshire brood hog. Sounds from other rooms penetrated the thin walls, guys ran down the hall at all hours, arguments broke out by the pay phone. Some days it was nonstop commotion and drama.

Since most of the guys were eighteen, there was no shortage of booze. Even better, they could drink legally in the bars. Grady had turned eighteen on August nineteenth and moved to Billings with Jake and Shiny the next day. He loaded his clothes, boots, toolbox, his favorite eight-track tapes, sheets, and a pillow into the Beast and headed west. His mom handed Grady a paper sack filled with sandwiches and chocolate chip cookies for the long drive. With tears clouding her emerald eyes, she said, "You be careful now. Write and let me know how it goes." He felt a stab in his heart, knowing how hard it was for her to turn her oldest son over to the big, wide world.

His mom found out about his dad's carousing during the spring of Grady's junior year in high school. The fighting had gotten worse and they agreed to call it quits. The night they sat down and told the kids about the divorce, Grady was devastated.

The way he'd been brought up, divorce was a bad thing. It sounded earth-shattering, terrifying. Was it his fault? Had he failed his mom, let her down? If he'd been a better son, would his dad have not wandered, not drank all the time? He'd bolted out of his chair and took off on foot into the fields behind the farm. Soon, the other kids joined him, confused and upset, blaming themselves.

His fears were realized, the foundation finally crumbled and his family sank into the deep dark pit, never to be whole again. It didn't take long for Grady and the younger kids to realize it was the best thing that could have happened. Their dad moved into the old Franklin Hotel in Wibaux, a rundown building turned into efficiency apartments. Living in town meant he could walk to the local bars after his shift at the scales. Without having to worry about driving home, he drank all the more. By the time Grady had finished high school, his dad had earned the disgraceful title of town drunk. It humiliated him every time he thought about it. All the other kids in school had a regular dad. Not a perfect dad, just a regular dad. The kind that worked hard, provided for their families, kept a job. And loved their kids. How come he'd gotten the short end of that straw?

His mom, bless her heart, found a house to rent in town. With head high, she kept her job at the drugstore and did her best to raise the kids. Dieter hired someone else to run the farm.

Only five weeks into living on his own, Grady found himself pinched for money. He tried calling Naomi at least once a week, but after paying off his first phone bill he knew he had to cut back. He wrote to her every other day during the first few weeks, but between school and working at K-Mart's Auto Center, some days he flat-out ran out of time. He promised her he'd come home once a month, but the drive from Billings to Wibaux was 257 miles and now he had to pay full price for gas at the pump like everyone else. Gone were the days of bulk gas prices on the farm. But there wasn't a day when he didn't think about her, wishing he could see her pretty face.

* * *

The last week in October, Grady counted up his change and decided he had enough to make it home. Trouble was, there was no quick way to get there. The full distance across Montana, east to west, border to border, was nearly equal to the distance from New York City to Chicago. He took off in the Beast as soon as Friday's lab session ended, thankful for a break from Shiny's annoying habits. The worst stretch was between Miles City and Glendive. He tapped the steering wheel in rhythm to "Honky Tonk Woman" by the Rolling Stones and pressed down on the gas pedal, thoughts of Naomi's blue eyes pulling him home.

He missed talking to her, especially on the swings at the city park in Wibaux. They'd probably hung out there a hundred times or more, side by side, talking, sharing ideas for their future. He had so much to tell her about school and the dorm and Billings. He couldn't wait to hold her hand, feel the silkiness of her skin. And even better, when they were alone, feel her lips pressed against his.

Thanksgiving was only four weeks away and he planned to come home again for the holiday. His mom's rented house had a good comfortable feel, one that came from being with family. The younger kids were doing better; Melinda was a junior now. He stopped in Wibaux long enough to throw his stuff on his bed, give his mom a kiss and a hug, and rush over to Beach to pick up Naomi. He laughed out loud, wondering how many times he'd made the drive between Beach and Wibaux, most times at breakneck speed. It didn't matter—7 miles or 257 miles—he'd do whatever it took to see her.

"Man, it's good to be home," Grady said, leaning against the yellowed vinyl cushion. He and Naomi were cozied up in a booth at Skelly's Truck Stop off the interstate in Beach, a burger basket in front of each of them. He was tired, but sitting next to her made every mile worthwhile.

"How's school going?" Naomi asked, taking a sip of her Coke. She looked as cute as ever, her long dark hair spilling over the shoulders of her pale blue sweater. He adored the gentle curves of her delicate nose and small mouth.

"Great. Did I tell you I'm one of the parts runners?"

"I think you wrote about it in your letter."

"See, the shop needs certain parts each day, depending on which cars are scheduled to come in and what needs fixing. Well, not everybody has a car, so I signed up to be a parts runner, even had to sign a contract," he said with a bit of pride.

"Uh-huh," Naomi said, listening as she ate her fries, one by one.

"I get to make the rounds, usually two or three places each morning. Jake goes with me most times." Grady took another bite of his cheeseburger.

"Is it different than high school?"

Grady nodded. "Big time. I mean, we're actually working on people's cars, fixing brake lines, water pumps, whatever. It's cool."

"How about the teachers?"

"It was funny—almost the first day me and Jake figured out which instructors were either gonna be hardnosed or pushovers. They all wear these white lab coats with the Eastern Montana Vo-Tech patch on the front. But right from the start we all liked Mr. Steiner the best; he's a good guy."

"How's it going with Shiny?"

"Oh, man, that dude is the biggest slob!"

"Really? I would have never guessed that about him."

"He's a good guy, but man, some days I could just choke the kid. Dirty clothes everywhere, smelly ol' McDonald's bags with stale French fries, pop cans—you name it. It's ten times worse than sharing a room with Kurt and Dean!"

Naomi giggled between bites of her burger.

"Want another Coke?" the waitress asked.

"Huh?" Grady asked, fighting back a yawn. "Yeah, sure." He turned his attention back to Naomi. "Anyway, I gotta go see Mr. Malone while I'm home."

"What for?"

"In our last semester we get to rebuild an engine, so I have to find one to work on. Malones have this old beat-up pickup parked behind their machine shed. It's perfect, a '67 two-barrel 283 Chevy. I spied it last summer when I worked out there. I hope they don't want more than a few bucks for it 'cause I'm running low on cash."

"So, what will you do with it?"

Grady sighed and reached for Naomi's hand. "We get to rebuild the engine," he repeated for her benefit.

"Then what?"

"I can put it in a car," he said with enthusiasm. "Won't that be cool?"

"I guess," she said. "Oh, did you hear? Dan and Marsha are engaged. Her diamond is kind of small, but it's a really pretty ring. It's all she can talk about."

"Yeah, Mom told me." Grady smiled and took her hand. "So, what was it you wanted to talk about?"

"Well . . ." Naomi shrugged and looked away. "You know, just stuff. It can wait until we go for a drive or something."

"Then let's go," Grady said, picking up the slip. "I'll go pay for this."

Naomi slid out of the booth and put on her jacket. Grady drove south of Beach out past Cemetery Road and parked on the shoulder. The cool October evening was damp and foggy, and a few snowflakes sputtered in the night sky. So far the Beast was hanging on, despite the miles he'd put on between Wibaux and Billings.

He slid his back against the door to face Naomi, the lights from the dash illuminating her face in a soft glow. Shifting shadows filled the crevices of the jagged crests beyond the car windows. Grady leaned over to give Naomi a kiss, the kind of kiss that came from being apart from the girl he loved. His passion for her had never waned, despite the great distance between them. He loved her, respected her, and believed unequivocally they would always be together.

Naomi pulled back and unzipped her jacket. "It's warmed up in here, hasn't it?"

Grady caught a hint of something in her voice. "I hadn't noticed," he said, leaning forward, eager for that first kiss.

She put her hands against his chest. "Wait."

"You expect me to wait when I haven't seen you for six full weeks?" He said it in a teasing manner, but he was partly serious.

Naomi paused and took in a deep breath. "I've got some things I want to talk about."

"Can't it wait?"

"Not really."

Grady settled back into the seat and tried to relax. "Okay, I'm listening." He put an arm around her shoulder, fingering her hair as it spread across his hand, the locks softer than the silky floss of a milkweed pod.

"I don't know how to say this, except . . ." Naomi cleared her throat and inched toward the passenger door. "This . . . it isn't working out the way I thought it would when you left."

Grady's heartbeat quickened. "What do you mean?" He took his arm away as she slid over.

"I love you and I want to be with you, Grady, you know that. But . . ." She paused and turned her face toward him. "I don't get to see you often enough. There're other guys asking me if I can date or if I'm going steady, and it's hard for me to say we're going steady when I never see you." She looked down at her hands in her lap and twisted Grady's class ring off her ring finger. She held it in her hands a moment. "I think it's best . . . well, that maybe we stop seeing each other."

Dumbfounded, Grady stiffened against the seat. "What?"

Naomi handed the ring to him, still wrapped in blue yarn that she'd added in order to make it fit her slender finger. "I want to give this back to you."

Grady stared at the ring, now in his hand. He didn't want it. How on earth had this happened? He had been so anxious to get back to Beach and see Naomi . . . and now she wanted to break up with him? How could she do that when he loved her, really *loved* her.

He gently lifted her chin and studied her deep blue eyes. One look echoed her words. His hand fell to his lap and he shut his eyes, afraid to breathe. He felt like he'd just been kicked in the gut by a bucking bronco. His mind cried, *no, no, no!* If only he could turn back time. He couldn't lose the one person in his life besides his mom whom he trusted and loved unconditionally—his precious Naomi.

"I want you to know I still love you and you'll always be special in my heart." Naomi's voice cracked as she fought back tears.

Grady's mind pleaded, *Stop, just stop, now!* But she didn't, and the wild mustang kicked again.

"I read somewhere that if you love someone and you let them go, if they come back to you, they're yours. If they don't come back, they never were." She gave in to her tears and put her face in her hands.

What a crock! Don't break up with me and then try to make it a God thing with some cheap Cracker Jack saying! That's a cop out! Grady knew they hadn't been able to see each other like he'd hoped, but he expected her to wait for him to get out of school. Was that so wrong? He still loved her and showed her his love as often as he could. Anger welled inside, to think he was going to lose his precious Naomi. He tucked the ring in his pocket and started the car, fighting back his own tears. "Well, I guess that's it," he said with a catch in his voice. He pulled onto the road and turned toward Beach.

Naomi pulled a tissue out of her purse and wiped her eyes again. "Yeah, I guess so," she said softly.

"I'll drive you home." A rare, cold silence settled between them. There was nothing else to say.

Grady pulled up in front of the Braden house like he'd done a hundred other times. He opened the car door and Naomi crawled out on his side, like she always did. She reached up and gave Grady a hug and a kiss. "Good-bye," she said through the tears. "I love you."

Grady sucked in a deep breath. "I love you too." He wrapped his fingers around hers and squeezed gently. She held his hand for a moment and then pulled away. He watched as she walked into the house without looking back. It killed him to see the door close and the porch light go off. He was so unprepared for this moment that he didn't know what to do. He came home to see *her*, to spend time with *her*. Damn it, he *loved* her! How could she do this to him?

What was the point of *anything* if he didn't have Naomi? He couldn't handle the thought of life without her in it. He drove back to Wibaux, his mind a wreck. He couldn't go home and face his mom, not yet. Not knowing what else to do, he drove to the Stockman Bar.

"Hey, Grady!" he heard Tom Lorentz shout the minute he stepped inside. Grady walked down the narrow tavern, oblivious to the crowd of Friday-night regulars. "You're lookin' awful down in the mouth," Tom said, already tuned up pretty good. "What's going on?"

Grady shuffled his feet, grinding an imaginary cigarette to smithereens with the toe of his boot. "Me and Naomi . . ." His voice caught. "She broke up with me tonight."

Tom swung around and patted the bar stool next to him. "Ah, hell, it's probably better anyway. You're too far away to make it work. Someone else will come along. C'mon, I'll buy you a Pabst." He pulled out a couple dollar bills and pounded a fist on the bar. "Hank! Give us a couple more down here."

Grady slid onto the bar stool and rested his elbows on the bar. He listened absentmindedly as Tom gave him the rundown on his recent break-up. "Damn them girls anyway, huh," Tom said, commiserating with Grady.

Grady was numb inside. He didn't want to go home, but he really didn't want to sit there with Tom all night. He was broken inside, devastated. He twisted the bottle and picked at the label between swallows, blocking out the sounds around him. For each beer he finished, Tom ordered another one.

Tom got up to use the restroom and Grady stared at the mahogany bar, a grand masterpiece of woodworking with beveled mirrors, detailed cabinetry, and built-in coolers. The back piece was thirty feet long and rose to the ceiling, far too magnificent for a dumpy joint in Wibaux. On each end a bare-breasted woman stood stoically, carved into the smooth reddish mahogany like seductive pillars. Grady heard stories of it being carved in France and ferried up the Missouri River by steamboat to Bismarck and then hauled in sections on horse-drawn wagons the rest of the way. "Some loser probably did it to impress a woman," Grady muttered to himself. "Look where that gets ya."

"What's that?" Tom asked sliding onto his stool.

"Nothin'."

"Hank, give us a six-pack for the road, will ya?" Tom said to the bartender at closing time. "C'mon Grady, let's get the Beast and take a ride."

Grady drove out to the south slab and parked. Even though a part of him wanted to die, he was glad Tom was willing to sit and listen to his sad story. After they finished off the six-pack, Grady took Tom home and drove to his mom's house. Ever since he'd left Wibaux for Billings he'd tried his best to do well in school, keep Naomi happy, and earn enough money to get through one week at a time. All with the intent of moving back to Wibaux after graduation to be with Naomi.

He felt lost, empty. Worse, he felt unloved. Worthless.

And more alone than he could have ever imagined.

CHAPTER TEN

Days turned into weeks, and despite the ache in his heart life moved on. It felt so unfair but there was nothing he could do about it. He went home again at Christmas, but it wasn't the same without Naomi. Billings was buried in snow, and on some frigid January mornings he could hardly get the Beast started. Second semester was underway. Grady was still at the top of his class; he worked hard and paid attention to detail. He and Jake made a great team and always placed second or third in the shop competitions. He bought the old pickup from Malones for fifty bucks, pulled the engine out, and sold the truck to a salvage yard in Glendive for thirty-five bucks. Not a bad deal. He and Jake had an agreement that Grady would buy all the parts for it since it was his to keep after they completed the course.

For once Grady didn't have to work at K-Mart on a Friday night. He opened the door to his dorm room and threw his backpack onto his narrow mattress.

"Hey," Shiny said, looking up from the foot of his bed. His long shaggy curls nearly covered his face as he bent down, feeling the pockets of a pair of dirty jeans.

"What's up?" Grady tossed his keys onto the small ledge and sat down on his bed.

"Stone's on his way. Said he just picked up some good stuff. Damn it!" he said, flinging the jeans across the room. "I know I've got five bucks somewhere." He grabbed another crumpled pair from the floor. "Wait, here it is," he said triumphantly, holding up a five-dollar bill. "Yo, baby!"

A knock sounded at the door. "It's open!" Shiny called.

Dave Stoneman came in and closed the door behind him. His tall frame filled up the dorm, his shoulders nearly as broad as the front end on their ol' '67 Jimmy. "Hey, Grady, what's up?"

"Nothing, man, just got out of shop." Grady slid over to make room for him.

Dave Stoneman was in the refrigeration class with Shiny and was revered at school for having already done a stint in the army. Every day at lunch a crowd surrounded him in the cafeteria to hear another crazy story from his army days that he made sound amazing and hilarious. Grady never knew anybody who could laugh at his own stupidity like Stone. His whole persona intrigued Grady; Stone made fun of himself and had the rest of them laughing so hard they were in tears. Grady always hid his own mistakes, afraid people would laugh *at* him, not *with* him.

"Time to party, I'd say," Stone said with a deep chuckle. He sat down on Shiny's bed and pulled up the wooden spool that once held Western Electric telephone cable and now served as a table. "Hey, wanna buy some crank?" he asked, eyeing Grady. He pulled out a package of rolled up cellophane from his faded jean jacket. His hair was greasy, like he needed a shower. It was strange because it always looked that way, even when Grady knew the guy had just showered.

"I dunno." Grady shrugged as Shiny plopped down beside him. "I'm running short on cash right now."

Stone cocked his head at an angle, his eyes like two slits of charcoal, always dark and cryptic. He opened the cellophane and paper like a magician with an array of fascinating tricks, Grady and Shiny watching in breathless expectation. "No problem, man. My treat this time." He inched forward, focused on his task, positioning the small mirror and plastic baggie filled with pieces of white paper, all folded identically. He picked up one of the mini-envelopes and unfolded it in slow, careful steps, pouring a chalky, chunky substance onto the mirror.

Voices neared in the hall and Shiny jumped up as if he'd been stung by a dozen bees. "Yo! That was close," he said, flipping the lock on the door.

Stone let his jacket fall behind him and pushed up the sleeves on his Henley. "You sticking around for the weekend, Grady, or are you running home to see that pretty cheerleader you keep bragging about?" Stone asked.

"She's history."

"What?" he asked, looking up at Grady. "I thought she was the one."

"We broke up." His voice was raspy, as though the words had to scrape over sandpaper in his throat to get out. "End of story."

"Okay, man," Stone said. "Shit happens." He took a single razor blade and chopped the chunk into a fine powder, whitish sand in color, then used the blade to scrape it into six lines. "Two for each of us, how's that?"

Grady sat across from him, hands clasped, thumping his thumbs against his palms.

"Grady?" Stone nodded to the mirror.

He'd been around Stone long enough to know exactly what it was: crystal meth, a dangerous and addictive metham-phetamine. He'd always had the sense to say no before. But that was then and this was now. "Yeaaah," he answered in a long exhale, his hands starting to sweat. "Why the hell not."

"Atta boy!" Stone exclaimed. "'Bout time you wised up, Son."

"Yeah." Grady gave up a slight laugh and mumbled under his breath, "That was when I still had something to live for." Some*one* to live for. Sometimes he woke up in the middle of the night seeing Naomi on a swing, but only swinging backward, never forward. She was in slow motion, her long dark hair parting from behind, covering her face. He didn't know what the hell it meant and right at this moment he didn't care.

Stone rested his elbows on his knees, studying Grady. "You know, for me it was either gonna be prison or the army, which in some respects ain't a whole hell of a lot of difference."

"Prison?"

"I kid you not," he said with a nod. His eyes lightened to a smoky gray, the signal of another Stone story.

Shiny piped up. "What were you goin' to prison for?"

"Felony assault on a cop."

"What?" Shiny whipped his head around, his long curls bouncing on his shoulders. "You assaulted a cop? Are you outta your mind, man? That's crazy!"

"I'm afraid that's the story of my life," he said, shaking his head. "I was in this bar up in Kalispell, followed a buddy up there after high school. We worked road construction, widening out one of the mountain passes. Anyway, one night a bunch of us stopped off at this little hick bar out in the boonies. Bunch of locals in there, crazy-ass mountain men who spend too much time alone." Stone paused and made eye contact with Shiny and Grady. "My girlfriend had just broken up with me so I wasn't in the best frame of mind, I'll give you that," he said, raising his eyebrows. "I think I bumped some guy on the way to the can, and when I came back through this guy lipped off and gave me a shove. It didn't take much in those days. I took a swing at him and next thing you know two of his buddies join in and it's three against one. My friends were long gone and I was in the fight of my life, taking blows like baseballs in a batting cage."

"Oh, man," Shiny said, rocking in place. "Sounds bad."

"Suddenly, I see another guy coming at me from the left," Stone said, lifting his arm, his voice escalating. "I don't have time to get a good look; it's like out of the corner of my eye, okay? I see this figure coming my way and assume it's another one of the locals. I was already outnumbered. I went into survival mode, grabbed a chair and swung it at the guy, crammed him good. Turns out someone had called the cops—that's who I knocked out cold. Busted his jaw."

"Oh, man," Grady moaned. "No way!"

"You can't go back and undo that, let me tell you!" Laughing, Stone fell back partway. "Went right to jail that night. When it was all said and done, they gave me the option, prison or the army. Basically, they wanted me the hell outta there." He lowered his voice and took a serious tone. "After all I've been through, here's the best piece of advice I can give you: live fast, die young, and leave a good lookin' corpse!"

"I like that!" Shiny said, thoroughly mesmerized by Stone's every word.

"Yeah, but you ain't good looking," Grady said to him.

"Don't matter," Shiny said. "That's intellectual right there, man. Scholarly."

"Worldly's more like it," Stone said. "I'm serious, man. I've been around the block enough times to know a few things."

"Words of wisdom, man!" Shiny reiterated.

"Hey, Grady, look at it this way," Stone said. "At least you didn't get a stint in the army for losin' your girl."

Grady shrugged, not sure his sentence was any better. His was a mental prison of screwed-up thoughts, frustrations, anger, misery, self-loathing. What could be worse than that? He watched Stone take out a dollar bill and roll it into a tight cylinder. He pinched it between his fingers and held it up. Grady hesitated. Stone was the kind of guy mothers warned their daughters to stay away from, a thug who made money selling tiny pills and powder that delivered a quick high. Yet, he carried a hidden quality, a distinction that Grady was drawn to.

He took the dollar bill from Stone's outstretched hand. He put one end at the end of one line and bent forward, pressing the other end against his right nostril. He shut his mouth and inhaled deeply, the powder going up his nose and into his bloodstream. "Whoa," Grady said, leaning back. A rush of adrenaline hit his brain instantly, a sense of power and pleasure mixed into one. A distorted haze settled on him and he relaxed, ready to experience it for all it was worth.

Shiny took a turn next. "Oh, man," he said in a blissful moan. "Dude, that's tough."

"This is some sharp cookin' right here, man," Stone said, bending over to take a line.

"Whoaah . . . outta this world, man." Physical buoyancy intertwined with heart-stopping pulsations rushed through Grady as his body absorbed the dangerous amphetamine. "Wow . . ."

A few minutes passed and they repeated the process. "Man, let's go have a beer or somethin'," Shiny said. "I gotta move!"

"Sure, man." Stone wrapped up his contraband and tucked it inside his long denim jacket.

Grady jumped to his feet, on fire to get somewhere, anywhere. His body wanted to move, to do anything but sit still.

Billings was known for a ton of country music hangouts, crammed most nights with cowboy rednecks in oversized hats and belt buckles. Grady and his group avoided the cowboy bars at all costs and followed Stone to a small crusty bar called the Vault, where a different type of crowd congregated. Grady had been there a few times already, a basement hideout with a seedy reputation. The Vault meant hard-core rock bands and marijuana smoke. Drug deals were common in the alley near the entrance. Riding the intense high, Grady couldn't think of a better place to go.

A banged-up door at the corner of a commercial building in the warehouse section of downtown provided access to the shoddy tavern. Grady swung it open and started down the concrete steps. The metal door swung shut behind Shiny, leaving them in near-pitch-black darkness as they descended downward. For an instant Grady imagined he was going down the old steps into the root cellar, down into the earthen cavity at the old farm. His heart pounded faster, the drugs playing tricks on his mind.

Grady pushed through another door and his eyes adjusted to the dim light. He glanced around the crowded bar, trying to calm himself. Jimi Hendrix's "All Along the Watchtower" blared from the jukebox, the arched light flickering as if the bulb was about to explode.

Grady brushed past a man on a barstool near the door. "Hey, man," he said to Grady. "Watch it." He had an unusually wide chin and short black whiskers like Brutus in "Popeye," and his teeth were stained and short like they'd been ground down. Grady gave a look that said "mind your own business" and continued past him. He bought three beers at the bar and handed a bottle to Shiny and Stone.

Shiny spied an empty table near the stairway. "Over here, guys," he said, waving them over.

"Negatory," Stone said, shaking his head. He nodded toward the back wall and pointed at a table in the far corner.

"What's wrong with the other one?" Grady asked, pulling up a chair.

Stone sat down across from him and lowered his voice. "Here's one of the most important lessons I can give you, dude. Look around you."

Grady glanced at the typical collection of tough sorts. Long-haired men in denim jackets with the sleeves ripped off, wearing fingerless gloves, a few men with the notorious *Outlaws* emblem on the back. One guy had a patch over his left eye and a faded bandana headband. Another dude's hair looked like he'd been in a fight with a tub of Vaseline. Scrawny girls in mini-skirts, dangly earrings, and tight, low-cut tops hung on their every word. "Yeah, so?"

"Listen up. You *never* sit with your back to the door," Stone explained in a low voice, gesturing with his hands. "You always wanna be able to see who's coming through the door, who's coming in and who's going out."

"What the hell for?" Grady asked, not grasping the significance of Stone's dissertation. Other than Brutus, the regulars barely gave the three vo-tech students a second look.

"Trust me on this one, man," Stone said with a serious expression. "It'll pay off for you someday." He leaned his chair back, tipping it on the back legs. He took a long look at Grady's face. "So, how'd you get that scar, man?"

Grady sensed the question coming. Most guys stared at it without asking, but guys like Stone always asked. "Got in a fight with a chainsaw and lost." He tipped his beer at Stone and took a swig.

"Must a been one helluva fight."

"It was."

"How far does it go?"

Grady lifted his long bangs. "All the way up," he said, touching the top of his head.

"Man, that looks serious."

"It was a long time ago."

Stone put his chair back down and clinked Grady's bottle. "Yeah, well, that's some scar, dude. Looks like you're lucky to be alive."

Grady nodded. "You could say that."

An hour later Grady, Shiny, and Stone went back to the dorm room. Grady liked the feeling he'd had all afternoon and evening. A stimulated sense of being; a warped sense of time. Insane thoughts wrapped and wound in strange sensations he'd never felt before, ones that kept him from thinking of Naomi.

As soon as they got inside, Stone unloaded the contraband onto the stool again. A tiny voice inside Grady cried, *Don't do it!* Then the voice was gone, leaving him alone to decide. He liked the rush . . . and wanted more, despite knowing it was the beginning of a one-way journey to a hell-fired ending. Grady hesitated, as though he were standing in front of deep chasm. His family was gone, his mom was four hours away, his dad a loser drunk, and Naomi was out of his life forever. His life was already in a pit. He may as well crawl all the way in and get a taste of what lurked at the bottom. "Hey, Stone, how 'bout if I buy some of that?"

Stone pulled out the Ziploc bag filled with folded white envelopes the size of an eraser, a grin forming on his face. "I knew you'd see the light sooner or later. I got a dime bag just for you."

Grady took out his wallet and pulled out two fives. "Here you go." He picked up the Ziploc bag. "Cool."

Stone swiped the bag out of his hands. "Whoa, man," he said with a laugh. "You don't get the whole bag! A dime gets you *one* of those." He took out one of the small folded envelopes and handed it to Grady.

Grady took it from him, nodding. "Yeah, sure. I knew that."

"I'll take one too," Shiny said, digging in a ripped duffle bag at the foot of his bed. "Here man, here's my ten."

Stone tucked the cash into his jean jacket and offered up a crooked smile. "You boys won't regret it."

"Where'd you get this stuff anyway?" Grady asked, staring at the envelope in his palm.

"Can't tell you that, man. Came from out of town."

By the time the weekend was over, Grady and Shiny had gone through twenty bucks worth of crank and had slept a grand total of three hours. The days and nights went by like flashes of lightning on his brain. Monday morning Grady sat in class half-dazed, not sure what to make of it. He'd drunk beer all weekend but hadn't felt drunk. It was like drinking water; it didn't seem to have an effect. "All right, men," Mr. Steinar said. "You've got your work orders. Get to work!"

Grady closed his notebook with a slap and followed Jake into the shop. He pulled his toolbox next to his Chevy engine and lifted the top. Jake stood next to him, watching Grady's every move. "What?" Grady finally asked. Irritated, he pointed to the engine. "Let's get at it."

Jake's eyes stayed on Grady. "You okay, man?"

"Yeah, sure," Grady answered, looking away. He picked up the ring spreader.

"You look like shit."

"Yeah, well, you don't look so hot, neither."

"I'm serious."

"So am I." Grady held the spreader in his hand, staring at Jake. They were in the middle stages of rebuilding Grady's Chevy engine, ready to put in the new oversized pistons and rings Grady had bought.

"You're moving slower'n a three-toed sloth, man."

"What are you, my mother?"

"Grady, listen to me."

"I got a better idea, I'll put the pistons on the connecting rods with the new rings," Grady said, picking one up in his hand. "And you can hone the cylinders. Make a good crosshatch, and I'll clean 'em and wash 'em out when you're done."

"Seriously, man, you look a mess," Jake said, picking up a drill.

"All under control." Grady knew Jake's athlete mentality kept him from putting anything into his system other than a few beers, but the last thing Grady wanted was a lecture of any sort.

* * *

Winter weekends developed a new pattern. Grady wholeheartedly adopted Stone's theory to live fast, die young, and leave a good-lookin' corpse. At least if something awful did happen to him, he could fulfill Stone's slogan to a T. His shoulders were still nice and broad even if he had lost a few pounds. Girls seemed to dig his long dark hair. One cute blonde told him he had "mysterious eyes"—whatever that meant. Regardless, he didn't have time to get too worked up about it. He enjoyed the flirting and having fun without getting serious.

Stone was the man of the hour and always had the necessary connections to fuel his desires. Crank, pot, hash. The man had a way of making it look harmless. Even tripping on LSD was ordinary, easy. Whenever he craved a purple microdot or an orange sunshine, Stone had him covered. Parties were wild, but no one was falling over dead from any of it. When he overdid it, he'd puke his guts out, sleep it off, and start over. One of the hazards, no biggie. Besides, there was nothing else to do as the harsh winter weeks softened into the spring winds of March.

Grady needed a fix badly, and called Stone to meet him in the little park up on Sacrifice Cliff. The sandstone rims, cut by the winding Yellowstone River, stood five hundred feet high and ran east to west along the northern edge of Billings, making an impressive backdrop for the city. The end of the walking trail in the park offered a full view of the river and downtown.

"Hey, man," Grady said, hopping out of the Beast and into Stone's car.

"What's up?" Stone asked, turning down the volume on his radio.

"I could use an orange sunshine."

"No problem." Stone made a quick survey around the parking lot and Grady copied. No other cars were within sight. "Got it right here." He pulled out an envelope from the inside pocket of his jean jacket. Inside were smaller baggies with even smaller pieces of paper folded to look like miniature envelopes. "Got some purple too, if you're interested."

"Don't matter." Grady watched him unfold one of the pieces, rubbing his hands together, ready to pop it under his tongue. He'd grown to like the intense high more and more.

"Here you go." Stone's dark eyes had the look of quarried granite as he handed over a tiny envelope.

"Party while you still can, right?" Grady's hands shook as he unfolded it and placed the tiny pill under his tongue, letting it dissolve. He wanted it to numb his mind before he had time to think about how unhappy and unsettled he felt. Stone took out another pill and put it in his mouth. Within seconds Grady was severed from reality and thrust in a whole new realm. *Oh, yeah, I need this.* This is what kept him from falling completely apart. Now he didn't have to think about school or disappointing his mom or Jake or his teachers, and it freed him from thoughts of Naomi.

Acutely aware of each and every thing around him, his mind raced at breakneck speed. One second he loved the feeling, the next he hated himself for giving in to the urge. Again. Maybe he'd be better off if he got out of the car and raced right off the edge of Sacrifice Cliff, like the young Indian braves had a century earlier. Would his freefall to the river below be more exhilarating than what he was feeling right now?

"Dude," Stone said, slapping Grady's shoulder. "What's going on?"

Grady shook his head. "I'm all screwed up."

"Nah," Stone said. "No worries. It's all good."

"I dunno."

"Let it go, man. Just relax and enjoy the ride." Stone rolled his head against the headrest. "Oooh, man . . ."

Grady's heart felt on the verge of exploding, the most exhilarating and frightening feeling meshed into one powerful sense. In the distance a giant thunderhead filled the sky, cottony white with a pink tinge at the top. Wind whipped the feathered grasses on the ridge in front of the car in constant rhythms. He rolled down the window halfway, letting the moist March winds blow in from the top of the rim.

Whenever Grady was high he noticed squirrels, song birds, noises he'd never paid attention to before. A crow cawed, but the sound was amplified a thousand times. It was a super-intense awareness, like being on the thin edge of genius and insanity. Sometimes he didn't know which side of the razor's edge he would fall.

"Dude!" Grady shouted. "Car coming. What if it's the cops? We gotta get outta here, man!"

"Whoa, relax!" Stone said in a calming tone. He watched in the rearview mirror as the beige Crown Victoria pulled into the parking lot about six car widths away. "Lay low."

"I can't take it," Grady said, his voice raspy and on the verge of tears.

Stone looked at him, his shiny hair combed back in one long swoop. "What's wrong with you, man?"

"I swear . . . I can't take it anymore." Grady turned, eyes darting, trying to get a look inside the other car.

"Relax," Stone said. "Just a couple a teenagers, probably gonna do it Daddy's car or somethin'."

"Oh, man . . ." Grady pressed on his thighs so hard he thought he would leave bruises. High on LSD meant Code Yellow at all times. Paranoid, watching for cops. Seeing uniforms everywhere, even when they weren't there.

For four strong hours his heart raced and his mind rushed, stimulating his brain with an intense awareness that left him wanting more. There was a part of him that needed to experience that crazed brush with the impossible, a vain attempt to placate cravings that were never fully satisfied, always wanting more, *needing* more.

And afterward, the downer. A rush of self-hate that kicked him square in the gut. By the time the acid had worn off, Grady went back to his dorm and crashed; his body collapsed and he wanted only to sleep a deep dark sleep.

CHAPTER ELEVEN

Grady still went back to Wibaux every so often, mostly to check on his mom. He'd tune up her car or Melinda's, fix things around her new place. His dad was still in his apartment, barely hanging onto his job with the state. Rumor had it that he'd shown up for work primed more than once, hardly a shock for anyone who knew Frank Kramer.

Grady had only called out of obligation and now here he was, mid-afternoon, on his way to meet him. "C'mon down to the Silver Dollar," his dad had said. "I'll buy ya a beer." Sure enough, Grady found his dad propped on the same stool, elbows on the bar. His right hand gripped a bottle of Old Milwaukee like he was Jack Nicholson and he was holding his Oscar for *One Flew Over the Cuckoo's Nest*.

"Grady!" Old Jack called. He'd been the bartender in the Silver Dollar since forever. "How you doin' kid?"

Grady waved a hello. "Doing good. Going to school in Billings."

Frank turned and patted the bar stool next to him. "Hey, you made it. Give my boy a Pabst, will ya, Jack?"

"Comin' right up," Jack said, drying a whiskey glass with a towel.

Grady slid onto the stool next to his dad. "How are ya, Dad?"

"Doing jus' fine." He turned with a stiff back to face Grady. "When you'd get home?"

"Last night."

Jack put the cold bottle in front of Grady. "Here you go."

"Thanks," Grady said, taking the bottle.

"You're lookin' mighty thin from what I remember you."

"Yeah, I miss my ma's cooking." Grady forced a laugh, avoiding Jack's pressing eyes.

"You better take care of yourself, kid," Jack said.

Grady took a swallow, wondering if Old Jack knew his secret, his habit. Being a bartender in small town, Old Jack knew a lot of people's secrets. *Paranoid.* Even when Grady wasn't high.

"Whacha home for?" Frank asked.

"We had a couple days off school, so thought I'd come home and check on Mom and the kids. Make sure their cars are running good. See who's around town, the usual."

"Ain't much changed around here, is there Jack?" Frank tipped his bottle up and downed the last swallow.

"'Cept the price of gas." Jack lifted the lid on his cooler and pulled out another Old Milwaukee, replacing Frank's empty. "Went up twenty-five cents, like nobody's business."

"Tell me about it. I just paid seventy-five cents a gallon coming home," Grady said, commiserating.

"It's gonna hit a dollar a gallon one of these days," Jack said. "We'll have to go back to the horse and buggy." He chuckled and turned to answer the phone.

"Hey, Grady," Frank said. "We should go fishin' next time you come home. Whadaya say?"

Grady studied his dad, the lines around his eyes deeper, more puffiness in his cheeks. His nose was so red and big it looked swollen—outward signs of an alcoholic. "You know, I'd like that," Grady said. "I live right by the Yellowstone, a fisherman's paradise for sure, but with school and work I hardly get out there." He nodded, thinking back to some of their fishing outings. "I miss it."

"Yeah, those were the days, weren't they?" Frank said with a slur. "But you know . . ." He turned on his stool, one arm propped on the bar, and faced Grady.

"What's that, Dad?"

"I s'pose I was hard on you kids and maybe I shouldn't a beat ya the way I did . . ." He paused to take another swallow.

Grady felt the hairs go up on the back of his neck. He waited.

"Maybe your ma was right . . . but look at you, damn near at the top of your class, I'd say you done okay. Must a given you some character along the way, don't you say?"

The anger, the hate he thought he'd buried, flew up like a squadron of Blue Angels, bursting through his veins at Mach speed. He wanted to get up and walk out. Make a statement, right here in front of his dad's drinking buddies. What kind of man could think all those beatings and whippings gave his kids character? He was sick, insane, the lowest of the low.

Grady stewed silently on his bar stool for another half hour as he listened to his dad's ramblings. He pushed his beer back, still half full. "Good to see you, Dad, but I gotta run. Gonna go meet up with some of the boys."

"Next time we'll go fishing . . ." he heard his dad call as he walked toward the door.

"Like hell!" he said with gritted teeth. Grady got as far as the sidewalk before erupting. "Grrrrr!" He leaned against the brick front of the Silver Dollar, pounding it with his fists. Unbelievable how the ol' man still defended his actions! Grady looked down Main Street as the late afternoon sun disappeared behind the tree line to the west. The laws of science were locked in place and nothing on earth could ever change the twenty-four-hour cycle: The sun came up, the sun went down, and Frank Engel Kramer drank himself drunk.

Grady's hands burned, scratched and red from the rough surface of the bricks. He watched Pistol Pete pull away from Wibaux City Hall next door. "There's the putz that won't do anything about Marvin Cook," he said under his breath. His mom had confided that the old rancher was trying to hit on her—to the point it was getting worrisome. She'd done everything possible to get him to leave her alone and nothing worked. She'd even complained to the police department, but Marvin Cook was still showing up at her door at all hours. Grady decided now was as good a time as any to take care of the problem.

He opened the door to city hall and walked inside. The young gal at the front desk pushed up her glasses. "Hi, can I help you?"

"Where's Mrs. Roisum?" he asked, looking around the front half of the small office building. Grady had been good friends with both her daughters in high school and her judicial title didn't intimate him.

She picked up the receiver on her telephone. "She's in her office, I'll see—"

"Don't bother," Grady said, cutting her off. He marched straight back to the door that said "Municipal Judge" and walked into her chambers.

Judge Roisum looked up from her desk with a look of surprise. "Grady, what are you doing here?" she asked, putting down a thick law book. Dressed in a navy suit, she looked every bit professional.

The receptionist poked her head around the door frame. "He didn't give me a chance to call you first."

"It's okay, Molly," Mrs. Roisum said, legal documents scattered in front of her. "What can I do for you? You look upset; have a seat." She motioned to the wooden chairs in front of her desk.

Grady paced back and forth between bookcases. "I'll just tell you like it is," he said, taking a deep breath. "If somebody doesn't do something about Marvin Cook coming after my mom, I swear I'm gonna beat the hell out of him myself."

"Grady, slow down," she said, motioning with her hands. "Calm down and tell me what's been going on."

"He's crossing the line, going over to her house, won't leave her alone," Grady said, still pacing. "She said she talked to someone at the police department, but it hasn't stopped. She's scared and I'm fed up with nobody doing nothing about it." He spread his hands on the edge of her desk and bent forward to meet her at eye level. "I mean it, Mrs. Roisum, I don't care what happens to me."

"I'll check into it, I promise," Mrs. Roisum said in a calming manner.

"It would be *appreciated*."

Back outside he glanced at the Silver Dollar, feeling slightly better than he had a half hour ago. His mom had always been there for him; this was the least he could do for her.

* * *

By the time the bright orange trumpet-shaped flowers on the honeysuckle vines burst with the sweet scent of spring, Grady's routine was a predictable combination of school, K-Mart, and partying. He wasn't sure how he pulled it off, but he hadn't missed a day of school or an exam, and his grades were

fine—all thanks to the pills and weed that got him through week
to week.

Grady's new favorite high was a Thai stick, a marijuana
joint wrapped in a string of diluted heroin or angel dust. The mix
of drugs sent him into a blissful, frenzied spin that kept him from
facing reality. Truth be told, he was willing to try anything
except shooting heroin. Many times he had watched the other
guys heat the spoon or put the band on their arm, but for
whatever reason, he drew a bizarre line in the midst of his
guttered lifestyle, one that kept him from putting the needle in
his own arm.

After another weekend of heavy partying, Grady woke up
feeling like death taking a shit. His head throbbed incessantly, a
minor hazard. Somehow he'd managed to be in class by 7:30
a.m., freshly showered and ready for the next section on fuel
systems and emission controls.

"C'mon Jake, ride shotgun with me for parts this
morning," Grady said, jingling his keys.

"Sure thing," Jake said, grabbing his jacket.

"Here's your list," Mr. Steinar said, pulling out a pen
from his front pocket. "You need one stop at QB&R for
electrical components, and then over to NAPA and Car Quest for
the rest."

"Good one, Mr. Steinar, that rhymes," Jake said with a
look of approval.

Mr. Steinar smiled and handed Grady the slip. "Got it,"
Grady said.

Grady and Jake lit up cigarettes as soon as they got in the
Beast. "Aaah, I needed that," Grady said, inhaling deeply.

"Grady, you should cut the hard stuff," Jake said, flicking
an ash out the window.

"Jake—don't." Grady cracked his window and exhaled.

"You don't see what it's doin' to you, man. Alan Coleman said he ran into you at Pizza Hut last Saturday night and you looked like a walking ghost."

He'd smoked a few Thai sticks that weekend with Stone and some guys he didn't know. "I had a bad night."

"Give it up, Grady . . . before it kills you."

"So, are you my mother?" Grady said angrily, tossing the butt out the window. "I'll get right on that." He turned onto North Twenty-Seventh Street to go up toward NAPA. He turned northeast on Fourth Avenue, a one-way thoroughfare in downtown Billings, the bright sun—still low on the morning horizon—nearly blinded him as he approached the next inter-section.

"Watch out!" Jake shouted.

Craaash! The Beast smashed into the side of a pickup, jolting the vehicles in opposite directions. He slammed on the brakes and his car screeched to a stop in front of the next corner.

"What the hell happened?" Jake asked, rubbing his head.

"I dunno!" said Grady, trying to figure it out. "I guess I didn't see the stoplight."

"Obviously you didn't see the pickup either."

"Man, which way did he come from?"

"Right there," Jake pointed to Grady's left.

Dazed, Grady looked up to see a man climb out of the pickup cab. The tall cowboy pushed back his wide-brimmed hat and rubbed his forehead, staring at his damaged truck. He started across the street and Grady got out to meet him.

"What the hell you doing, boy?" the man said in a deep gravelly voice. His belt buckle matched the size of his hat and he marched toward Grady like a rolling bulldozer.

Grady assessed the man's size and demeanor in three seconds flat. He stood at least six foot four and had the shoulders of a Denver Bronco linebacker. "I'm so sorry, sir! The sun was in my eyes; it was my fault. I didn't even see the stoplight," he said, waving an arm toward the intersection. "I don't have insurance, but I'll pay for it, I swear."

"You're damn right you will," the giant cowboy said, his eyes boring a hole through Grady like a spear.

Grady apologized repeatedly until the man calmed down. "Listen, I know people in the car business, real gearheads. I'll take care of it, I swear." Grady pulled out a pen and small notebook from his shirt pocket. "Here's my name and address. Call me tomorrow or whenever you get an estimate."

The man's face was partially hidden by the wide brim of his cowboy hat. He bent at the waist to make direct eye contact with Grady. "You're damn right I will." He took a look at the Bel Air, the front end completely smashed in. "Otherwise I know where to find you too."

"You won't have to, mister, I swear."

The man strode back to his truck and Grady melted into the side of his damaged car. "Oh, man, I thought that ol' cowboy was gonna kill me!"

Jake watched him drive away. "You better fix him up right or he still might."

Grady's heart sunk. "Damn it!" he said, kicking the tire. Judging by the damage, the Beast wasn't worth fixing. He had no money saved up, barely scraping by paycheck to paycheck. Not only would he have to pay for the truck, he'd have to buy a new car.

That evening he placed a phone call to the one person who never let him down. "Hey, mom."

"Grady, what a surprise. I was just thinking about you this morning. Praying for you, like I always do," she said with a genuineness that warmed Grady's heart. "Are you okay?"

The enormity of her love moved him and he was unable to answer. His mother was as good as his father was bad, complete opposite ends of the spectrum. "You remember saying if I needed anything to call?" he asked softly.

"What happened, Grady? You can tell me."

"I had a wreck this morning, T-boned a guy; the sun was in my eyes. It was my fault and I need four hundred fifty bucks to fix his truck."

"I have a little saved up," she said without a second's hesitation. "I'll send you a check."

"I'll pay you back, I promise."

"I know you will, Grady. I'm not worried about that. You better take care of this other man's truck and get right with him first. Then we'll worry about the rest. Is school going okay?"

"Yeah, just fine."

"How's Jake doing?"

"Good, he's good."

"I suppose you two are together all the time, huh?"

Grady hesitated. "Not all the time. We're working on my engine at school."

"Say, I meant to tell you . . ."

"What?"

"I don't know what happened, but that ol' Marvin Cook hasn't showed up at my doorstep anymore. He even came in the café the other day and didn't come to my counter. Sat at the table and let somebody else wait on him. I about fell over. Ain't that something?"

Grady chuckled. "It sure is."

"Well, you take care now."

"Thanks, Mom," he said, his voice softening. "I love you."

"I love you too. Call me again if you need to, you hear?"

"Yeah, I will." Grady hung up the receiver and turned down the hall to his dorm room. He would work double shifts, whatever it took, to pay back his mom.

CHAPTER TWELVE

Friday afternoon Jake and Grady cleaned up their lab and put away the toolboxes. As the school year neared an end, Grady's toolbox was covered in stickers from all the major vendors: Eddlebrauch, Hooker-Headers, Thrush Mufflers, Mac Tools, Holley Carburetor.

"You wanna hang out tonight?" Jake asked, putting away his torque wrench. "Go get a pizza and a beer?"

Grady respected Jake in many ways, but he wasn't fun enough for a Friday night. "Hey, I'd like to, but Stone's girlfriend has a friend in town and he asked if I wanted to go hear some music."

"Whoo, a date!" Jake said, razzing him. "Who is she?"

"No one I know," Grady said, shaking his head. "I guess you could call it a blind date. It's just, you know, Stone needs someone to make it a foursome."

"Sure thing, man," Jake said, locking his box. "Hey, take it easy."

Stone showed up at Grady's dorm room shortly before eight o'clock. "Whadaya say we do a couple hits before we pick up the girls?"

"Give me an orange sunshine," Grady answered, opening his wallet. "How much?" At $4.35 an hour, it took a lot of hours to support his lifestyle. So far he'd paid back his mom half of what he owed her and had bought a '74 Datsun pickup with American Racing white-spoke wheels, overhead cam, four-cylinder, five-speed.

"A dime will do it." Stone pulled out a small vial that held a collection of tiny pills and poured them into his palm. Grady picked up an orange-colored pill and put it under his tongue, and Stone copied. Within minutes Grady's mind was running like a 110-volt motor in a 220-volt circuit.

Still riding a sweet high, Stone and Grady picked up the girls at an apartment on Canvas Street a half hour later. "Grady, Michelle. Michelle, Grady," Stone said, making the introduction.

"Hi," Michelle said. She had a pretty face, short blonde hair, and hazel green eyes accented with a thick dose of green eye shadow. She looked cute in a green knit sweater that accented her eyes and fit snugly on her curves—definitely someone he could hang out and have fun with.

"Hey," Grady said in response. "Ready to go dancing?"

"Sure!" she said with enthusiasm. "Where we going?"

"The Vault," Stone said. "They've got a dynamite band tonight. I heard 'em in Bozeman one year. Their guitar player is from L.A. and, man, can he play a mean guitar; sounds just like Tony Iommi."

"No way, Black Sabbath?" Grady said.

"I swear. It'll blow you away."

"Sounds great to me," Nancy said, draping an arm across Stone, her long hair pulled back in a clip, a yellow blouse neatly tucked in her high-waisted jeans.

Stone parked in a neighboring lot behind a warehouse and they cut across to the alley entrance. Grady pushed the door and held it open. "Ladies first." The girls went through the entrance and the guys followed, descending down the dark steps.

"This way," Stone said, leading them through the crowd. They waited by the bar while Grady ordered a round. The band was in their first set, the music amplified through huge speakers on the stage. A smoky haze hung in the basement nightclub, crammed with diehards ready to jam.

"Hey!" Grady shouted, noticing some guys leaving. "Follow me." He grabbed the table and waited for Stone and the girls to make it through.

"Perfect," Stone said, glancing around.

Grady nodded. Stone could keep an eye on the stairway door and the band in one easy motion. He took the chair opposite Stone with the girls in between. "Man, I've never seen it like this in here before. Crazy!"

"Told ya they were good," Stone said.

They listened to the first set, a guitar ripping mix of Pink Floyd, the Grateful Dead, Jimi Hendrix, Cream, louder than he'd ever heard in a bar. The drum set was huge and the lead singer looked like he walked right off the cover of Rolling Stone Magazine. Long greasy hair, jeans with holes all the way up and down one leg, shirt wide open in the front that revealed a leathered, bare-skinned chest. Somehow the screaming guitar and pounding drums gave him supernatural powers to communicate with the band without ever opening his eyes or looking up, his long hair hanging in his face.

"Wanna dance?" Michelle asked.

"Sure, let's go," Grady said. They danced until the end of the second set just as Stone brought another round of drinks.

"I forget," Michelle said to Grady above the noise, "are you going to school?"

"Yeah, I'm at the vo-tech in town, auto mechanics. I've got less than three weeks left." Grady took a long swallow and set his bottle on the table. "Can't wait to be done with it some days."

"Yeah, I know that feeling. I started college last fall, but my dad got hurt and lost his job so I had to drop out because I couldn't afford it all on my own—" Michelle was cut off by a loud crash as beer bottles and a chair hit the floor behind them.

Grady looked up as a fight broke out at the next table. Three guys were on their feet, yelling and swearing at each other. Within seconds it escalated from shouts to fists. The tall guy in a black leather jacket shoved the heavier guy in a sleeveless jean jacket and knocked him into the table. All the mixed drinks crashed to the floor as a third guy in a fringed vest came at the tall man in leather. The guy in the jean jacket lowered his head and charged the other two, yelling at the top of his lungs, a look of madness in his eyes.

Grady put a protective arm around Michelle as the two guys in leather pushed the stockier man back. He caught himself and nearly knocked into Michelle before he turned for the door, just as Brutus the bouncer made his way over.

Grady eyed Stone and looked around. "Asshole! I wonder what that was about."

"Dirtball must 'a' pissed somebody off."

"Fight's over!" Brutus yelled and picked up the table. A scrawny brunette in a tight T-shirt came over to clean it off. The guys in leather picked up their chairs and flirted with the waitress as she wiped it dry. The band came back on stage and everything returned to normal.

The next set sounded another ten decibels louder and Grady leaned close to Michelle in order to hear. "Yeah, like I was saying, my summer after high school I went to L.A. to stay with a cousin," she said, scooting her chair closer. "My parents weren't too happy about it 'cause I used most of my graduation money for the bus ticket, but I didn't care. I wanted to do something fun after high school, you know?"

Grady nodded as the band started a rocked-out version of "Magic Carpet Ride." "Let's dance again," he said, pulling Michelle to her feet. After a couple songs Grady went to the bar. Every now and then there was nothing like a shot of Jack Daniels sliding down his throat. He wiped his mouth and bought another round of beers. "Man, I'd come back and hear these guys again," Grady said, handing a bottle to Stone. He tipped his beer toward Stone, signifying a great night.

Stone jerked his head up and Grady caught a look of horror in his eyes. "Grady!" he screamed at the top of his lungs.

Grady turned his head a fraction to see the barrel of a .357 magnum revolver eight inches away from his face. Aimed straight at him, it looked the size of a cannon. Time froze. *Oh, my God, he's gonna blow my head off!* Grady dove forward as the gun exploded in his right ear. A bright flash burst in front of him, followed by a deafening, *BOOM!* He reached across the table for the girls just as another round went off. Flash, *BOOM!*

A deafening ringing echoed in Grady's ears to the point he could hardly comprehend what had just happened. The band stopped. For three or four seconds the whole place went silent. Horrified, Grady stared at the crazed man still holding the gun. He recognized the jean jacket—the guy who'd been in the fight. The tall guy in the leather jacket who'd been sitting right behind Grady lay on the floor, his eyes blank and lifeless. Blood oozed from his nose and mouth. More blood seeped from the hole in his neck where the second bullet'd hit him.

It'd happened so fast, Grady couldn't think. The girls screamed. People yelled and started shoving like mad. Stone took one look at Grady and nodded toward the exit. Grady understood perfectly. They were tripping on acid and the next people sure to come down those steps would be cops. They had to get out of there—*now*.

Grady freaked. He grabbed Michelle by the arm and dragged her to the door, fighting his way through the crowd to get out. The girls had no clue that he and Stone were on acid. No doubt more than half the crowd and the band were tripping on LSD or crank. Everyone had the same thought as a frenzied stampede of people headed for the door.

Michelle cried as they made their way up the dark stairway, her shoes slipping on the concrete. Stone and Nancy pushed them from behind. "Hurry up!" Stone shouted at Michelle. "Go! Go!"

"Oh, my God! Oh, my God!" Michelle screamed over and over.

The screams reverberated inside Grady's head, echoing off one side of his skull to the other like a cavernous gorge. His heart pounded so hard he thought it might burst. *Oh, my God! That guy is dead! That would have been me if I hadn't ducked the very instant I did! It could be me lying on the floor in there with blood oozing out of my neck.*

Grady bolted through the door, dragging Michelle with him. Sirens screamed in the distance.

"C'mon, we gotta get the hell outta here *now!*" Stone yelled as soon as they reached the top. They climbed into Stone's Pontiac, tires screeching as he tore out of the lot. Grady stared at the single light illuminating the Vault sign until it was out of view.

CHAPTER THIRTEEN

Warm summer breezes brought a welcome freshness to Billings, a city bathed in the beauty of the surrounding Yellowstone Valley. Wildflowers bloomed on the high, flat tablelands of Big Sky Country where ranchers grazed their horses and cattle. Mountain bluebirds, black-capped chickadees, and western tanagers sang in appreciation of early morning showers. On clear days the snow-capped mountain ranges to the west were clearly visible, luring those willing further westward. The Yellowstone River was still running high from the recent rains, sandbars hidden by the rushing water that flowed northward to the Missouri River in North Dakota.

In a way Grady, too, carried a sense of newness, rebirth—saved from the dormant, decaying life of a druggie. The writing was on the wall: keep going down the steep, slippery slide with Stone, or break away—now. It was hard. He was shaky, on edge, and depressed at times. But he was alive . . . and right now that seemed like a good thing. More importantly, he couldn't betray his mom any longer. If she ever found out about the drugs, he wouldn't be able to face her. She'd always wanted the best for him and he owed it to her to go clean.

Grady graduated from vo-tech in June and took a full-time job with K-Mart as a mechanic. Making less than five bucks an hour, things were tight, but at least he had better things to spend his money on than a nasty drug habit. He moved out of the dorm and found an apartment not too far from Jake. It was a cramped one-bedroom in the upstairs corner of an older house, but the rent was cheap.

His appetite came back and he started sleeping better. Most days when he got home from work, he'd eat a snack and then meet up with Jake and some buddies later and eat again. Maybe now he'd have time to get out on the Yellowstone. If he went a ways upstream a riffle turned the river into a quick chute of deeper water, which was perfect for trout, and near Billings he could catch large walleye, catfish, and sturgeon.

Grady climbed the outdoor steps to his apartment door. He showered off the car grease and put a frozen pizza in the small gas oven. Made of white enamel, it was about one-fourth the size of the big stove in the farmhouse. He liked the convenience of turning the knob and having an automatic flame, but he missed standing next to that big ol' cook stove, the smell of wood burning, watching his mom stir up a scrumptious breakfast. A frozen pizza didn't come close, but it would quiet his rumbling stomach for the time being.

The phone rang and Grady picked up. "Hello?"

"Grady, man, how you doing?"

"Hey, Tom, what's up?" Grady hadn't talked to Tom Lorentz since the night Naomi broke up with him, his impromptu counselor with a six-pack to go.

"I've got a proposition for you if you're interested."

"What kind of proposition?"

"You heard how the oil companies are digging for oil in these parts, haven't you?"

"Sure, man, everyone's talking about the price of oil these days."

"I started working for Noble Oil six months ago and they're hiring."

Good for you, buddy. The idea of another move didn't interest him. "I already got a job." The oven door had a tight spring and Grady pried it open. Heat billowed around his face as he eyed the bubbling cheese.

"Does it pay over fifteen bucks an hour?"

"What?!" Grady let the oven door snap shut with a *bang*. "Are you serious, man? Fifteen bucks an hour?"

"That's *starting* pay, Grady, lowest man on the totem pole. You start as a trainee, but the rate they're adding people, I'll bet you can work your way up in no time. They're putting up these million-dollar rigs and digging holes like there's no tomorrow."

"Keep talking, man." Grady listened, pacing in excited steps as far as the phone cord would let him.

"It's like I said, oil prices are at record highs, so all these companies are forced to spend the money right here in the good old U. S. of A., rather than stay dependent on foreign countries that control the crude oil prices. One of 'em found oil clear back in 1951 in Williams County, North Dakota, and now a whole bunch of companies are back here looking for more. It's a competition between companies, a race to see who can find black gold in our little corner of the world."

By the time his pizza had burned to a crisp, Grady learned all he needed to know. He added up the difference in about three seconds flat, and at the end of the month threw his meager belongings into the Datsun and said good-bye to Billings. He got hired by Noble Drilling, an oil company based out of Oklahoma, and moved in with his mom and the kids in Wibaux on a temporary basis. The oil rigs were anywhere from 100 to 180 miles north of Wibaux, which proved to be a nightmarish long drive back and forth.

Within a few months Grady and Tom Lorentz pooled their resources and bought a house in Williston, Ground Zero for the oil boom. A midsized town of about ten thousand people tucked in the northwest corner of North Dakota, cheap apartment buildings sprung up on newly expanded streets and local businesses thrived as the oil companies and subsequent entourages moved in.

Experts claimed the nearby Bakken shale held as much as four hundred billion barrels of oil in a basin that stretched across several counties in the north and west parts of North Dakota, into Montana and Saskatchewan in Canada. Locals simply called it The Bakken. Because it pooled in a narrow river of dolomite between two layers of shale, it was extremely hard to extract. Rigs had lost many a pipe in the Bakken and most dug now in the Red River, Stonewall, Winnipeg, Nisku, Madison, or Interlake crude oil reserves.

Geologists used plat maps to find out who owned the land and mineral rights, and ranchers were more than willing to let crews put up a rig in exchange for royalties. Almost overnight derricks popped up like metal trees all over the region.

Grady's mechanical experience and schooling helped him the grasp the workings of an oil rig and the massive diesel engine that kept it all running. The derrick—the metal framework—held the components of the system needed to accomplish such a feat. The Kelly—a five-ton hexagonal steel member suspended from the swivel through the rotary table—connected to the topmost section of the drill pipe. Hooked to the massive traveling block—an assembly of pulleys and sheaves that moved up or down—it lowered the pipe into the hole. Hundreds of pipes were stacked in the pipe rack next to the rig, waiting to be added to the ones already in the hole.

The man in charge of Grady's new crew was called the driller. He worked the controls on the draw works and shouted orders out to the men. Like a choreographed action movie, everyone followed his orders in succinct, smooth steps. The motor man pulled the thirty-foot pipe up the beaver slide to the mouse hole until it was time to make a connection or add another joint of pipe to the drill string. The driller raised the Kelly and the crew moved in to their preassigned choreographed positions. Whenever the Kelly was disconnected from the drill string, it was pushed back to the pipe in the mouse hole and screwed together. The chain hand wound his chain around the tool joint of the pipe in the hole, and as the Kelly and new joint of pipe came out of the mouse hole, the motor man and worm stabbed it into the waiting drill string. As the trainee, Grady stayed within shouting range. He was there to do grunt work and whatever else he was told.

All said and done, it was a pretty simple plan: dig down ten thousand feet below the earth's surface one thirty-foot section of a pipe at a time. After roughly 350 sections of pipe, they'd have a hole two miles into the ground, and if all went well, gold at the end of it—in this case, black gold. A rig could drill down ten thousand feet and hit oil in as few as thirty days, but every so often they walked away with a duster.

Each oil rig had four assigned crews that rotated shifts: one crew worked from eight a.m. to four p.m., daylight tower; the next shift worked four p.m. to midnight, evening tower; the third crew worked midnight to eight a.m., morning tower, while the fourth crew had "days off." The operation ran 24/7 until it was time to rig down and move to the next location. It took fifty semis to haul one drilling rig—estimated at a whopping five-million dollars—to the next hole.

Grady felt good about the new direction his life had taken. And to top it off, he'd just cashed the biggest paycheck he'd ever seen. Working the rigs was physically hard, but he grew up knowing what hard work was all about, thanks to his dad's parenting attributes. Grady made one effort to go see his dad while he was staying in Wibaux. He went to the apartment and found it empty. Grady knew he had a fifty-fifty shot where to find him: the Silver Dollar or the Stockman. After a few minutes listening to the ornery ol' cuss, Grady'd walked out, disgusted as always.

Grady and Tom found a nice rambler on a corner lot with two bedrooms and the living/dining room all on one level. He appreciated his mom letting him stay with her while he and Tom looked for a house, but he was glad to be on his own again. Sharing a room with Kurt and Dean at nineteen about put him over the edge. Melinda was getting prettier all the time and starting her senior year. Kurt was a junior and thankfully using his restless energy to play running back for the Wibaux Longhorns. Dean was in sixth grade and liked riding bike to see his friends. His mom had her hands full, but a person would never know it by her demeanor: always happy, smiling, doing whatever it took to make ends meet.

Grady walked out to the garage to organize the back wall and put up shelving for his tools. Already he had guys asking if he could replace the shocks, brakes, or sway bar on their cars. The garage was a virtual disaster after the move and he hardly knew where to start. He opened the overhead door and leaned against the door frame, soaking up the morning sun. No more mountain views in the distance—this part of North Dakota was so flat you could see clear to Canada. He tapped a pack of Marlboros on his wrist and pulled the farthest one out with his lips. He positioned a Bic lighter at the end and flicked the tiny fork-spring three times before it emitted a large yellow flame. The odor of butane gas filled his nostrils and he stared, mesmerized by the dancing fire.

When he was five or six, he and his cousin Casper had gotten caught playing with matches under the porch at his aunt and uncle's house. Back then he thought Casper was the funniest name he'd ever heard, like Casper the ghost. Casper was a couple years older than Grady, the adventurous and mischievous sort. Grady really liked the kid and was always willing to go along with his ideas, good or bad. First they burned a few small twigs and then some grass, which caused enough smoke to alert their parents drinking and playing canasta inside. Before Grady knew what'd happened, his dad dragged him into the kitchen and shoved him into a chair.

"Give me your hands!"

Grady hesitated.

"Give me your hands I said!" he yelled even louder.

In innocence Grady unfolded his hands over the table, tears welling in his eyes. Something told him it was going to hurt real bad.

His dad popped out a Zippo lighter and waited until he had a nice flame going. Then he pulled Grady's fingers directly over it. "There! How do you like that?" The fire in his father's eyes was more intense than the actual flames.

Crying, Grady tried to pull his fingers back but his dad's strong hands were no match. "You wanna know about fire?" he said in a deep growl. "I'll teach you about fire!"

Grady's flesh turned white and his fingernails bubbled. The odor of burning flesh hung in the air. He screamed for help and by the time his nails had melted, his screams turned another pitch higher. It must've finally got the best of his mother, because he heard her call from the other room, "Frank, that's enough!"

His dad kicked a chair in her direction. "I'll decide what's enough," he said, spit flying, still gripping Grady's small hands.

"Frank, please!" Carol Kramer's voice pleaded from somewhere out of view.

"What do you know about discipline?" he hollered in a taunting tone. "Huh? If I left that job up to you he'd be nothing but a spoiled brat, and I can tell you right now, that ain't gonna happen in my house! This boy needed a lesson and I think he's learned it," he said like a proud master teaching an apprentice. "He'll never play with matches again!"

That particular lesson haunted Grady for years, especially at night. He'd wake up sweating, crying, flames leaping at him in his dreams. His dad was right; he didn't play with matches again. But the real lesson he learned was that dads can hurt their kids and no one will stop them.

PART III

CHAPTER FOURTEEN

Northwestern North Dakota, 1981

Grady stood on the crown of the giant oil rig a good 160 feet off the ground. He glanced at his watch: eight-thirty—just over three hours left on his tower. Right now the western sky was afire in brilliant streaks of orange and red as the sun nudged lazily toward the horizon. In another half hour the big flaming sphere would slip behind the ridge, covering the barren landscape in shimmering hues of summer's brilliant twilight. The day had been a scorcher, over ninety degrees—typical for August—and Grady's greasers were drenched in a stench of gray mud and sweat.

He pulled the grease gun strapped to his back around his waist and pumped a few squirts of axel grease onto the assembly of sheaves and pulleys mounted on beams at the top of the rig.

145

He liked it at the top. It was the only place on the large metal derrick where he could escape the constant drone and din of the compounded motors grinding 24/7 down below. When they were digging hole at a good rate, he'd climb to the top two or three times a tower.

He leaned back against the metal pillow block and scanned the rugged terrain that stretched out before him, a 360-degree panoramic view that stretched for a good fifteen to twenty miles. At least a dozen other rigs were visible in the near-dusk light. As Grady's eyes settled on the parched, hardened landscape, he couldn't help wondering why settlers were drawn to this area in the first place. He'd heard stories from ol' timers about folks who had come through with a wagon and what little they could carry, and of all the places on God's green earth, what made them stop and settle here. Only prairie grass as far as the eye could see, no trees to build a shelter or house. Settlers had to cut sod all summer long, stack it, fill in the cracks and holes, only to worry about what to burn all winter in order to keep warm. Then again, maybe things were much worse wherever they'd come from. Regardless, they must've been pretty damned desperate.

Nowadays ranchers had sporadic fields of summer fallow, wheat, and sunflowers planted in large sections. Every so often a giant patch of brilliant yellow faces stood out like bold droplets of the sun, poised proudly on tall green sticks. Herds of Texas longhorn, Hereford, Angus, and Galloway grazed on open ranges where the rough and rolling terrain made it impossible to grow crops. Maybe there was a certain beauty to the land. Some folks—namely oil company execs—were far more intrigued by what lay below the earth's surface.

In the four years since he'd started with Noble Drilling, he worked his way up from the lowest job of trainee to worm's corner, chain hand, motor man, and now derrick hand. Right now he was working on a new rig in Sheridan County, Montana, which bordered Canada on the north and North Dakota on the east.

Grady turned into the evening wind and waited. There, he heard it—the pretty tune of a meadowlark. Soon another responded, singing, whistling back and forth as they flew for cover in the evening. Tiny lights flickered in the distance from the other rigs; a few stars shone in the east as the evening sky began to darken one soft shade at a time. A half mile away a "see-sawing" hammerhead pumped crude oil on a former hole Grady worked two summers ago. Bright spotlights affixed to each rig stayed on 24/7, flooding it in a glaring white glow, attracting throngs of insects as evening settled on the land.

He took off his hard hat and rubbed his head where the sweat pooled in his hair. He wore it a little shorter now, just below the ear. The breeze at this height was nature's air conditioning and it cooled his muscled frame. At twenty-four years of age he was in the best physical shape of his life. He slid into the ass-lift, a climber belt hooked to a cable with a 110-pound counterweight. He put his feet on the side rails of the ladder and in a matter of seconds pulled himself down thirty feet to the boom pole, a section of four-inch drill pipe that stuck out twenty feet perpendicular to the ground.

Still ninety feet above the drilling floor, Grady stooped down and lowered his body onto the boom. He scooted on his stomach out to the end and pulled the grease gun around again. He gave the pulley a few good squirts and eased himself back the length of the pole to the girders within the safety of the derrick framework. More than once he'd used the Geronimo line to swing to the ground, but the tool pusher frowned upon the cheap form of roughneck recreation. He knew better to get on the driller's bad side and instead climbed down the ladder to the drilling floor in search of Kilowatt.

Donny Berg was the driller on Grady's tower, but everyone called him Kilowatt. He'd been an electrician for six

147

years before he started on the oil rigs and still did it on the side. At thirty-four he was one of the older guys on the crew, skinny as a pipe stand, but a good leader on their crew and liked to stop for a beer with the younger guys. His standing joke was that he was in no hurry to get home and climb in bed. "Have you seen my wife? Hell, she ain't the better half; she's the bigger half!"

Kilowatt had started to teach Grady about the proper weight to run on the drill string. Grady hoped that would be his next position. Who knew, maybe after that he'd even make tool pusher, the man in charge of all four crews and responsible for the round-the-clock operation. Tonight the geolograph steadily clicked off foot after foot as the bit dug deeper into the earth. Drilling through rock and shale at 7,000 feet down, it averaged roughly a foot every five minutes. The drill string—which was in fact pipe—held steady at 140,000 pounds and kept the weight off the bit that priced out at fifteen thousand dollars.

As the derrick hand, Grady was responsible for maintaining the mud. Technically, drilling "mud" was a liquid made up of saltwater, barite, clay, and starch. Large high-pressure reciprocating pumps circulated the mud down the hole, forcing debris to the surface and cooling the bit simultaneously. A large reserve pit built next to the rig held the mud and water as it worked through the system—sort of an on-site recycling program. Bore cuttings and sediments ended up in the reservoir. The further down they drilled, the more water he needed to keep the hole conditioned.

Grady checked the mud in the top tool room one last time for his tower. Tonight was the last in a set of six and he looked forward to having a set of days off. Evening tower was the preferred shift because the guys could still hit the bars before closing and sleep in the next day. After sundown the winds calmed and straight above him millions of stars hung in wondrous lace patterns across the vast night sky. He spied headlights in the distance; the relief crew was right on time.

Two royal blue rail-car-sized trailers sat on top of one another and served as the center of operations for each drilling rig. The driller had his office in the top doghouse, where he monitored the automatic driller that fed constant data at a set rate and recorded important indicators. The rest of the crew had their lockers and equipment directly beneath in the bottom doghouse.

Grady swung the metal door open on the top doghouse. "Tower's over," he shouted to Kilowatt above the noise. "Crew's coming. I'm going down to meet 'em."

"I'll be down as soon as I go over the drilling report with Tony," Kilowatt answered, studying a printout of the geolograph under the bright fluorescent light affixed to the ceiling.

Grady slid down the handrails and into the bottom doghouse just as Steve Brock, the derrick hand for the morning tower, stepped in. Grady unlaced his boots and unhooked his bibs while relaying the day's information, "Number One is back on the hole. I took it off because we washed out a liner and a swab head."

"What about Number Two?" Brocker was short and stocky and had an odd-shaped face that resembled a toaster, with small ears tucked close to his head on each side.

"It's good; nothing wrong with it tonight." Grady threw his hard hat into his locker and picked up the army surplus bag that held a week's worth of summer roughnecking clothes: two pairs of bib overalls, three sleeveless T-shirts, one long-johns top in case it got cool on an evening tower, half-dozen pairs of extra socks, and a dozen or two pairs of work gloves.

"Okay," Brocker said, putting down his cooler and duffle bag.

Grady changed out of his greasers into clean jeans and a T-shirt, and his good boots. "The mud's looking good. I've got sixty-two viscosity, a twelve-point-two weight, and my water loss is at ten."

Brocker nodded. "How's the salt water?"

"We had another five thousand gallons delivered around six, so you're good there. The mud truck was out this morning during daylight tower; you've got a full mud house. If you guys don't have a trip, you'll have a sleeper tonight."

"Sounds good to me."

"Knowing you, you'll be laying on the mud sacks by four o'clock," Grady said with a laugh. The mud house held stacks of one-hundred pound bags of clay that the crew rearranged into a couch or recliner when it was slow.

"Nothing wrong with that." Brocker laced up his boots and put on his hard hat.

Whenever Grady took a turn on the mud sacks, the constant rumble of the massive diesel engines put him out like a baby. He slammed his locker shut and stuffed his greasers into his duffle bag. He'd have to hit the laundromat during his days off. "See ya next week." Grady shimmied down the handrails on the half flight of metal steps to the ground. "Extreme!" he shouted, looking past the mud house. "Let's go."

"Right behind you," came a low voice. Extreme didn't normally work on Grady's tower, but Rob Teiner went to his grandma's funeral in Jamestown, so they were short a motor man. Extreme stayed over from the daylight tower and worked a double shift to fill in. He'd earned the unusual nickname because of his innate sense of adventure that led to extreme situations— on and off the rigs. Back in June he blew up an old schoolhouse with a homemade bomb big enough to get the feds involved. One of Extreme's roommates worked as a seismographer and word was that he gave Extreme a couple five-pound tubes of explosive gels. Bored one evening, he rigged up the abandoned schoolhouse and sent pieces of it flying for hundreds of yards. The entire building blasted to bits except the roof, which landed dead center in the foundation. According to Extreme it was no big deal—just having a little roughneck fun. Of course, the feds'd had a different viewpoint and the incident was tagged "under investigation."

One by one the men congregated next to the parked cars. "We've got an extra car tonight," Kilowatt said. "How you wanna work it?" Because of the extreme distances between housing and the rigs, the driller had the added responsibility of getting his crew to the rig. He drove to each guy's house, picked him up for his tower, and drove him home afterward. Instead of the usual five guys for one car, they had six guys and two cars.

"Who cares, I just wanna get home," Red said, a skinny kid from Fargo with bright red hair and a deep voice that didn't fit his boyish appearance. He was the trainee and brand new to the rigs.

"Yeah, I'm tired," Napper said. He moved up to worm's corner when Red got hired.

"I know one thing for damn sure, we're hittin' the bar when we get to town," Mike Bigsbee said, pointing a finger at Extreme. "We're on days off tomorrow. Time to take advantage." His large-framed glasses nearly reached the thin line of fuzz above his lip that he proudly called a 'stache.

"Quit wasting time B-S-ing and let's hit the road," Kilowatt said. "Worse than a bunch of ol' biddies in my grandma's card club."

Extreme walked around the front of the Buick. "What's in this thing?" he asked, tapping the hood.

"A 455," Grady said. "Why?"

Extreme took a drag on his Winston and tossed it into the dirt. "It's five to," he said, checking his watch. "I'll make you a bet . . ."

"Yeah," Grady said, inching forward. "What's that?"

Extreme exhaled and ground the butt into the gravel with the toe of his boot. ". . . we can beat you back to the bar in the Buick."

"No way!" Grady said. "It'll never happen."

Kilowatt stepped in front of Grady and stood face-to-face with Extreme, arms crossed. "You think you can outrun us?" Kilowatt and Extreme eyed each other like two gunslingers about to duel.

Grady gave Extreme a shove on the shoulder. "The Pontiac has a 389, a Super Chief. It'll outrun the 455 in a Buick any day of the week, and then some. You don't stand a chance."

"But the Buick's a seventy-two," Napper said, shaking his head. "The Pontiac's what . . . a sixty-eight?"

"Sixty-nine," corrected Grady.

"You on?" Extreme asked. "Or not?" His well-built frame stood on the ground as solid as the nearby derrick.

"Are you serious?" Red said. "It's almost fifty miles back to Grenora. You gonna race the whole way? *Fifty* miles?"

"You got a problem with that?" Extreme lowered his head like an angry bull about to charge and Red retreated a step.

"Sounds kinda crazy if you ask me." Red made eye contact with each man in the circle, silently begging for support.

"Who is this kid anyway?" Extreme said with his back to Red. He swatted a wide palm like he was getting rid of a nasty mosquito. "Maybe you're all like baby face here—"

"Just who you calling baby face?" Grady arched his back and stepped forward.

Kilowatt stared at Extreme. "That's it. You're on, man."

"All right!" said Grady, slapping his fist on the hood. "That's what I'm talkin' about!"

"Your ass is gonna be sorry," Extreme said, smiling.

Grady stopped in his tracks. "You better think again, wiseass."

"Oh, man, this is wild," Napper said with a chuckle. "If losers buy the first round, I'm riding with Extreme."

"Where does the race start?" Red hugged his lunch box to his chest like a security blanket and walked around the white Pontiac. "On the tar?"

"Hell no," Kilowatt said.

"You can't race on gravel," Red said, shaking his head. "There ain't room."

"Says who?" said Extreme.

"We've got eight, nine miles of gravel before we even get to tar!" Red exclaimed, fear dripping from his bulging eyeballs.

"More like eleven miles," Kilowatt said. He opened the driver's door and turned around. "Three to a car. Grady, Red, let's go!"

"But it's pitch dark!" Red shouted, frozen in his tracks.

Grady hopped in the front passenger seat. "Get in back, Red." Each roughneck had an unofficial seat assignment in the crew car based on rank.

The Buick pulled away with Extreme at the wheel, Bigs riding shotgun, and Napper in the back. Kilowatt started the Pontiac. "Red! Get in—now!" Red dove into the backseat as Kilowatt punched the gas pedal. The sedan fishtailed a few times, then straightened out as Kilowatt picked up speed.

"Whoa!" Red yelled, looking back.

"We ain't even started yet," Grady said.

"I didn't really want to race him," Kilowatt said, eyes fixed to the road. "Way to egg him on."

"Extreme has a way of getting under my skin," Grady said.

Kilowatt was silent and then a roguish smirk spread across his face. "What the hell, man. Let's beat the tar out of him," he said with a quick sideways glance at Grady. In a matter of seconds Kilowatt sped the Pontiac up to sixty-three miles an hour, leaving a trail of dust as thick as a late August dust storm.

A deep laugh escaped Grady's throat. "It's all good, man."

"I dunno . . . I can barely see his taillights."

"No worries. You're gaining on him." Grady eyed the faint red taillights through the brown wall of dust billowing in their headlights. "You got it."

The Super Chief flew off the ground a good twenty feet as they crested a small hill. It bounced hard, gained traction, and kept going. "We're eatin' their dust, Grady," Kilowatt said in a cool, even voice.

"There's a straightaway coming up in about a mile," advised Grady. "You can take him there."

Sure enough, the hills gave way and the headlights lit up a flat section of gravel. Kilowatt floored it again. "*Hang . . . onnnn!*" he sang, gripping the wheel with both hands. The Buick was within thirty yards, spitting a cloud of dirt skyward like a combine combing a wheat field after a long drought.

"Take him, now! Punch it!" yelled Grady as the Pontiac sped around the Buick with no room to spare. Grady and Kilowatt both let out a roar. "Get over, over!" Grady shouted. "Don't let him sneak by you on the right!"

"I think *you* should be driving this thing," Kilowatt said with a nod toward Grady.

Red whipped his head around. "They're right behind us!" Kilowatt kept the accelerator floored for two miles until they reach another section of low hills. "Oh, man, here they come!" cried Red.

The Buick sped by in a brown flash of choking dust and dirt. "That's okay," Kilowatt said. "We'll get 'em on the tar. I know I can outrun 'em."

"Now you're talking," Grady said.

As soon as they hit the intersection with the county highway, the Buick squealed to make the corner just ahead of them and the Pontiac echoed. Red's skinny frame slid across the silver vinyl seat, right to left. "Whoah . . ." Both cars laid a long line of rubber as they turned south and reached a steady speed.

Kilowatt glanced at his dashboard. "I'm doing ninety and we're not gaining."

"Pick it up a hair," Grady said.

Kilowatt pressed the gas pedal farther. "Okay," he said after a couple miles, "I can tell we're catching him now."

"Good work," Grady said. "Now, slide on over." Kilowatt eased into the left lane until he was running side by side with the Buick. "Look at 'em over there," Grady said, bursting into laughter. "Extreme's yelling somethin' fierce at Bigs. Oh man, can't you just hear him!"

"Should you be on the wrong side of the road like this?" Red asked in a nervous tone.

"Don't matter as long as there's no other cars on the road," Grady said calmly.

"Oh, man, my ma would kill me if she knew I was doing something like this."

"She won't have to if we meet another car." Kilowatt gave Grady a wink.

Grady grinned. "Ah relax, kid," he said. "This goes on all the time and we haven't lost anyone yet, have we Kilowatt?"

"Other than a few cars. Idiots that can't drive, lose control and roll a few," Kilowatt said, keeping a close eye on Extreme and the Buick.

For five grueling miles the two crew cars stayed neck and neck until headlights appeared on the horizon. "Car coming!" Grady shouted.

"I see him," Kilowatt said in a smooth voice. "I got time yet." He maintained the same speed with the Buick until the approaching headlights expanded in diameter and neared within a mile.

Half mile.

"Oh—Mother—Mary—" Red said in hyperventilated breaths.

Quarter mile.

155

With seconds to spare, Kilowatt jumped on the skids and swerved in behind the Buick's rear bumper as Red continued his impassioned plea to the Virgin Mary.

"Damn!" Kilowatt said. "We're behind him again."

"Tell you what . . ." Grady leaned forward with one hand on the front dashboard. "Wait until we come to that little section where it gets all hilly again. As soon as Extreme clears a hill, shut the lights off. When you come over the hill you can see his taillights and follow him, but he can't see you. He'll have no idea what happened and he'll start to slow, you watch. Then you can catch him and blow right by him, I swear, and he won't have a clue you're comin'."

"You gotta be shittin' me," came the deep voice in back.

"That's good," Kilowatt said, nodding. "That's real good. Now you're talking. Did anyone ever tell you you've got guts? Oooh, you're gonna make a good driller one a these days!" Kilowatt laughed and slapped the steering wheel. "Okay, okay, here we go."

"You gotta be shittin' me . . ."

Kilowatt turned serious and sat rigid in his seat, focused on the Buick's taillights.

"As soon as he clears this next hill." Grady sat sideways with one arm on the seat back, one hand on the dash, coaxing Kilowatt. "Okay, shut the lights down."

Kilowatt pushed in the knob and pitch black darkness filled in the space in front of the Pontiac. "This is more nerve-wracking than walking the divin' board in a thunderstorm." Long, dark seconds ticked past.

Grady watched the red dots slowly expand. "Relax," he said. "Keep your speed up! That's it!"

Kilowatt fixated his eyes on the set of red lights. "Whoa, they're slowing down, I can tell."

"Told ya!" said Grady.

"What if they think we had car trouble?" Red asked.

"That's the whole idea, dumb ass."

"Oh, man, I can't handle this," Red said in a deep moan, leaning over the front seat. "There's a car coming! Don't ya have to turn the lights back on?"

"That'll ruin our whole strategy," Grady said to Red. He turned to Kilowatt, "Just keep a close eye on it so they don't drift over into our lane. They won't have a clue we're here until we fly by 'em."

"Gotcha."

They rode in silence, eyes peeled to the roadway, watching the headlights get close and closer. *Whisshhh,* the car went by them. Grady turned to watch the car swerve in its lane. "Probably freaked out Ole and Lena."

"Damn! This is takin' a while to catch 'em," Kilowatt said.

"Can you push it any faster?"

"I've been doing close to ninety for four, five miles now."

"Here's comes another car," Grady said.

"Damn," Kilowatt said. "The square dance somewhere must 'a' just ended." He gripped the steering wheel, watching the headlights approach. *Whoosssh!*

"Watch now, you got it," Grady said. "We're gaining on them, we're almost there."

"I've got a straight shot up ahead," Kilowatt said.

"Yup, I see it. Okay, floor it!" Grady shouted. "Now!"

Kilowatt hit the gas and pulled to the left side of the road. He laid on the horn and blew by the Buick at eighty-nine miles an hour. Grady, Red, and Kilowatt let out a roar that nearly busted the windows. *"Yaaaah!"* Kilowatt flipped the headlights on and pulled into the right lane.

"Oh, man, they're way back there now," Red said, looking through the back window.

"Not for long, I'm sure," Kilowatt said, easing back slightly. "Oh, that felt good!" He squirmed in his seat, watching his rearview mirror.

"Can you just hear Extreme? I bet he's going crazy!" Grady said, slapping his thigh.

"Here they come!" Red shouted. "They're gainin' on us."

"I see 'em." Kilowatt adjusted the mirror slightly.

The Buick pulled up right behind them and then pulled into the opposite lane. "Keep it going!" yelled Grady, keeping a close eye on their competitor.

Extreme ran nose to nose with the Pontiac for a half mile but couldn't take the lead. "Oh, here comes a car!" said Grady. "He'll have to pull back."

"Damn!" yelled Kilowatt. "I think he's gonna get by me!" He gripped the wheel tightly, eyes focused on the road.

"Hang on! Keep it up!" Grady pounded the dash in encouragement.

For several long seconds the Buick and Pontiac ran head-to-head. The oncoming car neared at a steady pace. At the last possible second Extreme pulled behind, bringing another round of cheers from Grady and his car mates. As soon as the car sped by, Extreme gunned it again and pulled alongside the Pontiac.

Back and forth, neck and neck, the race continued another twenty-seven miles until they crossed from Montana into North Dakota. Lights from Grenora glowed in the distance—a tiny town hardly more than a bump in the road eighteen miles south of the Canadian border. "We're almost there," Grady said. "Don't let up, whatever you do!"

"There she is," Kilowatt said, referencing the Grenora Bar, a small dive of a joint.

"Keep it up," Grady said through gritted teeth as the bar came into view. "You got him!"

Kilowatt slowed down just enough to make the turn into the gravel parking lot first, the back end swerving in the sand. He slammed the brakes hard and stopped just short of the wooden rail in front of the rundown building. "Yeaaaah!" he shouted, shifting into Park.

Grady let out a roar and pumped his fist. "Oh, man, Extreme's gonna go off! You watch—he'll work a double again next week, just to take you on again."

"He don't scare me," Kilowatt said, killing the engine. He lowered his voice and leaned toward Grady. "I don't care what they call him. That punk kid is gonna be in a world of hurt from what I hear."

"Really?"

He nodded and held his forefinger to his lips. "Doing time. You don't blow up a building that size and get away with it," Kilowatt said with a nod toward the Buick as it pulled up next to them.

Grady and Kilowatt got out of the Pontiac, howling and yipping, giving each other high-fives in a show of their newly claimed victory. "Man oh man, that was sweet!"

Red leaned forward, hands on his thighs, face as pale as a ghost. "I can't believe we made it . . ."

Extreme jumped out of the Buick and slammed the door. The layer of dust covering the Buick was so thick the car looked like it was wrapped in peach fuzz. "That damn piece of junk let me down!"

Bigs and Napper hopped out the passenger side. "Man that was close!" Bigs shouted.

"I shoulda had you that last mile," Extreme said, kicking more dirt onto the Buick. "Next time, man. I swear." His tone left no doubt that he was dead serious.

"Yeah, well, this time you're gonna buy me a beer," Kilowatt said. He slapped Extreme on the back and they walked inside.

Grady sat down at the bar beside Bigs, thirsty for a cold one after their heart-stopping ride. "Gimme a Pabst," he said to the bartender, pointing behind him, "and he's buying."

"Hit me up," Extreme said, approaching the bar. "Same thing." He guzzled half of his bottle and wiped his mouth. "Damn piece of crusty metal," he muttered, pulling out his wallet. Napper joined them at the bar while Red headed straight to the restroom, hands clutched at his gut.

Kilowatt took a quick swallow and looked at his watch. "Well, I'll be danged, boys. We set a new record." Grinning, he tipped his bottle at his crew.

"C'mon, Grady, two out of three." Bigs nodded toward the pool table in the back.

Grady surveyed the patrons in the small-town bar. All locals; no crazies as far as he could tell. "Sure, man. Rack 'em and I'll break." Bigs took the first game; Grady won the second but scratched on the eight ball in the tiebreaker.

"Hey, how about buying those two a drink?" Bigs asked, nodding toward two girls in the corner booth.

Grady did a quick overview. The gal with reddish brown hair was keeping time to a Bob Seger song on the jukebox. She must've sensed they were watching, because she looked right at Grady and smiled. "Sure," he said, sliding off his stool. "I'm in the mood for a little sweet talk.

CHAPTER FIFTEEN

Like most of the roughnecks, Grady tipped a few brews after their shift, but he didn't like hanging out in bars. The incident at the Vault still taunted him, always in the back of his mind like a dark shadow about to explode in his ear. He drank just enough to take the edge off from time to time and steered clear of places where a crazed man with a Smith and Wesson would choose to even a score.

Grady dated now and then, but he hadn't found anyone special enough to make it serious. His mom still held out hope for him and Naomi to get back together. She always filled him in on the latest Wibaux-Beach news, typical small-town gossip. Who got married or had a baby. Who got divorced or lost a job. Melinda got married right after graduation and moved to Grand Forks with her husband. She already had a little girl, who was her spitting image. Kurt worked at Hornbacher's grocery store in Fargo; Dean was the only one at home with their mom.

Right now Grady's life revolved around the twenty-four-hour cycle of an oil rig. There was a good camaraderie among the roughnecks and he fit in well. The schedule freed him up to enjoy the great outdoors: fishing both summer and winter, hunting in the fall, and catching snakes in between. His favorite fishing spot was a sandy section on the Missouri River south of Williston nicknamed Little Egypt. Other times, when he and Tom ended up on a long change at the same time, they'd drive down to Wibaux to chew up their days off. They were assigned to different rigs and some weeks hardly saw each other.

Grady was stretched out on the couch watching a fuzzy episode of Outdoor Sportsman. No matter how he twisted the rabbit ears, he couldn't get a clear picture.

Tom came through the back screen door, letting it slam behind him. "Hey, Grady!" he called from the kitchen.

"In here!"

Tom leaned against the door frame. He'd filled out since high school, his shoulders pronounced and broad from his days throwing chain and lifting mud sacks. "You wanna run down to Wibaux with me?" His T-shirt had a big grease stain in the front and hung loose over his jeans.

"What's up?"

"I gotta help my folks fix fence tomorrow and Ma wants me to bring down a case of Mason jars."

"Anything to help out Miss Myrtle," Grady said without budging from his comfortable position. Myrtle Lorentz was a character in her own right, always spoke her mind. Originally from Arkansas, she seemed to have a sixth sense about things in life.

Grady and Tom packed a duffle bag for the road trip and locked up the house. Tom cranked down the window in Grady's Datsun and rested his forearm on the open frame. After a quick stop at Albertsons for Myrtle's jars, Grady deposited a dozen paychecks at his bank.

"What in the world?" asked Tom when he saw all the pay stubs.

"I got a call from some sweet-sounding southern gal in payroll, asking me to deposit them."

"What were you hanging onto them for?"

"No reason; just didn't think it mattered. Got plenty in my account, that's all." Grady pulled away from the bank. "Hope that makes Miss Daisy Duke happy now."

Tom's head whipped sideways. "Do you s'pose that's what she looks like?"

Grady frowned and spit out the window. "I talked to her; I didn't see her, dumb ass."

"Yeah, well I'd like to see her. Daisy Duke, I mean. I'm in love with her, ya know. Long hair, long legs."

"You're pathetic, you know that."

"Hey . . ." Tom paused to light up a Marlboro. He took a long drag and blew the smoke out the window. "Let's take the back roads. Maybe we can find somethin' to amuse us on the way."

The smoke triggered a nicotine urge and Grady reached for his own pack, tapping it on the dash. "I'm game."

The strong August sun smothered the open landscape in a stifling blanket of heat. Streaks of varied wisps of white clouds created a tic-tac-toe image against the soft blue sky. Grady crossed over a wide section of the Missouri River; the muddied water rippled in the afternoon wind, whitish buttes hugging the water on the north side. A few determined fishing boats clustered around a gentle bend of the river, out of the wind. He drove south of Williston and turned east on Highway 200, which cut through the tiny town of Cartwright. Here and there pink patches of sweet clover poked their heads above the tufts of prairie grass. He turned south again on a county road just before the Yellowstone River, where a bed of cattails filled a low spot in the ditch, heading south of Highway 68. Down around the little village of

Trotters, Grady crossed the state line into Wibaux County in Montana.

"Hey, cut through this pasture," Tom said, pointing to the two-rut trail. "There's an abandoned shack back in here I wanna show you. I bet it's been there over a hundred years."

"How far back?" Grady drove over the cattle guard and turned down the gravel trail. A cloud of reddish brown dust puffed out from the back end of the Datsun.

"Two, maybe three miles. It sits behind a set of buttes. I didn't know it was there until last year, when I was hunting pheasants back here with my dad."

The rough trail followed a sloped ridge into the lower part of the pasture. "Whoa!" Grady said, looking straight ahead. "Look at that!" He eased off the gas pedal as a whole slew of snakes crawling every which way moved across the gravel en masse.

"Holy Schmoly!" Tom leaned forward, brushing back his bangs to get a good look. "Have you ever seen anything like that in your life?"

"Them suckers must be heading back to their dens already." Grady braked and stopped the truck. The moving mass of sandy brown reptiles almost made him dizzy as he watched them slide and curl and twist their way across the rock-hard ground.

"Man, I've never seen a whole bunch together like that!" Tom said with a gulp.

"Me neither. You know what this means." It was a slinking, slithering challenge Grady couldn't resist. He killed the engine. Hides sold for two to three dollars each, but that was only part of his motive. He enjoyed the pure thrill of it.

"Time to catch a few?"

"Absolutely. I can always sell a few hides or cook up a few. Besides, I need a new one for my aquarium." When Grady was a kid he watched Marlin Perkins and Jim Fowler on *Mutual of Omaha's Wild Kingdom* every Sunday and studied how they handled snakes. Bull snakes were abundant on the northern prairie and good for practice, but he preferred the challenge of catching the deadly rattlers. He learned if a rattlesnake was going to strike it would draw its body into an S-shaped coil and lunge forward, mouth open, the long hooked fangs ready to deliver the venom into its victim. The trick was to push the head down with a shovel and grab the head in one swift motion. His tactics had paid off 'cause he'd caught dozens of rattlers every summer and never been bit.

Grady and Tom hopped out of the truck and grabbed the shovels Grady kept in the back end for just such an occasion. They followed the snakes across the road into the pasture, shovels held low, ready to defend against a possible strike. In all his years hunting snakes, he'd never seen so many in one cluster. The ground swam with innumerable shades of brown and green, slinking and twisting in every direction.

The prairie rattlesnake varied from light brown to green, with a yellowish belly. Dark oval blotches with light-colored borders ran along the center of its back. The blotches became cross bands on the back part of the body and rings around the tail, and most rattlers were thirty to forty inches in length. He knew the normal striking distance of a rattlesnake was only half the snake's body length, which helped him anticipate the snake's strike.

Grady spied a decent-sized one and followed it around a small patch of brush. Within seconds the snake coiled and jerked forward in a strike. Grady was ready. He aimed the shovel head at the snake and pushed its head to the ground. He kept the head pinned down and reached behind the shovel to grab the head. Its mouth opened, exposing the flared blackish tongue. Grady grabbed the head and lifted the shovel in one swift motion. "Ah hah! Gotcha!" he said triumphantly, letting it dangle at arm's length.

He carried it to the back end of the pickup and dropped it on the wheel track. Stunned, the snake tried to coil. In one swift motion Grady severed the head with the shovel before it had the chance. He threw the body in the back end of his truck and ran to get the next one. It didn't take long to work up a sweat in the hot August sun. Within a half hour he'd caught nine snakes to Tom's six.

Grady noticed one slithering under a sage brush and moved in for a closer look. His adrenaline surged as he eyed the size of it. "Tom! Get over here!"

"What?"

"Look at this one," he said, pointing to the sage. "Hold back a minute."

The rattlesnake curled and coiled, the head and tail up, on guard. *Chhhhhhst! Chhhhhhst!*

"Whoa, man. Get back!" Tom shouted, waving Grady back.

"No way," Grady said, taking a defensive pose, inching forward. "He's mine."

"Grady, no!" Tom retreated a few steps, wiping his hands on his jeans in nervous gestures. "That one's a monster. Let him go."

Grady stared at the huge snake; it had to be five, maybe six feet in length. He'd never seen one that big on the prairie before. "I'm gonna get him."

"Forget it, man. He's too dangerous."

The snake slithered a few feet and coiled again, head bobbing, moving, eyes bulging, its rattle in constant motion, *Chhhhhst! Chhhhhst! Chhhhhhst!* "I ain't gonna kill this big daddy; he's a keeper!" Grady held out his right arm, the shovel in ready position as he inched closer in slow, cautious steps. The snake stretched out to its full length and then coiled up in a double circle, like a vertical figure-eight. Grady froze. He waited several long seconds as the snake defied gravity and held its stance, the rattle buzzing. Its mouth opened, exposing the long tongue and the fangs. Grady eased forward, eyes locked on the head as it bobbed.

In one swift movement he took aim and pushed the shovel straight down against the head and picked it up. "I got it!" he said triumphantly. Tom was right; it was a monster, damn near six feet long. The black eyes bulged even farther; its red tongue speared outward. The striped marks across its face looked like war paint.

"Oh, man!" Tom said, backing away. "Watch him, Grady. He looks like Satan himself."

The snake curled its heavy body, shaking Grady's arm like crazy, its brute strength surprising him. The snake fought to free itself, twisting and turning his long yellow belly. "Damn, he's heavy!" yelled Grady, guessing it weighed eight pounds or more. He lost his grip and the snake hit the ground. "Holy cow!" Grady said, shaking his arm. He jumped back, keeping a close eye on it as it slithered for cover. "I swear I ain't never seen one that big!"

"You're lucky he didn't get you, Grady." Tom stepped back again, eyeing the ground. "That one creeped me out, big-time."

"Oh, he ain't gettin' away that easy," Grady said. He spied it heading for a crevasse near some rocks. "We ain't done yet, big boy," he muttered under his breath. Grady positioned the shovel behind its head and in one quick movement, sliced off the head. The eyes bulged out and the tongue went limp as the body curled and twisted on the ground.

"Whoo!" Tom shouted from ten yards back. "You're crazy, man."

Grady picked up the heavy carcass and carried it back to the truck. "I'd rather have kept him alive, but he ticked me off. Guess he'll make a nice pair of boots for someone." He tossed it in the back end with the others.

Within the hour Grady and Tom had caught nineteen snakes. The truck bed swam with headless reptiles, slithering as though they still had heads. "This will put me at an all-time high," Grady said.

"Oh, yeah?"

"I'm up to dang near fifty snakes this summer," he said with pride. "But I need one more," Grady said. "I want one live one to bring home." He kept an old dryer drum in the back end of the truck to transport live snakes and used a hubcap for a cover. His last catch of the day was a nice-sized rattler that Grady thought was rather cute. He dropped the little guy—maybe three feet long—into the dryer drum to take home for his aquarium.

"Guess we better get out to your ma's or she'll wonder if we're ever gonna show up."

Grady drove to the far side of the pasture and waited while Tom opened the gate. As soon as he turned onto the section road he saw an old structure, the wood nearly black from years of weathered beatings. "There, that's it," Tom said. Two stories tall, it was only one room deep and two rooms wide, the windows long gone, the base sitting on a stone foundation. A century ago it had been someone's home, standing alone on the prairie as seasons came and went. An abandoned shell of what once held the hopes and dreams of early settlers, mostly Scandinavian immigrants, forced out by drought or blizzards— either one sent many a settler back east.

Grady's Datsun thundered along the section road another twelve miles. Fresh-cut hay bales from the summer's second cutting rested in the field. A dozen horses roamed the next section, filling up on clumps of buffalo grass, tails swishing the flies off their rumps as Grady neared the Lorentz farm.

Tom carried the case of jars to the house and Grady followed him inside with the hope of getting something home-baked. Myrtle usually had fresh-baked chocolate chip cookies that were the best he'd ever eaten—better than his own mom's.

"Lands sakes, here's my jars!" Myrtle Lorentz exclaimed in her southern drawl, each word coated in sweet honey. "Thank you, boys, ya'll saved the day. I've got peaches up to my ears in here and didn't have enough jars for 'em all!" Tom put the case on the floor. The kitchen counter was buried under crates of fresh peaches and canning supplies, the fruit's sweet aroma filling Grady's nostrils. "I already done canned thirty-six jars of these blasted things." Myrtle had on a blue and white sleeveless cotton dress, with her short, wiry curls pinned up in the heat of the day. She had an apron tied around her waist, dirty and stained from a full day's work.

"Ma, you gotta come out to Grady's truck," Tom said with urgency. "You'll never guess what we found. We went through Benson's old place, remember?"

Myrtle's eyes grew big as silver dollars and she put both hands on her hips. "You boys find ya some snakes?" she asked with excitement in her voice.

"C'mon," Tom said, leading her out the front screen door.

The snakes were still slithering and crawling all over each other in the back of Grady's truck bed. Myrtle gasped, her eyes locked on the headless reptiles. "A snake will never die till the sun goes down," she said, wagging her forefinger at the boys. "You mark my words. As long as their bodies are warm, they'll keep slithering till it gets dark." She lowered her voice and tipped her head at an angle. "Then tonight, after dark, they'll stop. You watch 'em when you get home and see if what I say is right."

"I believe you, Mrs. Lorentz," Grady said. Something in her voice told him she wasn't fooling when it came to snakes.

"E-gads!" she said, watching them slither. "What are you gonna do with all of 'em?"

"We'll probably eat the smaller ones. Roll 'em in flour, little salt and egg, and fry 'em up in oil. It tastes just like chicken, very lean," Grady said. "The bigger ones I'll skin and sell the

169

hides. They're paying two or three dollars at the gun shop in Glendive."

"C'mon in the house." She waved the boys up the steps to the back door, where a black cat curled up against a dented cream can filled with lavender and pink petunias. "I've got half a peach pie from yesterday to give ya."

Filled up on pie and milk, Tom said, "Let's get going before Ma decides the fence can't wait 'til tomorrow."

"Wibaux?"

Tom nodded. "May as well."

Grady rubbed his chin and looked at Tom out of the corner of his eyes. "Let's hit the Stockman and make a few bucks."

"How we gonna do that?"

"We'll stop home and get my snake jar."

Tom roared in laughter. "Oh, boy!"

"The rodeo's in town, it outta be packed with redneck cowboys."

"I know where you're going with this."

"Hopefully, Mom ain't home. She freaked out on me last time I had a snake in the house."

Grady dropped off his duffle bag and left a note that he'd be home for supper. He switched the snake from the dryer drum to the jar and drove downtown.

Main Street Wibaux buzzed with the hot, dusty rodeo fever. Cowboys and cattlemen were everywhere. Pickups and horse trailers choked the streets between downtown and the rodeo grounds on the south end. Cute girls with feminized cowboy hats and colorful shirts smiled and waved at Grady and Tom as they walked the sidewalk to the Stockman Bar.

New owners from California had remodeled the historic bar, added rock music to the jukebox, and served fancy drinks like the Black Jelly Bean and Robin's Nest instead of just beer. The younger crowd loved it and word was the Californians were making money hand over fist, especially when the Little Britches Rodeo came to town in August and nearly tripled the population.

Grady carried the square glass gallon jar under his arm into the bar. The lid had holes punched so the snake could breathe and it was safe to transport. He pushed his way through a line of cowboys at the bar, clustered the way they did on the chutes at the rodeo arena. These were the cool rednecks, the kind who could tolerate rock music, versus the uncool ones that migrated to the back with the country crap-o-la.

Grady put his jar on the mahogany bar with Tom standing at his side.

"Hey, whacha got there?" one young cowboy asked, tipping his hat toward the jar. Grady's little fella slithered in slow, constant circles. The cowpoke looked twenty-five, and his blue plaid shirt fit tightly over his broad shoulders.

A second cowpoke, a skinny kid with his belt hooked on the last notch, leaned in and asked, "Where'd you git him, man?"

"Just caught him today." Grady pushed the jar a little closer to the cowmen. "Me and my buddy here."

"You shoulda seen 'em—snakes everywhere," Tom said, his chest puffed out as he described their daring venture. "We caught nineteen of 'em."

"No way," one of the cowpokes said.

"One was huge. What?" Tom slapped Grady's shoulder. "Eight-, ten-pounder?"

Grady nodded. "And at least eight feet."

"So, where's that one?"

"Headless . . . in the back of my pickup."

The skinny cowpoke pointed to the snake and took a drink of his beer. "So, what are you doin' with him in here?"

"I'm gonna make some money off him," Grady said with conviction.

They looked at each other with skepticism and laughed. "Oh yeah? How you gonna do that?"

Grady leaned over the top of the jar and pointed his forefinger at the cowpoke. "I bet you five bucks that you can't hold your hand against the glass, right here," he said, pointing at the side, "when he strikes." He stood back and let the boys get a closer look at the snake as a few more cowpokes gathered around.

The first cowboy put down his glass and pushed the wide brim of his hat back. "Okay, I'll try it."

Grady pulled out a five-dollar bill and laid it on the bar. "Here's my five, let me see yours."

"Got it right here." He dug his wallet out of the back pocket of his dust-covered Levis and counted out five ones and slapped the bills on the bar. As soon as he put his hand against the jar, the snake buzzed its tail and coiled in a tight circle. A second later it struck the side and the cowboy jerked his hand back like he'd touched a scalding hot branding iron. "Wait now! Hold on just a bull-doggin' minute," he said and raised his arms to protest. "Let me try that again. I wasn't ready."

"Sure thing," Grady said, patting the money. "Put down another five."

He filtered through the dividers of his leather wallet. "I only got three bucks left."

"How 'bout a beer, then?"

"Sure thing." He put his knuckles against the jar and the snake hissed. Its beady black eyes bulged as it coiled and struck the glass like lightning. His hand flinched back and he shook it as though he'd been bit. "Damn! I thought I could do it the second time."

Soon a couple roughnecks Grady recognized from one of the other oil companies wanted in on the action. "Let me try that!" one of them shouted, pushing forward.

"As soon as I get my beer from Tex here," Grady said.

"What do ya want?" the cowboy asked, shaking his head in disbelief.

"I'll take a Pabst."

"I'm next," the roughneck said, shoving the cowboy out of the way. "How much?" he asked with a bulge of snuff in his bottom lip.

"Five bucks," Tom said, serving as Grady's accountant.

The roughneck tucked his Rolling Stones T-shirt in a little farther into his Lee's and rubbed his hands together. "Working up for it," he said. He sucked in the tobacco juice and handed his money to Tom. "Okay, here goes."

"Here he comes, right through the glass!" someone shouted and the whole bunch burst into laughter.

"Gotcha!" another roughneck yelled.

One cowpoke with a red bandana and a white cowboy hat offered up his best rattler imitation. *"Hissss!"*

The roughneck pressed his hand against the jar as the snake slithered in a circle, its brown and greenish body in constant movement. The second it struck the glass, his hand jerked back faster than the cowboy's. "Aaah!" he shouted. "Shit!"

"Let me try that," his friend said, a crisp five-dollar bill already on the bar.

Smiling, Grady glanced up as an older cowboy came through the front door—older in the sense he was in his forties and looked like he was up to his hocks in money. He wore an oiled buffalo-hide cowboy hat, a shiny belt buckle, and black-and-cream-toned snakeskin boots. He took one look at Grady's jar and headed straight to it. "Hey now, boys, this looks like fun."

Grady could tell the rich cowboy and his friend must've already hit all stops in Wibaux. Grady made thirty bucks off those two alone before the bartender made him take his slithering moneymaker out to the truck.

Grady and Tom were still in the Stockman, talking stupid with their newfound friends, when the front door opened.

"Comin' through!" someone hollered. The nose of a chestnut quarter horse poked its pretty brown head through the front door. The young cowboy in the saddle pressed his heels into its side, urging the horse forward.

"Eh-haw!" someone called.

"Make room!"

Clomp, clomp, clomp, the horse's shoes clomped across the wooden floor as the kid rode it straight through the long, narrow bar and out the back door into the alley, followed by a round of whoops and loud cheers. Riding horse through the Stockman Bar was a tradition that went back to the days of Pierre Wibaux and Teddy Roosevelt, especially during rodeo when young cowboys were far from home and primed for a dare.

"C'mon, Grady," said one of the roughnecks. "Your turn to get the next round."

"Hold your horses," Grady said, nodding to the back door. He pulled out his wallet and waved at the bartender. Grady figured he raked in about sixty bucks with his snake jar. Not bad for a night in ol' Wibaux.

CHAPTER SIXTEEN

Grady and Tom chewed up a couple days in Wibaux, which made their moms happy. One night Grady treated his mom and Dean to supper at the Shamrock, hands down the best supper club around. Dean ordered the shrimp dinner and his mom giggled through the entire meal, watching Dean stuff himself with six colossal-sized shrimp, a giant baked potato, salad, and Texas toast. As they left the Shamrock, they bumped into Frank heading into the Stockman Bar next door. The awkwardness of the moment eased when Dean—all smiles and wide-eyed— bragged to his father about how much he'd eaten and Carol validated his every claim. Frank then asked Grady to go fishing. It was hard to say no face-to-face, especially since he'd only seen his dad a handful of times since he moved to Williston.

Frank's favorite fishing spot was a little lake about twenty-five miles south of Wibaux. "We should get in a couple hours' worth, wouldn't you say?" he asked.

Grady glanced at the sky as they carried their gear across a dusty, crooked path to the water's edge. Silver sagebrush and lavender aster made a nice combination, sprouting from the crooks and crannies of the cracked earth. Frank led Grady to a spot on the bank that faced west and they each threw a line.

"Nice and calm today," Grady noted.

"Maybe that will help our cause."

"I found a place in Williston where I like to go. It's a nice sandy spot on the river."

"I hear you're doing real good on the rigs these days," his dad said. "Made another move up the ladder, is that right?"

Grady nodded, watching the late afternoon sunlight flicker like the finest sterling silver against the smooth water. If he didn't know any better he'd think that was a compliment. "Yeah, I'm a derrick hand now. Only job above me is the driller."

"Which company you working for?"

"Noble Drilling."

"Some of the boys at the Silver Dollar said that's a good company to work for."

"Most of the time."

"Well, I'd say you done pretty good there, Son," his dad said. "Must be the way I raised you, huh?" He laughed and put down his rod to light up a Winston.

Grady watched several Northern Pintails fly across the width of the lake and glide to a smooth landing on the water. Once again his dad had to take credit for something Grady accomplished. A short-lived compliment if there ever was one.

"Say, did I tell you I caught four nice walleyes last time I came out here?"

"Pretty nice." Grady fixed his eyes on the ducks, watching them flap their wings, beaks tipped into the water.

"Took 'em home, fried 'em up. Ate every single one." Frank reached into the cooler. "Want a beer?"

"Sure, I'll take one."

He handed an icy bottle to Grady and took another one for himself. "Here we go, that's what I'm talking about . . . got a tug on my line." He put down the beer and reeled in a nice smallmouth bass. Frank took another worm from the bucket and sent his line flying into the sun. "This is a good spot in the winter too. Did a lot of ice fishing out here, all the way into April this year."

"You remember that time I was about twelve or thirteen and I dropped the ice bar through the hole?"

"That was out here?"

"Right over there, if I remember right," Grady said, pointing to a small bay on the south side. "In fact, I don't think I've been out here since."

"Was that when I made you dig it out of the lake with a magnet?"

"Yup. The minute the ice bar slipped through my hands and into the water you said, 'How many times do I gotta tell you to put that damn rope around your wrist!' You drove all the way back to the Co-op in Wibaux and borrowed a magnet and a rope and another ice bar. Then you made me chop another hole and put that magnet in there until I got it up to the surface."

Frank let out a roar. "The damn thing was caught under the ice."

"You made me take off my jacket and stick my arm in that freezing water until I could get it turned enough to pull it through the hole."

"Did you ever forget to put the rope on the ice bar after that?"

Grady shook his head. "Can't say I ever did."

"There you go. Lesson paid off then, didn't it."

Grady grinned. The old man had him on that one. They fished from the bank until sundown brought streaks in every imaginable color this side of heaven and the temperature cooled as though on cue. Afterward, they drove into the Stockman and Grady bought his dad a hamburger.

Something in the stars was aligned right on this night. They'd each caught a half-dozen nice-sized bass and walleye, and for once their evening together ended without incident.

* * *

Grady and Tom made it back to Williston in time to catch the Rush concert at the State Line Club—a popular bar just inside the Montana state line. They picked up a couple girls to bring along and it turned into a great night. The outdoor crowd went crazy when the popular Canadian band played an extended version of their new single, "Tom Sawyer." It was Grady's first true rock concert and an awesome one at that.

Grady carried his Igloo cooler and duffle bag into the bottom doghouse, recharged from his days off and ready to get back at it. He was on evening tower and it was a few minutes before eight o'clock. He brought a thick T-bone with some sliced onions, green pepper, potatoes, and seasonings, wrapped up nice and tight in aluminum foil for dinner. Some time midtower he'd throw it on the cylinder head on motor number one and let it slow cook a couple hours, ten times better than a can of Dinty Moore chili or stew, like he had most days.

He licked his lips in anticipation and changed into his greasers. A bold Noble logo covered the front of his hard hat, along with a cockeyed collection of Gulf, Baroid, Reed, Schlumberger, and other stickers from mining and engineering specialists. As soon as he stepped outside, the low rumble of the diesel engines escalated to a full-blown roar, and dark fumes hung above the rig.

"Grady!" shouted Kilowatt.

"Yo!" He looked up toward the drilling floor and Kilowatt waved him up. Grady's hard hat jiggled as he ran up the steps and met him at the control panel. "What's up?" he asked, adjusting the strap on his bibs. Freshly washed, the strap had twisted around the metal hook at least three times.

"Just read the geolograph," Kilowatt said in a loud voice, pointing toward the top doghouse. "She's really slowing down the last two, three hours. Time to trip out."

"You got it, boss."

"Spread the word," Kilowatt shouted above the engines in a hard hat and safety goggles. "We're right at ten–one hundred this morning. She'll be a long one."

Grady looked over the railing and spied Red on the ground. Grady cupped his hands around his mouth. "Red! Round up the boys—now! We're trippin' out!"

"Yes, sir!" he yelled in response, and turned back to the doghouse.

Time was money in the world of oil drilling and it was critical to replace the worn-out bit in as little time as possible. Ten–one hundred meant 10,100 feet of pipe stands had to be pulled out—the reverse process of drilling—and stacked in one long, smooth process. If they didn't hit a snag or run into problems, a good crew would be able to do a round trip—pull out all 10,100 feet of pipe, change the bit, and get the pipe back into the hole—within their eight-hour tower.

Within minutes Rob Teiner, Napper, Red, and Bigs joined Kilowatt and Grady on the drilling floor. "We're two miles in, men, so she'll be a long trip," Kilowatt said, wiping the sweat from his brow with a stained work glove. The evening air was dry and still. "Rob, get rigged to set the Kelly in the rat hole. Red, you help him. Let's rack 'em and stack 'em!"

Grady made sure the hole could be filled with mud so when the pipe came out of the hole it would keep the formation pressures in check. He grabbed Napper by his bib straps as he walked past. "You know the drill, Napper. Bypass the shale shaker and shut it down. I'll open the gates in the number three mud tank. You get number two and meet me back up here."

"You got it, Grady." Napper climbed down the stairs, heading to the shale shaker on mud tank number one.

Grady opened the sediment gates in the last two tanks to allow the mud to get to the pump, since there would be no down-hole circulation. He walked by way of the motor house through the pump house and into the mud mixing room at the end of number three. He shut off the mixing hopper and mud guns used to stir and condition the mud in tank number three. Then he raced up the ladder of the mud tank to open the gates. He looked over and watched Napper pull the gates open on tank number two.

Grady met up with Napper at the junction of the number two and three tanks. "Looks like Kilowatt's ready," Grady said. "Let's get up on the drilling floor and pull some pipe outta the ground." He guided Napper along the top of the mud tanks toward the shale shaker, double-checking to make sure the gates were pulled and there was enough mud to fill the hole. It wasn't that he didn't trust Napper, but it was his habit to make sure things were set up right before they starting tripping. Napper was still learning, but Grady liked the kid's work ethic.

They reached the drilling floor just as the crew broke off the Kelly from the drill string. Grady walked to the pipe stand and opened a valve to the mud line running to the blowout preventer below and closed the valve to the Kelly. This allowed the hole to fill as the pipe was pulled out. If there was a blowout, Kilowatt could hopefully control it.

"Red, you're in the wrong damn spot!" shouted Kilowatt, motioning him over in frenzied hand signals. "Hook that cable around the Kelly so Rob can pull it back with the cat line!"

Red stepped back and followed Kilowatt's orders. "Like that, boss?"

"Yeah. Now get over to the rat hole and help Bigs stab it in."

The five-ton Kelly lowered into the rat hole. Rob grabbed the hook release pole and released the Kelly bail from the cow's cock while Kilowatt lowered the traveling block to disengage the bail.

Grady spotted Red standing right under the elevator, looking down and not up, a critical mistake for newbies. "Red! Look up!!"

"Damn it, Red, pay attention!" shouted Kilowatt as Red scrambled backward awkwardly, trying not to lose his balance. "That's right where you'll be laying if you don't watch what's going on! The action is above you—that's where you need to be focused. I darn near pushed that hard hat of yours right down on top of your shoulders, boy!"

"Yes, sir!" he called, fear and confusion etched across his baby face.

As soon as the hook cleared the Kelly, Rob slammed it shut and opened the swivel lock on the cow's cock. Bigs rotated the elevators 180 degrees and Rob locked the swivel again.

"Turn 'em back around, Bigs. We gotta lay two joints down before trip-out," Kilowatt said.

Bigs looked at Rob, who promptly shrugged his shoulders and unlocked the swivel again. "I knew that!" he said with a grin. Rob's sweaty T-shirt clung to his muscled chest, biceps bulging as he pointed to the drilling floor.

When the pipe was pulled out of the hole, much of the sediment that hadn't yet made its way out would settle back down to the bottom of the hole, along with bits of formation knocked off during the trip-out process. It was necessary to lay down at least two joints of pipe on the beaver slide before tripping back in or they'd slam that brand-new fifteen-thousand-dollar bit into a pile of gravel and start a whole new set of problems.

Grady made a quick stop in the bottom doghouse to grab a sandwich out of his cooler. "So much for my steak dinner," he grumbled, packing it back into the cooler. Tripping pipe meant he'd be working ninety feet up on the diving board all tower long; he'd be lucky to grab a bite of the sandwich, and only if he kept it tucked in the front of his bibs. He couldn't even leave his post to take a dump without having to shut down the whole operation. That was too big of price to pay—usually a couple rounds at the bar—unless he was dying sick.

He grabbed his water jug and headed to the ladder on the derrick. "See you back on the bottom," he shouted to Kilowatt.

"Sounds good," Kilowatt answered with a nod at the draw works.

Grady started the climb just as Bigs threw the heavy chain around the first pipe, reversing the direction of its spin. "Here she comes!" he hollered as Red jumped back.

"You better watch that chain, boy," Kilowatt shouted to Red. "That's dangerous stuff, right there." He flipped the gear on the draw works, a hoisting mechanism with the drum that now spooled in the drilling cable as the pipe came out. "Showtime, guys; nothing but ink on the geolograph tonight." he called out. A solid blue triangle on the geolograph printout meant the rig kept running through the complete trip.

Grady climbed up the side of the derrick to his position on the diving board ninety feet above the drilling floor and tied his water jug against the framework. He hooked the safety belt around him and grabbed the rope, waiting for the first stand to come out of the hole. Even fifteen stories up, the air was already warm.

Grady positioned one foot on the diving board and the other on a piece of three-inch pipe that slid back and forth, keeping a watchful eye on the crew down below. Verbal communication wasn't possible. If he needed to get their attention, he had to take a wrench out of his bibs and bang on the pipe, and vice versa.

He watched as Kilowatt raised the first stand of pipe out of the hole. Rob attached the tongs with Bigs assisting. As soon as the joint broke loose, Bigs kicked off. Napper kept the tongs bit on the top pipe to keep it from rotating until it disengaged. The spring popped it out and Rob guided it over to the gator back.

Eyes fixed on the pipe stand, Grady waited for the top of it to reach him. Adrenaline rushing, he gripped the rope in his gloved hand and leaned forward again, held by the safety rope. As soon as it neared his reach, he swung his rope out and pulled the stand in. "Come here," he said in a deep growl.

As soon as the bottom hit the gator back, Grady opened the cast elevators from up on top. Timing was crucial. He pulled the pipe stand out of the path of the traveling block and pivoted on his left foot. He got in position behind it and grabbed the pipe with his left arm, walking it back down the diving board to the alley. From there he worked it into the first open 'finger', the temporary hold for the pipe stands until the bit was changed and they started tripping pipe back in the hole.

As the elevators came down, Teiner latched the locking elevators around the joint in the slips and Kilowatt threw the draw works into gear, lifting it off the drilling floor. Within one minute the next pipe stand was on its way out of the hole. Once again the crew below pushed the bottom of the stand onto the gator back while Grady pulled the top with the rope.

With quick grips he pulled the slack out of the rope to get it as close in as he could. "C'mon, c'mon," Grady said, coaxing the ninety-foot pipe stand toward him. "I gotcha now." The safety belt rubbed against his hips as he stretched his arm and grabbed the pipe, guiding it through the alleyway and into the open fingers.

Down below Napper slipped on the mess of mud and water that came out of the hole with the pipe and ended up on his ass. Grady watched them work in choreographed steps, their voices drowned out by the engines. Bigs unwrapped the chain and Napper guided the bottom of the ninety-foot section of pipe to the gator back. Grady stretched out his back as he waited for the next pipe. They had four pipe stands in the fingers and roughly three hundred plus to go . . . and then do it all in reverse.

* * *

Working on the rigs meant exposure to extreme elements both summer and winter. On December 23, 1978, Grady worked the morning tower on a rig in Plentywood, Montana, when the actual temperature was sixty-three degrees below zero, with the wind blowing at fifty miles an hour. Only to be outdone on February 14, 1980, in Dagmar, Montana, when they endured a week of minus-thirty- to minus-forty-below temperatures and the wind chill was a record one hundred twenty-three below zero.

Another time they were snowed in on a rig for seventy-eight hours straight. The roads were completely drifted over and relief crews couldn't make it out. Each guy had only brought one day's worth of food in their coolers, not expecting to be stuck there for three solid days. On the second day, they tore through every locker in both doghouses, looking for anything to eat. Things were looking mighty desperate, and by the third day they warned the trainee he'd be the first to go if it got that far. Fortunately, the roads got plowed and the next crew car got through before it came to that.

Roughnecking had its dangers too. Many a man lost a finger or had a chain snap and hit him in the face. One of Grady's good friends lost his left arm when the traveling block came down and cut it off at the bicep. One time Grady was working on the A-leg and lost his balance. He fell horizontally fifteen feet down to the drilling floor, arms flailing to catch something, anything. Instead, he landed chest-first on a three-foot-high piece of two-inch angle iron. His body draped over it in momentum, bounced off, then he landed flat on his back, unable to breathe. He coughed hard and spit up blood as the crew rushed to his side. His ears rang and he couldn't focus; their voices sounded far off as if they were in a culvert. A constant ringing echoed loudly in his ears; the floor vibrated beneath him from the motors as he struggled to breathe.

Luck was on his side that day—they were only twelve miles outside of Williston, the closest he ever worked to town. Kilowatt rushed him to Mercy Hospital in Williston as soon as they got him loaded into the crew car. The ER doctor asked what happened and Kilowatt explained how Grady fell fifteen feet onto the angle iron.

"That can't be," the doctor said. "If he fell that far, a piece of angle iron would have gone straight through his chest."

"Well, Doc, I saw it with my own two eyes. The man fell straight down, hit it right here," Kilowatt said, touching his sternum.

The doctor stepped to the side counter and picked up Grady's bibs, which the nurses had cut off, and felt with his fingers. "Well, I'll be . . ." He pulled out Grady's wallet from the front center pocket, studying it close up. "Look at this." He held it in front of Kilowatt and Grady. Centered in his wallet was the "L" imprint from the angle iron.

Grady speculated that maybe, just maybe, there had been more than luck involved that day. His ribs had broken loose from the sternum on both sides and he suffered multiple green-twig fractures in his ribs. He was a hurtin' unit for three days in the hospital—couldn't cough or laugh, much less have a smoke. When Grady got home, the phone was ringing as he walked in the door. He winced as he reached for the receiver. "Hello?"

"Hey, Grady."

"What's up, Mom?"

"How are you doing? A little birdie told me I should be praying for you."

The sound of his mother's voice brought an instant warmth. "I'm doing okay. Got a little dinged up at work; nothin' too bad." He had no idea how she knew to call him, but it happened every time he got hurt.

* * *

Grady poked his head into the mostly empty refrigerator. He pulled out a package of Oscar Meyer sandwich meat and took a quick sniff. "Good enough," he said, taking out a few slices. The label claimed it was Smoked Ham, but most of it was gristly and fatty. Not like the juicy, mouthwatering hams he had as a kid. He had to admit his dad sure knew how to smoke up the best tasting meats. The last time Grady had gone down to Wibaux, he found out his dad had moved out to California, where his sister Vera lived. At least now Grady was spared the embarrassment of running into him stumbling drunk at the Silver Dollar or Stockman Bar.

Grady slapped some Miracle Whip on four slices of bread and added a little onion and cheese with the ham. He wrapped both sandwiches in plastic and tucked them in the cooler with a six-pack of Pabst. He drove south of Williston about nine miles, past a farm site cluttered with broken machinery and two junky trailer homes, to a place along the river nicknamed Little Egypt. It was real sandy there, an oddity among the clay and weeds and rock-hard mud buttes. He carried his pole and cooler about a quarter mile from the road to the shoreline.

He picked a spot on the water not far from a big section of cattail reeds that spread into the river like a bronze bucket of spilled paint. No one else was within sight. He took out a sucker minnow and stabbed it on his smelt hook. Grady used a Mitchell 300 with a six-and-a-half-foot Ugly Stick that had given him pretty good luck over the last couple summers. He slid on a red and white bobber and pitched his line into the river downstream as far as he could. The big plastic bobber plopped into the water and floated lazily in the breeze.

Two broad-winged hawks soared gracefully overhead, rising and falling with the air currents. The cattails bent their heavy heads, side to side, back and forth in perfect unison like a marching band at halftime. It was late afternoon, his favorite time. He caught a whiff of sweet clover and drew a deep cleansing breath. Times like this he could let his thoughts wander—the perfect anecdote after a tough go on the rigs.

Last year he bought a '66 Chevelle and painted it '72 Royal Blue Metal Flake. Man, was that baby sharp! The interior was in great condition, nice bucket seats. He was thinking about buying a new Hurst shifter for it one of these days. Then again, maybe he should put on a new set of tires.

The minutes passed without notice as he contemplated his options. Tom had helped him build a second garage, 24'x24', next to the house, so Grady had a bigger place to work on cars. He put in a wood stove and used it year-round. The Chevy engine from school went in a '66 half-ton Chevy pickup he found in a cowboy ghetto—a field with junk vehicles—between Williston and Wibaux. He tore the engine out and built his own motor mounts for it. The truck had a straight-six and three-on-the-tree. Later on he swapped out the other engine at a junkyard for parts he needed on the '66 Chevelle.

Grady felt a tug on his finger. He sat up, reeling in the ornery fish as it twisted and slapped on the surface, splashing a prism of crystal-like droplets in a gentle arch. He won the tug-of-war easily and tied the nice-sized northern onto his stringer.

He rigged up his hook with another minnow and pitched it into the water, gazing up at the sun. A couple good hours yet till sundown—just enough time to solve all the world's problems. He leaned back against a clump of soft earth and closed his eyes, absorbing the warmth of the sun on his chest. Maybe, if he felt like it, he would fire up the chainsaw next week and get a load of wood ready for winter. Last year he went through two cords in the garage. Then again, he thought, as he opened his eyes a sliver and watched a golden eagle hovering over the water looking for prey, winter seemed a long ways off.

Another favorite pastime was to drive over to Minot—as in Why-not-Minot, the catchy phrase attached to the North Dakota town so outsiders could pronounce it right. He liked watching the big B-52 Stratofortress bombers take off from the air force base north of town. Nicknamed BUFF, for Big Ugly Fat Fellow, it amazed him how those big planes could fly under the radar undetected, maybe a hundred feet above the earth. Many times when Grady was out hunting he'd hear a high-pitched whistle and, just like that, *whoosh!* two or three of those big birds would fly directly overhead, close enough for him to see the wheel wells and Bombay doors.

Yeah, there were times he got a little lonely, but for the most part he liked the freedom he had to come and go as he pleased, nobody telling him what to do or when to be home. Some of his friends were married and had kids, and that was fine for them. Grady had dated one girl in Williston for six months straight, but he wasn't interested in getting tied down, and that was the end of that.

A couple hours passed and, before long, Grady had five nice northerns on the stringer. The sun was leaning westward in a brilliant shade of blaze orange. At times like this, God's creation simply amazed him: the rugged beauty of the land, the incredible abilities of the Sandhill cranes and Canada geese that migrated all the way to South America and back. Many days they filled the skies over the plains, horizon to horizon in their familiar V-formation, their honking heard for miles.

Something told Grady he was merely an observer, watching from the outside in. A rebel that didn't quite measure up to God's standards. No, not with all the sins he carried. Besides, it was safe to say he probably wouldn't live past twenty-

five, twenty-seven at the most. Car wreck, accident on the rig—
something was bound to get him sooner or later. In fact, the last
time he tried to get a nice-sized rattler out of his dryer drum he
dropped the lath he was using to hold the head. The damn thing
lunged at him and bit his thumb. He barely made it to the
hospital in time to get the shot of antivenom. The first twenty-
four hours he had been on neurological watch in case his heart
stopped; nurses checked his pulse every five minutes. His whole
arm swelled up and stunk like crazy; his fingers looked like thick
black sausages and stayed that way for four days. The smart-ass
foreign doctor told him he could've just as well put a stick of
dynamite up his butt and lit the fuse for trying to keep a rattler.

At times he felt like he was living testimony to Stone's
old line, "live fast, die young, and leave a good lookin' corpse."
Yup, the odds were stacked against him. One way or another,
he'd go out in a blaze of glory.

PART IV

CHAPTER SEVENTEEN

Los Angeles, California, 1988

Grady entered his second-floor apartment on Cherry Avenue in desperate need of a cool shower. He lived in the heart of Long Beach in a narrow strip of city blocks that divided the good from the ugly. North and east a ways sat quiet little neighborhoods with nice houses and late model Cameros and Camrys. But only another mile south and west of the railroad tracks, things took a turn for the worst—a section of town where trouble came calling day or night.

Grady stood in the shower stall letting the water beat against his bare skin, cooling his tired muscles. Lately he'd made way too many stops at In-N-Out Burger and El Pollo Loco. Right on cue a low rumble erupted in the pit of his stomach. Thankfully, Sarah was on her way over and promised to pick up groceries and make dinner. He dried off and put on a clean pair of jeans and a Lakers T-shirt.

The entire Los Angeles basin was stuck in the throes of another smog-filled weather pattern and his apartment was as stuffy as an old box car. One day, when the haze was so thick he couldn't see two blocks down the street, he had gone outside to have a smoke. He opened a brand-new pack of Marlboros—he was up to two packs a day by then—lit one up and took a drag as he walked to the local dairy. It wasn't a real dairy like in the Midwest—just a little corner store where people picked up milk and bread. Grady took a long, thoughtful look at the mix of smoke and dirt that had settled at street level and suddenly realized what a fool he was, paying for packaged sticks of nicotine when he could breathe in the same stupid stuff without lighting up. He threw his cigarette down, crushed it with the toe of his boot, and had never lit up again.

That was the second good thing that came from his move to California. The first was meeting Sarah. She was gorgeous and smart and plain-out fun to be with. They met at the gym one afternoon when they were both working out. Her friendly smile and sexy curves caught his attention right off—in reverse order, of course. He tried to fake that he had some culture and took her to the Moscow Ballet performance of "Swan Lake" for their first date. The gimmick worked. They fell in love rather quickly and were even talking marriage. For the first time in his adult life he felt a sense of happiness within reach.

Grady pushed open the single living room window, his only hope for cool air, since the apartment didn't have air conditioning. He put on a Stones album and fed the two remaining oscars in his aquarium. After the move, he had traded in his pet snakes for a twenty-six-gallon aquarium and stocked it with a nice variety of fish . . . until the aggressive oscars ate all the others. Admittedly, he didn't have much in the way of decent furniture or décor. He had hung a few framed prints on the bare white walls—a bighorn sheep, an elk, a set of whitetail deer— reminders of his hunting days back in Montana. He stacked up some cinderblock and one-by-ten lumber to make a shelving unit for his albums and stereo. He didn't have a couch yet, but he bought an oversized wicker frame Papasan chair with a bold blue pillowy cushion. Whenever he sat down in that baby it was like sinking into the depths of the Pacific Ocean, usually while watching the Angels or Kings on his nineteen-inch color TV.

The apartment complex consisted of three large buildings positioned U-shaped around the swimming pool. His unit faced the pool and the neighborhood flower shop, and across Cherry Avenue he had a magnificent view of the K-Mart parking lot. Down a little farther was an El Pollo Loco and a train trestle. Once in a rare while, when the smog lifted, he could see the tops of the mountains and downtown L.A. from his bedroom window.

Hard to believe he'd been in Los Angeles four years already. The oil boom in the Dakotas had gone bust in the mid-eighties and the roughnecks fled Williston faster than a windswept prairie fire. Tom ditched him as soon as things started to slow down, so Grady bought out his half of the house rather than lose all the money he'd sunk into it. At first he was angry about buying out Tom's half, but later decided it was a way to salvage their friendship and hopefully make a good investment. When it became apparent he wouldn't have a job any longer, Grady knew his options were limited. With a full mortgage weighing on him, he broke down and called his dad out in L.A. "Plenty a work out here," his dad told him. "All's you need is a welder's certificate and you'll be set. They're paying big bucks. I know a guy who can get you started." Two months later Grady was in California and had passed his welder's exam. He became certified through the Ironworkers Local 433 and could weld on anything except boiler pipe. He went straight from working the rigs in North Dakota to welding steel beams on the high-rises all over the Los Angeles basin.

Looking back, it was ironic that he followed his dad to L.A.—one of the crazy twists in his life he never would have predicted. So far it had proved to be a good decision. When his dad first moved to California, he lived with his sister Vera in Azusa for about a year, working odd jobs at the storage facility she managed. But, old habits die hard, and he drank as hard in California as he had in Montana. Vera soon learned her brother did more drinking than working, and since Vera's husband liked to tip a few, Grady's aunt'd had more than she could handle with two drunks under one roof. Sometimes she'd called Grady late at night to elicit help in getting his dad to stop drinking. Like his ol' man would ever give up drinking. Was she nuts? It was the whole laws of science thing: the sun went up, the sun went down, and his ol' man drank. Didn't matter if he was in Montana or California. "You can't change the laws of science, Auntie," he muttered, sinking into the Papasan.

Grady leaned his head back, letting his mind wander. Last year his aunt bought a piece of property with a dumpy trailer out past Palm Springs in a little town on the Salton Sea, where his dad lived now. Not really a sea at all, it was in fact California's largest lake, formed in the early 1900s when an overflow of the Colorado River flowed into an oblong-shaped desert sink. Basically a below-sea-level trough of water higher in saline than the Pacific Ocean, thirty-five miles long and fifteen miles wide. The salinity allowed speedboats to go even faster than on fresh water, and developers with dollar signs in their eyes billed it as the California Riviera, promising investors boatloads of money within fifteen years. Instead, the little towns went bust before they'd ever gotten started.

The whole area was the most bizarre place on earth. Grady went out there a few times to see his dad, and on a good day it was nothing but a big stink hole. Frank lived in Aunt

Vera's trailer and bartered for odd jobs in exchange for cash—most of which went for booze. About every two or three months, right on cue, Grady would get a call from him, "The fish are biting, Grady. C'mon out."

The last time Grady had forced himself to drive the four solid boring hours it took through the desert, his dad had been drunk the whole weekend. It was no different than when he was a kid, and he could hardly stand to be around him.

A knock at the door startled him and he jumped to his feet. "Hey, babe," he said, giving Sarah a kiss on the cheek.

"You sleeping?" she asked. Her deep brown eyes, pale skin, and natural blonde hair made a striking combination that stirred him every time he laid eyes on her.

"Nah, just resting my eyes. Long day." He took the heavy sack of groceries from her arms. "What are you making?"

"Lasagna and salad," she said, kicking off her red sandals. She turned her head and flashed Grady a soft smile. "Is that okay?" She looked especially cute in a red V-neck sweater, white jeans, and a pretty beaded necklace made with red stones.

"Sounds perfect. Want a pop or something?" he asked, following her into the kitchen.

"In a minute. Ralphs was packed; I stopped at the one on Long Beach Boulevard and got behind some crazy lady who decided she wanted a different package of sliced cheese than the one in her basket. She took off to the back of the store and literally disappeared. Who knows, maybe she was making out with the produce guy or something, but she never came back." Sarah waved a hand over her head. "And the clerk stands there talking to the bagger like I'm invisible or something." She reached a slender arm into the bag and pulled out cheeses, noodles, sauce, and hamburger. The kitchen was small and narrow with cheap imitation cupboards. She took a deep breath and leaned a hip into the counter. "Then, as I'm coming up San Antonio Drive, this kid in a big ol' Suburban just about rear-ended me at the light. I swear he was gonna hit me. Thank goodness the light turned green. I hit the gas like a bullet." Her bottom lip protruded slightly as she finished her dramatic tale.

Grady grinned. "Sounds like I've got a lady in distress." He opened the double bottom doors and took out a large kettle. "Want some help?"

"Oh, thaaaanks." She wrapped her arms around Grady's neck and kissed him with a long, full kiss. "You're so good to me, babe." She grinned, her brown eyes catching his before she turned back to the task at hand.

"Hold on there a sec," Grady said, rubbing his lips. He reached for her waist and pulled her in close. "How about some more of that?"

Sarah leaned into him and pressed her lips against his. "There, how's that?"

"Now you're talking," he said, feeling Sarah relax in his arms. This time he let her feel his passion. "We could always skip dinner."

She gently traced his upper lip with a bright red fingernail. "Yeah, and then you'd be crabby. No thanks."

"Me? What about last weekend down at Shoreline Village. You whined half the day that you were starving." He tickled her ribcage, holding her tight.

"Grady, stop it!" She tried her best to pry away his strong hands. "That's not fair," she said between giggles. "Now stop it!" She giggled again and pressed into his chest. "I hadn't eaten all day and you promised we'd grab a late lunch at Stefano's. I didn't realize just how late it would be. Now go," she said, squirming free, "change the album; I think it's over. I'm making dinner, remember?"

They'd been seeing each other steady for over six months. In his eyes, she was a knockout. Her curves were shapely and firm from working out, but she wasn't wrapped up in her own looks. Her simple blonde hairstyle framed her high cheekbones, giving her a fashion-model profile at times. He loved her spontaneous spirit, and in truth, Sarah was the best thing that ever happened to him.

They'd driven out to Lake Havasu in Arizona and camped a few times. Lately Shoreline Village in Long Beach was their favorite hangout, mostly because it was only two miles away and affordable. They could grab a sandwich or salad at one of the casual outdoor restaurants along the busy beachside near the Queen Mary. The big ship drew throngs of tourists year round. Sometimes he and Sarah hung out there just to people-watch. They liked taking a walk around Parker Lighthouse or up the beach, sometimes on the pathway, other times barefoot in the waves. At night the marina and harbor glistened in glowing, festive colors from the restaurants, hotels, and shops that lined the water's edge.

"Hey, babe, is Wade still dating that hot little secretary to that *supposed* movie producer?" she asked, licking the tomato sauce off the spoon.

Grady shook his head. "Nah, he's already chasing some other pretty thing with long legs and a short skirt that came into the construction office last week. Man, his neck cranked around so fast I thought his head was gonna come off."

Sarah laughed, stirring the hamburger in the skillet. "Sounds perfect for him. That man is the biggest flirt of all time. Come here, babe," she said, looking at his forehead. She reached up and ran her fingers through his bangs. "Piece of fuzz or something." With working in the hot desert sun, he shaved his sideburns short and kept his hair cut short around the ears. His long thick bangs were a thing of the past, and each year, whether he liked it or not, he noticed his hairline receding ever so slightly. "He'll never settle down with just one woman."

"He's not as smart as yours truly, now, is he?"

Sarah grinned, nodding. "You got that right. So how was work?"

"Same old, same old." Grady was working on the Library Tower in downtown L.A., a brand-new skyscraper touted to be the tallest building between Chicago and Hong Kong at seventy-three stories above ground. Designed by Henry N. Cobb, the building derived its name from the Los Angeles Central Library across the street that had undergone a major redevelopment following two disastrous fires in 1986. Grady liked the unusual design of the tower, a series of overlapping spiral cubes that created a building both circular and square. Below ground were two parking levels that stored their equipment as they began adding floors, one by one.

Sarah put the pan of lasagna into the oven. "How high are you now?"

"Fifteenth floor already."

"I don't get it—why do you have to work in the evenings so much? Kinda messes up our free time."

"That's just how it works. We have to stay two floors above the raising gang, so they can put the steel up."

"But isn't that creep Tank on the raising gang?"

"The one and only."

"What if he starts hassling you again? He was such a jerk when you worked on the Fox Plaza."

"Make no mistake, he certainly lives up to his reputation. We're doing the lowly hoisting equipment and he's the almighty structural guy, right to the core. Came at me a couple days ago; started in again, same old shit."

"What happened?"

"He started out like always, 'You guys got it so easy; you don't know what real ironworking is. You bunch of wusses, you never worked a day in your life!' Finally, I had it up to here with him." Grady thrust his chest out and drew a line at his throat.

Sarah's eyes widened as she grabbed a Coke from the fridge. "Up fifteen stories?"

"Where else?"

197

"Grady! I've heard the guys talking; everyone else is afraid of him."

"Well, I was sick 'n' tired of his mouth. I said, 'You know what, shut the F up.' And it was on from there."

"Oh, Grady." Sarah shook her head slowly as she listened.

"We're like the same height, but that dude's got a forty-two inch chest, no fat. Like a tank, ya know. He's one tough ironworker. I got right in his face and told him that I know what hard work is, told him I worked the oil rigs and could work him under the table any day. He's like, 'big blankety-blank deal.' Of course, we used a lot of words I know you don't want me to repeat. Finally, I said, 'What are you trying to prove, man?' He said, 'I'm trying to prove I can kick your ass.' So I said, 'You name the time and place.' " Grady's back stiffened as he relayed the incident, his voice deep and raspy.

Sarah covered her mouth with her hand, her brown eyes filled with fear and worry.

"He said, 'Three o'clock—in the parking lot,' and I said, 'I'll be there.' He said, 'Do you realize who you're F-ing with?' I didn't budge. Just stared him down and said, 'Were you born an asshole or do you do it as an occupation?' He said, 'I consider it my job.' I said, 'Well, you deserve a raise.' So that was it, all set, him and me in the parking lot at three o'clock."

Sarah's mouth dropped open. "Oh, my goodness!"

"Then he said flat out, 'I'll kill you, you—' And you can fill in the blanks, and now he's staring me down."

"Grady!"

"All the other guys are trying to get me to stop, and I pushed 'em off. I told Tank right to his face, 'You might kill me, but I guarantee you, you won't forget me. Before I go down, I'll gouge out an eye or tear off an ear, but, buddy, you'll remember me the rest of your life.'"

"I don't know if I want to hear anymore," she said softly.

"This was like at ten in the morning. All day everybody on my crew kept saying, 'What the hell you doing? You crazy? That dude is mean!' Which didn't help my mind-set, let me tell you. But I was so blasted mad, I didn't care."

"I can't believe you're even here, telling me all this." Sarah took a deep breath. "Grady, you can't go back, he might kill you or—"

"It's okay, let me finish," he said, gently rubbing Sarah's arm. "He came by, 'bout two-thirty, and asked if we were still on. I said, 'You damn right we are.' Then he sorta stared at me for a few seconds and said, 'You're the first person that's ever stood up to me, face-to-face, and hasn't tried to knife me in the back. I give you credit for that, man.' It was like I earned his respect by standing up to him. And after that, everything was cool. We all went down to the bar after work. He bought me the first beer and we sat there for a couple hours bullshitting."

Sarah folded her arms, shaking her head. "You're not serious!"

Grady nodded. "And it's a good thing, 'cause he would 'a' cleaned my clock. I mean, he's called Tank for a reason. He's so solid, I swear his shadow weighs twenty pounds." He paused in thought. "It was strange in a way. The next day I was sitting on some decking at lunch and he sat down next to me, asked how I got my scar, so I told him my story. Then I asked how he got this weird knob of skin by his right eye. He told me how he tried to stop his ol' man from beating up his mom when he was a kid. He'd grabbed his .38 and his dad got his .32 and they were going around the house real slow-like, hunting each other. He came around a corner, just peeked to see where his ol' man was, and his dad fired a shot. The bullet hit him in the sinus and exited on the right side of his eye. I told him he had a hard head, and he laughed."

Sarah wrapped her arms around his waist and looked into his eyes, gently running her fingers through the hair near his temples. "You scare me sometimes, Grady. It's like you have no fear. I don't understand it." Her voice was smooth and soft as she rested her head against his chest.

He hadn't meant to freak her out; he was just telling it like it was. "It's over," he said, smoothing her short, silky curls. "Nothing to worry about."

CHAPTER EIGHTEEN

As soon as Grady had moved to the Los Angeles basin, he had no trouble finding work. Construction companies erected skyscrapers all over the valley in a mad race to surpass each other. Certified welders were as sought after as the next blockbuster movie script. As soon as one job ended, Grady hopped in his truck and drove around until he spied a crane in the air and hired on at the next job site. He'd been working the Library Tower job a few months and figured the job should last nearly a year.

His mom hadn't liked it when he moved to California. Too far away, she said. The first year she called nearly every week. "Don't tell me how high up you're working; I don't wanna know!" she'd blurt out at the start of every phone call. She'd remarried and moved to Beach, and was working day and night to help her husband run the motel in town. Melinda and her husband, Gary, had three little girls and had moved to Glendive. Carol was excited to have her granddaughters so much closer. Judging from the last pictures, all three were each as cute as a bug's ear. Kurt had just gone through a divorce and shared an apartment with Dean in Fargo temporarily. They were rarely all together anymore. A few years back, his mom had told him Naomi had gotten married, so at least she didn't bring up the two of them getting back together anymore. It was just as well. Naomi probably had a houseful of kids by now. He hoped she was happy; she deserved that much.

Grady unwrapped a four-piece chicken dinner from El Pollo. No homemade dinner with Sarah tonight, although she was supposed to call. He took a big bite of chicken just as the phone rang. "'Bout time!" he said jokingly as he swallowed.

"What?" It was his dad's voice.

"Oh, hey, Dad."

"What's up?"

"Not much. Eating dinner and waiting to hear from Sarah."

"You still seeing that cute little blonde?"

"Yup."

"Listen, I want you to come out this weekend. There's somebody here I want you to meet."

A sharp tinge in his temples quickly spread across his forehead like cracked glass and he wished he hadn't answered. This was the third Friday in a row his dad'd tried to get him to come out. "I dunno, Dad," he said, rubbing his forehead. He wasn't in the mood to drive out to the desert and watch his ol' man get bombed.

"C'mon, she's really somethin'. I told her all about you and she can't wait to meet you."

Grady paused, debating. He was running out of excuses. "Sure. I can come out this Friday."

* * *

Grady found he missed the change of the seasons in Montana. For so much of the year Southern Californians endured

202

constant heat—often triple digits—and it wore on his nerves. He turned the radio to KLOS, his favorite rock station, as he followed I-10 east through L.A. to Palm Springs with the AC cranked on high, winding south through one hundred and eighty mind-numbing miles of desert wasteland to the Salton Sea.

Dead fish lined the lakeshore, and dilapidated trailers were a fixture up and down the gravel streets, with randomly placed homes-on-wheels that made the Salton Sea resemble more a ghost town on Mars than a riviera of any sort. Driving through Salton City was like witnessing the remnants of a lost civilization. Next door to his dad's place stood a corroded shell of a '57 Chevy pickup, and beyond that a collection of rusty relics: iron drums, a broken lawnmower, and half of an aluminum fishing boat. "Looks like a shitty dumping ground," Grady muttered as he pulled up to the green and white trailer. Beads of sweat lined his brow the minute he stepped out of his Toyota pickup.

The silver screen door squeaked as it swung open. "It's about time," Frank said.

Good to see you too, Dad. Grady took a deep breath and released it slowly. "Traffic was bad coming out of the city. It's a long haul coming out here."

Frank stood on the wooden step, holding the screen open, sporting a narrow mustache—sort of a distinguished Clark Gable look. "Throw your stuff in here. We gotta go." He had on a new pair of jeans and a plaid short-sleeve shirt with the trademark pearl snaps. His dark hair, now streaked with gray, was combed back neatly.

"What's the rush?" Grady grabbed his small duffle bag from the front seat.

"Chandra's got supper ready, and I know she likes to eat on time." Frank pushed the door shut behind him and motioned Grady to get in his car. Even though it was past six-thirty, the temperature was still over one hundred degrees. They drove a mile down the littered street to a collection of trailer homes bordered by a solitary row of palm trees, the tips of their long feathered branches scorched and crisp from the hot sun. Frank parked next to a newer gold sedan under a carport. The white trailer had a nice skirt around it; coral hibiscus and a flowering cactus accented the short driveway. Bright red bougainvillea grew up one side of the carport, offering much sought-after natural shade. Colored patio lights were strung on the corner of a small deck off the front door. Must be the high-buck part of town.

A disturbing stink in the air clung to Grady's throat and he coughed. "Dad, what is that smell?"

"Aah, you know. Every so often all the fish die off. After a while you don't even notice it," he said with a laugh.

Grady's eyes widened. He wanted to say, *are you kidding?* He coughed again and spit. Sweat pooled along his back as he followed his dad up the steps. Standing next to him, Grady noticed the puffiness in his dad's face and hands, eyes red and glassy, visual reminders of his lifelong habit. It quickly reduced his dad's image from dashing movie star to a man with no purpose in life except to find the next drink. Grady may not have everything in life figured out but at least his own goals were better than that.

The door opened and an attractive woman with a gregarious smile and fire red hair with lipstick to match greeted them. "Hi, Frank!" she said. Her iridescent eyes darted from Grady to Frank, and back to Grady. She touched Frank's arm and smiled. "This must be Grady then. Oooh, I've heard so much about you."

"Hello," Grady said, shaking her hand.

"This is Chandra," Frank said, sounding proud.

Dressed in bold purple slacks and a flowered blouse, the fiftyish woman reached for Grady's hands and flashed a pretty smile. "I'm tickled to pieces to meet you." Her voice gushed and she squeezed his hands before letting go. "Oh, my, my! Don't you look just like your father!" She laughed and slapped her thigh. "You could never disown this boy, could you?" she said to Frank.

"He's a handsome devil, isn't he," he said with a nod.

"Oh, you!" Hundreds of freckles danced on her face, her pale skin glistening in the sunlight. "C'mon in, both of ya, before y'all melt!"

Grady stepped inside to the instant relief of air conditioning, the fan running on maximum. The place was neat and orderly. Mauve drapes were pulled across the front bay window to keep out the penetrating sun. Framed pictures of who Grady assumed were grandchildren filled the shelves of a silver bookcase.

"This is such a treat to have y'all come all the way out here for dinner," she said, wiping the back of her neck. "Oh, my hair's so doggone thick, I sweat up a mess the minute I step outside that door. Goodness! Hang on there and I'll pour us something to drink."

Now it made sense. She must like the bottle as much as his ol' man. And her voluptuous curves and slender frame only made the prize that much sweeter. She was a looker—he had to give his father that.

Grady watched Chandra through the opening to the kitchen, expecting to see a bottle of Jim Beam or Jack Daniels. Instead, she pulled out a large pitcher from the refrigerator. "Is ice tea okay with you, Grady? Or would you rather have milk with dinner?"

"Um, tea is fine," he said with a glance at his dad. Frank busied himself at the table, putting out cloth napkins at each place setting. Chandra poured three glasses of tea and handed them to Frank.

"Perfect timing, by the way. Supper's all ready. There's not much going on way out here, so we like to eat right on time, don't we, Frank?" Her colorful outfit hugged her curves as she passed Frank the serving bowls and a bread basket. "Go ahead and sit," she said, shooing with her hands. "Both of ya, you're makin' me nervous standing there."

His dad sat down and Grady joined him. "Smells mighty fine," Frank said, scooting his chair up to the table.

Chandra grabbed two thick hot pads and opened the oven. "I hope you like chicken," she said, placing a Corningware baking dish onto an owl-shaped wicker pad in the center of the table.

"Listen, a single guy never turns down a home-cooked meal. This looks delicious," Grady said, eyeing the baked chicken, potatoes, gravy, and buttermilk biscuits.

"Should we say a blessing?" Chandra eased her purple hips into the chair and reached for Frank's and Grady's hands. Grady followed her lead and bowed his head. "Dear Lord *Jesus*," Chandra said with dramatic emphasis, "we come before you and ask for your blessing upon this meal. I thank you, Jesus, for bringing Frank's boy out here safely, and we just ask that you bless this time together and give us nourishment from the food you placed on our table this evening. In Jesus' *pre-shusss* name, amen."

"Amen," Grady and Frank said in response.

"Well now, dig in," Chandra said, passing the potatoes to Grady. "Take a big helping. Your father's told me what a hardworking young man you are, welding on those big skyscrapers in Los Angeles, doing such a fine job, from what I hear. Here's the butter if you need it," she said, picking up a pale pink oblong dish with a stick of creamy butter on it. "Tell me a little bit about what you do. Frank said you're working all over the valley, is that right?"

Grady scooped two big spoonfuls of potatoes onto his plate and passed it to his dad as Chandra handed him the gravy. "Oops," she said, wiping the table cloth. "I spilled a smidge.

Don't worry, I'll put some detergent on it right after supper." She studied Grady, waiting for his answer.

"Oh, well, there's not much to add. I work for the ironworkers as a structural welder on the rises. Do whatever the boss tells me, that sort of thing." He chuckled and took a bite of potatoes. "Our crew works on the hoisting equipment—man-lifts, material elevators, Chicago Boom, stuff like that. All over L.A."

"The real tall ones?"

"Yeah, I worked on the Taco Bell building in Irvine; it's a pretty cool-looking building. The Fox Plaza Tower in Century City—that one was thirty-four stories. It's kind of cool because it has different setbacks and glass that give it a unique look."

"I think I've seen that one on TV," Chandra said with a hint of excitement.

"Actually, they filmed a Bruce Willis movie there when we were building it. My foreman was a technical advisor for the film."

"Really?"

"They filmed most of it at night; it's something about terrorists that take over a skyscraper. Their crew set the charges to blow out the glass and film a scene, and then the next day we reset the glass. Whenever they needed to do a retake, we had to find a window with the same exact frame. We always worked a few floors above where they were filming. It's supposed to come out next month, in July. It's called *Die Hard*."

"That's so interesting," Chandra said. "So, what do you do? As a welder, I mean."

"Depends on the job; each one is a little different. For the Fox Plaza Tower I worked for Harmon Glass, welding the clips that hold the curtain wall—that's the glass and stone on the outside of the building. Now I work for Bymac on the Library Tower, which is completely different. Our crew has to keep the man-lifts or construction elevators two floors above the building. We 'jump' or raise our towers in the evening when the rest of the ironworkers are already done for the day. I weld the supports that hold the tower sections to the building and jump the towers and cages. We also have to keep the cranes that haul the material up into the building climbing as the building goes up. It's a lot of welding and hauling cables and counterweights."

"Interesting, very interesting," she said, nodding. "Frank, you better be proud of this boy."

"You bet."

"So, tell me all about your girlfriend. Sarah, is it?"

Grady was surprised how much his dad had already told her. "We've been together over six months. It's getting pretty serious. She went home to see her folks in Wisconsin and told them we're . . . you know, thinking about a future together."

"That's wonderful, Grady. Isn't it, Frank?" said Chandra, and his dad nodded.

Grady took another helping of chicken and potatoes. "How about the two of you?" he asked, pointing his fork. "Where'd you two meet?"

Chandra's eyes lit up as she stirred a spoonful of gravy into her potatoes. "Well, your dad was in Jake's General Store one day. Of course, I went in there to get some groceries and he was at the bar. He walked right up to me and started a conversation. He's not shy, this one! Course, neither am I! Maybe that's why we make a good pair." She giggled like a schoolgirl and smiled at Frank. "But we're taking it one day at a time, aren't we, Frank?"

His dad grinned and shrugged his shoulders. "Somethin' about that red hair, I don't know, she hooked me good."

Chandra blushed an inflamed shade of pink that clashed with her hair and lips. She reached across the table and placed a hand on Frank's arm but fixed her eyes on Grady. "Oh, he's a good man, this one here. Grady, I have to tell you how he fixed up Mrs. Kelting's deck. It was about to fall right off the front of her trailer, and your dad went over there and spent three full weeks working in that hot sun. It's like brand new again. She's well into her seventies and can't afford much these days. Oh, she was so happy." Chandra turned to Frank. "Didn't you?"

Grady buttered another biscuit, watching his father. Frank pushed back his chair and reached for a toothpick, tapping his fingers on the table.

"And what about Doc Hampton? Frank fixed his car when it broke down over in Balsam Lake. Didn't even think twice about it. Drove over there and got it running within the hour. Doc couldn't thank him enough. I tell you, this man has made a world of difference for a lot of people in this town. You can probably see folks around here don't have much money. Some are just scraping by as best they can. Frank is always willing to do what he can to help them out. That's just the kinda man he is. You must be pretty proud to call him Dad."

Grady felt his back stiffen and a piece of chicken caught in his throat. He swallowed and the chicken lodged, forcing him to cough hard a couple of times.

"You okay?" she asked.

Grady nodded and took a gulp of ice tea, eyeing his father's redheaded bombshell with added suspicion. Was the woman a half bubble off center? Or was the cheese starting to slip from the cracker? Either that or she must be such a boozer herself that she can't tell the difference.

"Enough about me," Frank said, clearing his throat. "Chandra's the one everyone around here is crazy about. She knows everyone in town and then some."

"Well, that's 'cause I been living here a lot longer than you."

Grady cleaned his plate and pushed his chair back from the table.

"Grady, what do you say we help Chandra clean up the table?"

"Sure thing. By the way, thanks so much for dinner; it was delicious." He stood and patted his stomach. He hadn't eaten that good a meal since the night he ordered the Cajun rib-eye at Parkers Lighthouse down at the Shoreline Village with Sarah for their three-month anniversary. Grady took the plates from his father one by one and passed them to Chandra in the kitchen. Frank put the cactus-shaped salt and pepper shakers on a tiny ledge above the sink and collected the napkins. In all his years growing up, Grady couldn't remember a single time his dad'd helped his mom clean the table, and now he was more than eager to help. Interesting. *Just wait till they bring the booze out.* He was surprised he hadn't seen it yet.

"Let's put these in the dishwasher," Chandra said. She whirled in a flurry of activity, all the while talking about her three grown children and six grandchildren back in Oklahoma.

As soon as the tablecloth got a dose of spot remover and the kitchen was back in order, they moved into the living room at Chandra's suggestion. She and Frank took a seat side by side on the gold and orange flowered couch. Grady surveyed his options and sat down in the rust-colored recliner directly across from them. He thought about asking to watch the Angels game, but a large window fan blocked the view to the small television.

"So," Chandra said, slapping her lavender thighs, "what about you, Grady? Tell us, what's the *most* important thing going on in your life right now?"

What the hell kind of question was that? "Work, mostly," he said with a shrug. "I'm still paying on my house out in Williston, back in North Dakota." The room was quiet except for the ticking of the wall clock above his head. He opened his mouth—maybe he *should* ask to turn on the Angels game. The team was out in Kansas City starting a three-game series with the Royals and, if he remembered correctly, Stew Cliburn was pitching.

Chandra leaned forward and rested her elbows on her knees. "Your dad's told me about all the times you've been hurt through the years. As a kid, with the chainsaw—"

Instinctively, Grady touched his nose. He glanced at his dad, who didn't offer any comment.

"—and it sounds like you had a couple bad incidents working on the oil rigs."

"Can't deny that," he said, wondering where on earth she was going.

Her voice softened. "You know what you need, don't you?" Her eyes sparkled a brilliant shade of green, like the Caribbean waters plastered all over travel posters. She paused, Grady thought, for dramatic effect.

He could hardly stand the suspense. "What's that?"

"You need Jesus in your life, Son. There ain't no doubt about it. Don't you see?" she asked, her voice going up in inflection. "That's why all these awful things have happened to you."

Her words hit him like a lead bullet out of Smith and Wesson at close range, sending shards of shame right through his heart. She spoke with an authority that Grady didn't quite know how to take. His gut churned and he wished he hadn't eaten that last helping.

Chandra placed a hand on each hip and laughed. "Now, don't be looking at me like that! I'm only speaking the truth. Listen here, I've lived a lot longer than you and I'm telling it like it is." She lowered her voice to a whisper. "Are you going to church these days?" Her eyes gleamed like two turquoise nuggets, settling on Grady as she waited for an answer.

Feeling trapped, he cleared his throat and loosened his shirt at the collar. "No, ma'am, I've moved around a few too many times lately." He adjusted his position in the cushy recliner again. Despite the air conditioning on high, his underarms suddenly felt sticky.

"You know what you need? You need to take that girlfriend of yours and make her your wife, settle down and have a few kids."

Grady eased back in the recliner, surveying his options. There was no escape. Chandra and his dad sat directly in front of him, only a few feet away. Man, it was going to be a long weekend.

She took a deep breath and continued. "You need a *home*," she said and stressed the word, "and God in your life, Son." She edged closer to Frank, patting his arm. "It's like I told your dad when we first spent time together. You can't get too far in life without God. Frank here's a good man; I can see that."

Grady's eyes locked on Chandra, who seemed a cross between Tammy Faye Baker and Scarlett O'Hara. "He's been helping a ton at my church. It's a real small Baptist church out here, you know. We're all so thankful to have him; the whole church feels blessed that he's able to do so much for us."

Grady didn't mean to be rude and stare, but he couldn't help himself. It was too bizarre to think she was actually speaking about his father. And with such conviction! If he was a stranger and didn't know better, he might believe her.

She waved an open hand above her and lowered her voice to nearly a whisper. "It's like God sent us an angel when Frank moved out here. And I believe . . . well, let me put it this way— we're gonna work through these couple issues he has. He even came to church with me last Sunday."

Grady's jaw dropped as he dug his fingers into the armrests. Frank winked and smiled sheepishly. The strict, ritualistic German Catholic father who insisted the whole family attend mass week in and week out stepped foot inside a Baptist church? Not even a regular Protestant church like Lutheran or Methodist, but *Baptist!* Were the planets out of orbit? Or had aliens replaced his father with an imposter? How else could anyone explain Frank Kramer drinking ice tea at supper and willfully sitting through a Baptist church service?

Grady was speechless. He wanted to ask what color glasses this woman was looking through—or better yet—what she was smoking to come to that conclusion, but one look at her smile outlined in bright red and her sparkling eyes . . . he couldn't burst her bubble.

"Now that we've met, it's like we're family. Listen here, Grady," Chandra said, "I want you to know, I'll be praying for you."

The only thing missing was a choir of angels singing alleluia in the background. Grady cleared his throat, stifling back a growl. *Give it a rest, lady.* He faked a smile and stared blankly through the lace sheers drawn across the living room window to the desert landscape beyond. Gusts of dusty wind blew through rusted-out cars; dying palm trees stood defiant against the torrent of blowing sand, branches dried and brown. Down the street, the door of an abandoned shed rattled nonstop.

There was only one logical explanation—the whole world must be coming to a vicious, wicked end.

CHAPTER NINETEEN

The weekend stretched on far too long for Grady's liking. He could hardly wait to get out the stinkin' sinkhole or salt sink—whatever the hell it was called—and took off for L.A. first thing Sunday morning. It boggled his mind to think how his dad was working this woman, fooling her right down to her religious core. Other than the church and Jesus stuff, she seemed like a decent woman, but, lordy, she had no idea what she was in for. Part of Grady wanted to tell her what the real Frank Kramer was like, but he figured she'd find out soon enough.

Saturday night the three of them had gone down to Jake's General Store so Frank and Grady could shoot pool. He and his dad each had a couple beers, but Chandra only drank iced tea. Here he'd pegged her for a boozer, but after the weekend, it sounded like the only thing that made her high was Jesus Christ. And boy, she'd let him know about that!

Grady got back to the valley just in time to grab a sandwich at Jimmy's Sports Bar and catch part of the rubber game between the Angels and Royals. He had to admit, living in

Los Angeles was exciting at times. For the first time in his life he lived close enough to attend professional sports games. It was so cool to drive right over to Anaheim Stadium and watch a game with the guys from work.

Monday morning Grady drove from Long Beach to Anaheim, ready to start the prep work for the "jump" that evening. The jumps were staggered, so they'd bring up the man-lifts the first night, the material hoists the next night, followed by the Chicago Boom the third night, a process they worked weekly.

Grady pulled into the Bymac yard in Anaheim shortly after six-thirty a.m. He liked this shift because he missed the worst part of rush hour. Right now he worked only seventeen miles from his apartment, so he took the Toyota most days. Otherwise he took his 650 Kawasaki CSR when the job site was farther, so he could weave in and out of traffic.

He parked his truck next to the bright yellow Bymac van that he and Wade drove to the work site. "Mornin'," Grady called to Wade. He grabbed the bucket that held his welding hood, leather sleeves, welding rod, and tools.

"Ready to hit the road, man." Wade Jackson stood beside the van with a paper coffee cup in his hand. "The van's loaded."

"Oh, so today you're in a hurry, is that it?" Grady said, putting his bucket in the side door. "What—the Dodgers lose last night?"

"Course not. This is their year; I can feel it."

"Nah, their bullpen's not deep enough." Wade was a Dodgers fan and Grady liked the Angels, so most mornings they traded stats from the previous night's games on the ride to the job site and argued about which team was better.

The massive Library Tower work site took up a good two-thirds of the city block, carved deep into the earth, the perimeter blocked off with orange construction barricades. Traffic buzzed around all sides, oblivious to the work in progress. A temporary walkway was in place to protect pedestrians at ground level. Three large cranes reached to the sky, one behind in the 'hole' and two next to the structure at ground level.

Grady and Wade crossed the dirt-filled yard as a derrick operator hoisted I-beams from semitrailers and set them on the working floor. Dust flew up from a bobcat that passed in front of them.

"I need to stop in the office," Wade said. "Not sure if they're going up two floors today. That'd be my guess."

"Sounds about right."

"We're gonna need that sixty-five-ton crane to get the tower sections stacked up," Wade said, talking over the noise. "I wonder what the availability on that is. Friday it was tied up all day."

Grady followed him into the contractor's office in the building next door. Wade made a beeline to the newest secretary and sat down on the corner of her desk. By the look on her face, she didn't seem to mind one bit. At six foot three, with a chiseled frame and jet black hair, Wade was by all accounts a real lady-killer, despite missing all four fingers on his left hand.

After working with the man for nearly three years, Grady had watched him work his charm on the opposite sex more times than he could count. He swore it was like an addiction for Wade; instead of a morning caffeine fix, Wade needed to have his ego stroked by an attractive blonde with plenty of cleavage. There was no doubt Wade's ass would be glued there at least fifteen minutes.

Grady cursed under his breath and retreated to the restroom, irritated because they had work to do. He found a box of fresh donuts in the coffee area and spent a few minutes bullshitting with one of the engineers. He stalled a good fifteen minutes and rounded his way back to the front office. Wade hadn't budged one iota, other than to lean in a little closer. A puzzled look crossed his face as though there was some complicated, convoluted system to figuring out the crane schedules, something he could have done within minutes.

Grady pissed away another fifteen minutes by the coffeepot making small talk, getting more antsy by the minute. "Hey," he walked up to Wade and slapped his shoulder. "Let's get going. We've got a crew coming in half an hour."

"Relaaaax. This is serious stuff here." Wade winked at the secretary, who was by all accounts drop-dead gorgeous. "Jen has it just about set for us."

"Whatever." Grady looked at his watch. He was done babysitting Wade. "I'm heading down to lube the Chicago Boom draw works."

"Take the buckets down, will ya? I'll be right there," Wade said without taking his eyes off his blonde bombshell.

Grumbling under his breath, Grady felt like a stupid trainee carrying both tool buckets to the tower. He went down to the machinery room deep in the center of the substructure, the same hole that would eventually house the elevator shaft. Nearby electric motors rumbled like a dozen freight trains coming through a tunnel all at once.

Grady wanted to make sure the truck had dropped the skid earlier that morning. He rounded the corner and saw the corner of the machinery room sitting at an angle. "Good," he said, putting down the buckets. "At least that's in place."

The machinery room housed the draw works and a three-hundred-horsepower motor. Because of the narrow space, the driver's only option was to drop it kitty-corner to the bay. Much like the draw works on the oil rigs, the skid held miles of cable on a spool that ran the high-speed man-lift. The first order of business was to align the twelve-ton skid with the elevator bay. The skid was a good fifteen feet long, seven feet wide, and seven feet tall—not really a one-person job. He would need to swing the front end over a good fifteen feet for starters.

Grady walked around it a couple times, sizing up his options. "Never say never," he said, rubbing his chin. He grabbed a twenty-ton come-along and chained the winch end to a base column of the building and the other end to the skid. Using a cheater pipe, he put as much of a strain as possible on the come-along. The skid didn't budge.

Next, he grabbed a six-foot pry bar and poked it under the skid, trying to get it to slide. No luck. He searched through a crate in the machinery room and found a tube of grease. He spread grease on the concrete floor along the base of the skid, so if he did get it started, the iron box would slide a little easier. He tried lifting it again and still nothing.

Within minutes he'd worked up a major sweat and attitude. "Damn it anyhow!" he shouted, but his words were drowned out by the rumble of the engines. He kicked an empty tool bucket, digging through the pieces until he found a long piece of pipe. If Wade was down here where he belonged, they'd have it done by now. He put the pipe over the pry bar for more leverage and shoved it under the skid. He gripped it with both hands, then bent at the knees and gave it everything he had. He felt a *pop* in his lower back. Pain shot up his spine like a flame and then faded. He straightened up slowly, not sure what to make of it. Within seconds, sharp shooting pains followed.

"Grady! Where'd you go?"

"In here!" he called above the motors. Wade's frame turned the corner and he stood in front of him. "You done socializing finally?"

"Gotta make the most of every opportunity, you know."

"Help me get this damn hoist in line, would ya?"

Wade tipped his head, eyeing Grady. "Hey, you aren't looking so good."

"Just pinched something in my back. No big deal."

By eleven-thirty Grady had so much pain shooting down his leg he couldn't stand. "Damn it anyhow! Grrrr!" he said through clenched teeth. He couldn't straighten and gripped a column for support.

Wade dropped his pry bar. "We need to get you in somewhere, now."

Grady grimaced, arching his back. "Oooh, ooh," he said in quick breaths. "Take me back to my truck. I'll get in with my chiropractor. Get a tune-up." He'd strained his back more than once since he joined the ironworkers. Whenever it flared up, he made an appointment and went in for an alignment, kinda like servicing a classic car.

Grady eased himself into the van for the ride back to Anaheim and drove directly to his chiropractor. He undressed and went through the standard routine and X-rays.

"Get dressed and I'll write up a review," Dr. Stan said, a middle-aged man with graying hair and a long skinny nose. The man didn't have much of a personality, but he knew how to work Grady's back. "I'm sorry, Grady, but you've got more going on than I can help you with. I've set up an appointment with an orthopedic surgeon, day after tomorrow."

Grady endured two miserable days without hardly any sleep and arrived at the appointment early. The doctor listened as Grady recited his symptoms. "Well, I read the report from your chiropractor and I can tell you right now, he's way off base," the surgeon said. "You've got a herniated disc; that's why you have the shooting pain going down your butt cheek into your heel. It's the L5-S1 disc. It's either herniated or extruded."

Grady took a deep breath. "Whatever you gotta do, I need help *now.*"

"Have you always been in the ironworkers?"

"No, I've only been doing this about four years."

"What'd you do before that?"

"Worked the oil rigs, back in Montana and North Dakota."

"With big heavy equipment to move, I'm guessing?"

"Between that and working on cars, moving engines in and out."

The surgeon offered a pretentious nod. "I think it's safe to say you've abused your back more than once, young man."

Grady shrugged. "It happens, part of the job."

"Well, I'm afraid this is more serious than you think." Dressed in pale green scrubs, he stared at the X-ray. He wheeled his chair over and pointed to the skeletal picture of Grady's spine. "Right here, you've completely blown out two discs, S2, S1, L5, L4, right between L5 and S1, and the disc between L4 and L3 is herniated. See this bone, it sticks out on each side, and this one is cracked. There's cumulative trauma built up over time, and with the strain from this most recent incident, it blew out."

"Got any good news?" Grady asked with a forced laugh.

"I'm sorry to be the one to tell you this, but you are done ironworking, Son." He pushed the chair backward to the desk and scribbled in the folder.

Grady gritted his teeth, his emotions ready to boil over. *I'll decide when I'm done working, Doctor.*

"I'll have my assistant come back and she'll set you up for physical therapy. You need to start that right away. It'll help with the pain and strengthen the core of your back. We can't—"

"What about surgery?" Grady asked, interrupting him. "Isn't there something you can do?"

"You need to go through the physical therapy first. We want to take a conservative approach; surgery is always the last option. And you'll need to check with your insurance, make sure you're covered for long-term disability."

Long-term disability. The doctor's words burned in his ears, numbing his brain. What the hell was he talking about? He'd be back to work within the week; he *always* was, no matter how bad he'd gotten hurt through the years. "I'm with the ironworkers."

"Well, you should have good coverage then."

Grady left the clinic with an appointment slip for the California Spine Institute in Long Beach. "They better have some answers," he muttered between clenched teeth. Long-term disability was *not* an option.

* * *

Six long months after the injury, he was nearing the end of his physical therapy program. The regimen meant trips to the center every other day for hours-long therapy sessions. According to the therapist, the intent was to open the vertebrae and create a vacuum to draw the nucleus back inside the disc. They put him in all kinds of strange contortions and so far none had helped. Every day he was still bothered with pain in his back.

The first few weeks hadn't been bad. He'd been free to meet Sarah for lunch dates every other day, kinda like being on a long change on the rigs. Only, one day stretched into the next, and each one was filled with intense, sharp pains. By the second month it started affecting his relationship with Sarah. She got upset when he couldn't sit through a movie or a long car ride to the desert. And he didn't have as much money to spend on dates.

Sure, he was cranky at times. Moody, frustrated. He didn't want to be that way, but the pain was so overbearing at times, he couldn't help it. In a way, he shouldn't have been surprised when she wanted out. She was tired of his limitations—both physical and financial. She'd said in so many words she was tired of taking care of him, running him to appointments, putting up with his mood swings. Before he knew it she called it quits. He couldn't blame her, really, but he missed her.

There was somewhat of a distraction in October when the Dodgers made it into the postseason and World Series. Even though he was an Angels and American League fan, he felt obligated to cheer on the other hometown team in the postseason. It took extra effort to watch the three-hour games, most times from a standing position. But it helped pass the time. The most memorable moment came in game one of the World Series. With the Dodgers losing 3-4 in the bottom of the ninth, Tommy Lasorda had sent in the injured Kirk Gibson as a pinch hitter. Gibson had injured both legs in the National League Championship game against the New York Mets when he made a spectacular catch, and he hadn't been expected to play in the World Series. Somehow he worked an 0-2 count from Dennis Eckersley to 3-2, and smacked a backdoor slider over the fence in right field. The stadium went wild as he hobbled around the bases in pain, pumping his fist in jubilation as his teammates stormed the plate. Grady had watched the replay of his trot around the bases at least a dozen times, admiring the man for his bulldogged attitude and determination.

He was determined too, determined not to give in to the crippling pain. He tried his best to maintain his sanity. It irritated him to no end that instead of going to work every day, he went to the clinic for treatment every other day. He hated not being able to work. He collected disability, but it wasn't the same as a full paycheck.

Grady sat in the waiting room of the spine center. He arrived early, mostly out of boredom. He picked up the Long Beach Gazette and scanned the articles. The local school district short on money, the library needing an update, another crime spree on the south side, sand sculpture contest on the beach, car show in Belmont Shore, and so on.

"Volunteer Cuddlers Give Time and Get Rewards." The caption caught his attention and he started reading. "Statistics show that premature babies held by parents or volunteer cuddlers frequently develop faster and are discharged sooner. Francia Gibbs has been a surrogate grandmother to some forty-five prematurely born babies in the neonatal intensive-care unit and Long Beach Community Hospital. 'The main job is to simply hold the infants; some are in the hospital for weeks or months and mom and dad can't always be there,' says Nurse Lois Fisher. 'Nurses may be busy feeding babies or starting IVs for an entire shift. When these little ones are held, they are calmer and can relax. We can always use more volunteers to fill the shifts.' "

Grady finished the article, studying the picture of a premature infant being held by a woman in a rocker. He had to admit, it was a good idea for people who had time on their hands.

"Graden Kramer," the nurse called.

It took him a moment to stand.

"They're ready for you," she said, holding the door open for him. "Down the hall all the way, third door on the left."

Once again he went through every contorted position they came up with, bending, twisting, doing repetitions as instructed. When the session ended, he exited the suite and pushed the button for the elevator. He stepped in and leaned his head against the paneled wall, shutting his eyes. Anger shot through him in fiery unison with the pain, attacking his strained spine. *Why did this happen to me, God? Why?* He remembered Chandra's accusation. Was it true? Had he gotten hurt all these years because he didn't have God in his life? Why had she said that to him, when she hardly knew him? It annoyed him to think she might be right. How else could he explain why he'd been close to death so many times in his thirty short years?

The worst, of course, was the chainsaw. He'd come within a heartbeat of not surviving that day. And he'd cut it pretty close that time he got bit by the rattler. Plus the shooting at the Vault. Then the fall on the rigs, when his wallet had stopped an iron post from spearing his chest. Shortly after he moved to L.A., he had wiped out on the I-10, cruising in and out of rush-hour traffic on his 650 Kawasaki. He had lived clear up in Azusa back then and for six months straight drove his motorcycle back and forth to work without a helmet. Three days before the accident, his boss had handed him a helmet, begging him to wear it. After the crash, there'd been nothing left of it except shattered fragments of fiberglass. That made five times, right there.

He thought of the caption printed under his picture in his senior yearbook: *Don't take life too seriously; you may never get out of it alive.* Was that some sort of precursor? Was God trying to get his attention? Or were the injuries and accidents a forerunner to eternal life in hell?

The way he was taught, Catholics were the ones going to heaven. Not the holy-roller Protestant types. He attended mass at Saint Cyprian Catholic Church on all the holy days and holidays now, even went on a men's retreat once. He cut back on his drinking and made sure he never drank and drove. Didn't that count for something?

The elevator opened and a petite lady with snow white hair stepped in, her skin peach-fuzz soft and wrinkled like one of those Chinese Shar-Pei dogs. She wore the familiar pink of the volunteers and smiled at Grady as she grabbed the handrail. "How are you today?"

Grady offered a faint smile. "Could be better."

She lifted her chin, eyes twinkling. "Or could be worse, right? It pays to think positive and be thankful for your blessings." Her voice sounded old but wise. She shifted, putting all her weight on her right side and Grady noticed the prosthetic leg.

"Or could be worse," he said, nodding.

Two weeks later, Grady was at the spine center for another routine appointment. In the mess of pamphlets tucked in a large multibox holder on the wall, a photo of a tiny infant on the front of a shiny pink paper caught his attention. He pulled the pamphlet out of the slot. "Cuddlers give their time and love to little ones who need it most." It was the same program he'd read about in the Long Beach paper.

The image of the newborn stayed with him long after the therapy session. A few days later, Grady stopped at the hospital and went to the information desk. A pencil thin gal in light green cotton scrubs who barely looked college age looked up from her paperwork as Grady approached the desk. "Can I help you?" she asked in typical receptionist politeness.

"I saw the pamphlet for the Cuddler program." He glanced down the shiny hall and took a deep breath. "I'd like to volunteer."

A look of surprise crossed her face. "You do?"

Grady dug both hands into his pockets, fingering the seams inside. "Yeah."

"Um, that's great. Just fill out this application and then Steve Davidson will call you. There's an interview process and stuff."

Grady nodded. "Sure, yeah."

The girl swung her ponytail and poked her chin with the cap of her pen. "Hey, I think it's way cool you want to do that."

CHAPTER TWENTY

Grady somehow endured another six months of physical therapy without any sign of progress. The insurance company for his workman's compensation agreed to cover a discectomy, which meant having muscle tissue removed from the lamina above and below the affected disc. Retractors would hold the muscle and skin away from the surgical site, giving the surgeon a clear view of the vertebrae and disc.

Strike One.

With no relief from the pain, Grady followed that with a laminectomy surgery. This surgery removed bone and ligaments in order for the surgeon to see and gain access to the disc without damaging the nerve tissues. The idea was to relieve pressure on the nerve roots, but again it didn't take away the pain.

Strike Two.

In between the surgeries, doctors offered epidurals, which helped, but only short-term. For the longest time Grady held out hope that he could go back to work, but when he passed the one-year mark, he started to have doubts. The stress took its toil emotionally, physically. Dealing with the pain day in and day out changed his whole personality, consuming him at times. He missed working, missed feeling *normal*.

The worker's compensation people told him it was time to find a new career. In order to determine a good fit for his skills, they put him through a battery of tests. The first one was so basic Grady termed it "stupid school." Someone poured a bunch of bolts in a tray and he had to figure what went where. *D-d-duh, dumbbell.* That took all of four seconds. The next one was a box of bolts, nuts, and screws. A picture on the box showed the parts as they should look assembled, which took less than five minutes. Didn't they get that his back was messed up, not his brain?

The next great idea from the team of doctors and therapists was water therapy. Instead of going through his routine in the gym, now he followed a new regimen in the pool three times a week. Although it didn't cure his pain completely, he discovered one important fact: when he was in the water, his back didn't hurt. As soon as he got out, the pain returned.

He was no rocket scientist, but he wasted no time in finding a place he could be in the water without it costing a fortune. Leave it to California's state park system to include underwater state parks. Crystal Cove Underwater State Park between Laguna Beach and Corona del Mar on the Pacific Coast Highway was the closest to his apartment. The underwater park stretched for three miles along the Pacific Coastline and into the ocean a half mile, covering eleven hundred acres offshore. The park was open from six a.m. to sunset, and he discovered if he got there early enough, especially on week days, he could park on the highway for free.

The morning air was cool as Grady grabbed his duffle bag and walked down the lengthy wooden stairway made from railroad ties that led to the beach. With over one hundred steps down the steep hillside, maneuvering down them was the hardest part of his day. The sun was up and the salt smell of the ocean permeated the waterfront, a refreshing contrast from the traffic and congestion surrounding his apartment. He relished the quietness of the early morning, with only a few fishermen standing along the rocky sections, usually looking for kelp or rock bass. Some mornings he chatted with them or waved a hello.

Waves rushed ashore, one after the other, their constant thrush onto the beach soothing. *Whoosh . . .* a short pause, then *whoosh . . . whoosh . . . whoosh.* He put on his wet suit and stuffed his clothes into his bag. He brought a twelve-inch Subway sandwich and a jug of ice water, and tucked his things in the shade under a large rock. This early there were only one or two people walking the beach, usually looking for shells. So far no one had ever bothered his things when he was out in the water.

Grady sat down at the water's edge and put on his fins and mask. He grabbed his Hawaiian sling by the lanyard and started into the water, completely encompassed by blue: blue sky, blue water, blue waves. The swells weren't too bad this morning; it always depended on the tides. He spied the landmark rock sticking out of the water and entered to the east of it. Closer to the rock, the bottom was uneven and shallow and caused him once to bash his shins. He'd learned the hard way that it was better to swim out first and then over to the rocks. Scotchman's Cove contained enough rocks and reef to make the dive interesting for an entire day.

Sometimes the surges were so strong that they pulled him in the opposite direction for quite a distance. The first time he got caught in a riptide, he was so scared, sure his carcass would end up floating backside-up in Hawaii. Natural instinct was to swim to shore, but then his brain kicked in. *Wait, swim parallel to the beach,* and eventually he swam out of it.

Grady kicked his fins a few times and swam down, deeper into the water. The reef system held an ecological wonder of sea lions, thresher sharks, harbor seals, kelp, and dolphins. He took his time, watching the opaleyes, lobsters, and anemones gliding past him effortlessly. Starfishes were plentiful, and every so often he even saw octopus, sea hares—the species were endless.

He floated in the ocean water, letting the ebb and flow of the waves carry him, rocking him like a little baby. It was the one place Grady had true peace. No noise. No pain. Sunlight filtered through the green-blue water above him, illuminating sunrays and garibaldi—a bright orange fish, his favorite to watch.

After a good hour of relaxed swimming, he cocked his handheld speargun. He'd read up on the fish and game laws and knew which species he could kill inside the park. There were plenty of options, like kelp bass, rock bass, sargo, tilapia. The spear had a five-foot tether, and he used a small mesh bag tied at his waist to hold his catch until he got back to shore.

Fish always faced the direction the water was moving. Grady kicked his fins to swim with the water, then turned and shot his spear at a sargo, piercing it in front of the dorsal fin. It seized up as he pulled the tether in and took it off the spear. Three or four sargo and tilapia in his bag would make for a nice dinner when he got home.

Grady came out of the water around eleven o'clock and made a stop at the park facilities, his body exhausted. He ate half of the turkey and provolone sandwich and put the other half back for a midafternoon snack. He sat in the sun to rest, admiring the beautiful view all around him: huge rugged rocks in strange dark shapes protruded out of the water like giant sea creatures.

The meeting of powerful waves against the land intrigued him. Rocks in strange formations washed smooth from the constant battering of waves; white foam raced up with each wave, running high up the shore and trickling back. Other times, when he walked farther south, the shoreline was all sand, polished and smooth. Many times he stayed and watched the sunset before heading home, mesmerized by the orange-red glow of tranquility, until it disappeared behind the water's edge. Nature's beauty at its finest. He only wished he had someone to share it with.

* * *

"I've reviewed your application and it looks good," Steve Davidson said. He was small in stature, only about five foot nine, with a thin build, but fit and muscular. "It's my policy to meet potential volunteers for an interview before I do the background check. If everything comes back okay, then we'll do a second interview. Make sense?" He looked at Grady out of the corner of his eye; his tanned face remained expressionless.

Grady nodded. He'd worn his nicest brown slacks, a tan button-down shirt, dress shoes, hoping to look presentable. Even trimmed his beard nice and short. "Sure, however you want to do it." They were in a small office next to the quiet room for nursing mothers in the neonatal unit. Nothing more than an oversized closet, it had a small table, two chairs, file cabinets, and a bulletin board with notes pinned to it.

"Just so you get an idea where I'm coming from, I was in the FBI for thirty years. Investigative work, so I know how to dig into people's background. If you're hiding anything, I'll find it." He remained sober faced. No smile, no hint of humor.

"Not much to find. I've never been in trouble of any kind." Grady offered a nervous laugh.

Davidson looked at Grady over the tops of his reading glasses. His eyes were a light hazel, almost clear. "I hear that all the time. So tell me about yourself. Where you coming from? What's your story?" He leaned back in his chair and folded his sun-soaked bronze arms.

Grady took a deep breath. "Well . . . grew up in Montana, small town right on the border with North Dakota. After graduation I went to school in Billings for a year. From there I went to Williston, North Dakota, and worked on the oil rigs until that industry went bust. Came to California in eighty-four. My dad lives out here, in Salton City. I passed my welding test and worked for the ironworkers until I hurt my back."

"What happened?"

"Popped a disc in my lower back in 1988 working on the Library Tower downtown. I've been going through P.T. ever since. I've had two surgeries, but neither one solved the problem."

With his gaze still fixed on Grady, he said, "Go on."

"I go to P.T. every other day, depending on which program I'm on. The doctors told me I need to find a new career. I can't work physical jobs like I always have, so I'm in vocational training right now."

"What are you doing now?"

Grady shrugged. "Other than my physical therapy schedule, that's about it. I'm single, never been married. No kids. The rest of my family is still in North Dakota and Montana."

Steve studied him for a moment. "So why do you want to do this?"

"I've got all this time on my hands; just thought it would be something good I could do."

Steve leaned forward, resting his elbows on his knees. "You gotta level with me, okay? Why would a thirty-one-year-old single man want to sit in a rocking chair for four hours once a week and hold premature babies? You hear what I'm saying?"

Grady nodded and lifted his shoulders in a shrug. "That's it. I've got all this time to fill. I don't have forty, fifty hours on the job anymore, no family around. Just wanted to volunteer. Last year I got involved with the Catholic Big Brothers through St. Cyprian and I've been assigned a little sister, actually. I'm the

231

only person in the Los Angeles County program with a little sister instead of a little brother."

He cocked his head, his colorless eyes boring into Grady. "Why's that?"

"They gave me pictures of a girl and two boys and let me pick. The girl had a birth defect; her right eye was in the back of her head, twice as far back as normal, and she'd been through a bunch of surgeries to move the eye forward. She still doesn't look 'normal' and has some learning disabilities. I picked her because I know a little bit what it's like to have people staring at your face." Grady pointed to the bridge of his nose.

Steve studied Grady's face, nodding. "What happened to you?"

"Chainsaw, when I was nine."

"Sounds bad."

"It was."

"So, you're in the Big Brother program now?"

"Yup, I listed them as one of my references."

"I'll give them a call."

"Sure, that's fine."

"Smoke?"

"Used to. Gave it up when I came to California. Decided I get enough crap in my lungs with all the smog in the air." Grady smiled, hoping to lighten the mood, but the former agent's face remained as serious as if Grady had just confessed to murder.

"Drink?"

"Here and there, not too much. If I go out with guys from work, sure, I'll have a few. But around the apartment, no. Besides, I'm on a pretty tight budget. Don't have much extra for booze these days."

"Any felony arrests?"

"Nope," Grady said, thinking back to Extreme and some of the other roughnecks.

"Police records?"

"No sir."

He handed his pen to Grady. "Give me the contact information for your 'little sister': parent name and number." Grady scribbled down the names and numbers.

"Anything else?" Steve asked with another long stare.

"Like I said, don't have a lot of money. Mornings you can find me down at the Crystal Cove Underwater State Park; I go snorkeling down there. I don't have any back pain when I'm in the water, so I go out there several mornings a week." Grady shifted in his chair and offered up another smile like a white flag. "And it's free."

"So, why this one? I mean there're lots of volunteer programs out there."

"I don't know . . . it just caught my attention. With my back the way it is, I can't do anything physical. It's close to my apartment. I thought it would be something I could handle." He stopped. He didn't know what else he could say to convince the man.

"So, you want to hold babies?"

Grady crossed his arms, then uncrossed them to hide the expanding sweat spot under his arms. "Yeah."

"That's it?"

"There's no motive, man, other than giving back. I've been through a lot. I used to own my own house, had a wad of money in savings back in North Dakota. Now I'm scraping by month to month, but I have all this time, you know? I feel like I should do something positive with it, give back somehow." *I'm trying to volunteer here, damn it!*

Steve flipped his folder shut and laid his pen on top. "Okay. I'll dig into your packet, make some calls. If there's anything out there, I'll find it: arrests, evictions, civil orders. You hear me?" He stared at Grady, waiting, and Grady nodded. "I'll give you a call when I'm done." He stood and stuck out his hand.

Grady stood and shook his hand. "Sure, man." He walked out of the hospital feeling like a criminal awaiting his sentence.

* * *

Grady endured a couple bad weeks in a row, desperate to find answers from a new set of doctors. In a weak moment he'd told his dad how bad things were, so his dad and Chandra were on their way to Long Beach for a visit. The drive to the desert was too painful to make, so he hadn't seen much of his dad since he'd gotten hurt. While he appreciated their concern, he wasn't set up to have company. His apartment was too small for them to stay in, so Chandra made reservations at a nearby motel.

"We're right on Long Beach Boulevard," she told Grady. "It's not as expensive as some of those other places."

As soon as she gave him the address, Grady said, "Chandra, you might want to change your reservation. That's not in a good part of town."

"We'll be fine, Grady," Chandra said, then threw out her typical response. "The Lord will protect us."

Grady hung up, shaking his head. "Don't come calling me when you get robbed," he said to the telephone.

To Grady's surprise, Chandra and Frank had gotten married a few months earlier in a small ceremony in their Baptist Church. Yes, *their* Baptist Church. The one-time Catholic had converted to Baptist. He called Grady one Friday night with the good news. "Grady, when I was a Catholic, I went to Catholic high school. Did I ever tell you I almost became a priest?"

"No, Dad."

"I spent a lot of time in the church, praying all the time. I did all the sacraments and rituals. I was *the* Catholic, you know?"

"Uh-huh."

"Here all that time I was a Catholic, I never knew for sure where I was going when I died. Now I've started reading the

Bible and I know for sure. When I die, I'm going to heaven. I've been forgiven, Grady, and I'm going to heaven."

Unmoved, Grady grunted a response. *You're thinking pretty doggone highly of yourself. You might want to step back in case that ol' lightning bolt comes out of the sky and wipes you out. Let's not forget about your drinkin' days, Dad. A beer in your hand every single day when we were kids. Fishing trip, family picnic—it didn't matter. Or how about when you whipped us kids for leaving a gate open or not hanging up our coat? How 'bout the yelling and fighting with mom—or even better, screwing around behind her back? You might be foolin' yourself, ol' man, but God knows the real you, and I don't think for a second he wants you in heaven.*

Grady paced his eight-by-ten-foot living room floor, trying his best to put aside those feelings before he and Chandra showed up. Part of him was happy for his dad. At least now the man had a different goal every day besides getting drunk. Chandra'd made it clear that if Frank Kramer wanted to marry her, he had to give up the bottle. And to the shock of the extended Kramer family, Frank did it. He finally "saw the light," as she loved to put it. At the same time it almost bugged Grady that Chandra was right. She'd gotten him to quit drinking when no one else could. Now she was working on him to give up the cigarettes, but the ol' stubborn German wasn't quite ready to let go of all his vices.

Frank and Chandra arrived at Grady's apartment about three in the afternoon. Right away he noticed something different about his dad. At first Grady couldn't decide what it was, then he realized his dad's face was slimmer and tanned. He was more easygoing, much more relaxed than Grady ever remembered. They took Grady out for dinner and bought him a few groceries, only to go back to their motel and discover the next morning that someone had broken the car window and stolen the radio, their tapes, and his dad's toolbox in the back.

"So much for the Lord's protection," Grady muttered when they called with the distressing news. Needless to say, it shortened their trip to Long Beach, and they left in a rush to get back to the safety of Salton City.

* * *

Grady returned to the Long Beach Hospital for his second interview with Steve Davidson. He swore that if the man came down on him as hard as he had the first time, he'd get up and walk out. So what if Davidson had been in the flippin' FBI? Grady didn't need to get hassled by an egomaniac for simply trying to volunteer.

Nervous sweat trickled down his back as he walked down the shiny hallway, his shoes echoing on the tile floor. The air conditioning felt refreshing after a morning in the stuffiness of his second-floor apartment, the cool air tingling his bare arms. He approached the nurses' station and offered up his best smile. "I have an appointment with Steve Davidson."

"Right through that door," a nurse said, pointing.

"Thanks." Grady tapped on the open door and walked in. "Hi, Steve. How are you doing?"

"Great. Have a seat; you're right on time." Dressed in a white short-sleeve shirt and white slacks, Steve waved a hand to the cheap plastic chair with metal legs that resembled a moonwalker.

He sat rigid against the hard plastic, hands clasped, ready for another onslaught of tough questions.

"Well, Grady, I made all the calls, ran a full FBI background and fingerprint check, followed up with your references, the Big Brother coordinator. Everything checked out," he said. "You're clean as a whistle."

Grady felt his body relaxing. "Told ya," he said with a smile.

"I don't take any chances," Steve said, motioning to the neonatal nursery sign. "These babies are pretty fragile. You gotta admit it, you don't exactly fit the profile of the average cuddler."

"I s'pose not."

"I'll add your name to the schedule. I'll have you shadow with me—"

"You volunteer too?"

"I founded the program in Long Beach, modeled it after one out east." He leaned back and stretched his arms.

"Interesting."

"I didn't want to sit around and rust after I left the FBI." Steve allowed a faint smile to cross his face. "Check in at the nurses' station each time you come in. I'll go through the procedures with you until you get comfortable," he said. "Listen, I know you're in a tough position right now. Hurt, out of work. That's not a good row to hoe. Here's a little good news. Every time you volunteer, you get a voucher for a free meal in the cafeteria. Contrary to public opinion, it's pretty decent food."

Grady smiled and nodded. "Thanks."

"Welcome aboard. Here's your badge to get through security at the front doors. I'll see you Saturday morning. You need to wear all white; that's our policy," Steve said, extending his right hand, "I look forward to working with you."

* * *

The past two years had been a blur of vocational training, continued physical therapy, and living with constant pain. He saw every doctor the worker's compensation insurance company recommended and other doctors on his own. Grady faithfully went down to the Long Beach Community swimming pool at five a.m. and swam a mile every morning, Monday through Friday. His therapists had stressed the importance of building his abdominal muscles to help strengthen his back and he had taken it to heart. Thirty-five laps in the pool equaled a mile and he swam it five days a week.

He never missed a Saturday with his babies, rocking the morning away with a fragile infant in his arms. Some were so small they fit in the palm of his hand. Holding those little ones, so innocent, so completely dependent, fulfilled him in an unexpected way. They *needed* him. And truth be told, he needed them. Probably more. He didn't understand it all, but he could feel his heart changing, softening. Maybe it was time to shed the fearless self-sufficiency he'd always relied on. He was at peace during those moments when they were snuggled against his chest, heartbeats in rhythm.

Grady signed up for a brand-new six-week regiment of physical therapy at a pain management program that scheduled full days of group therapy at Long Beach Community Hospital. He arrived at seven a.m. sharp, as the instructions stated. The therapist outlined the details of the program, including vocational rehab. Once again he held out hope for a positive outcome.

When noon rolled around, his therapist escorted him to the dining hall for lunch. About ten minutes later a group of patients arrived from another wing. One by one he watched as grown men strapped in full-body wheelchairs were pushed up to the tables. Grady could see they didn't have the motor skills to even sit up on their own. He eyed one of the staff members. "Brain injuries," the therapist said, positioning a young man's wheelchair.

Grady felt himself straighten in his chair as he surveyed the rows of wheelchairs. None of the men could hold a fork or spoon to eat; several had drool running down their chins, eyes blank, hands curled into a tight fist. A Hispanic man, probably the same age as Grady, sat limp in his chair. The man's mom stopped by to feed him lunch, and Grady wasn't sure he even knew she was there. It was sobering to watch her feed spoonfuls of Jell-O to him. Unresponsive, he stared into space, oblivious to his mother's comments and questions.

During the lunch hour he learned several were victims of motorcycle crashes. One younger man who barely looked eighteen had taken a bullet to the spine, two were car accident victims, another had crashed into a cliff while hang gliding. It was clear most of them were completely unaware of why they'd been pushed into the dining hall for their noontime meal, let alone what day of the week it was or that it was 1990. Grady glanced up at the staff. Busy with their patients, they didn't make eye contact with him, but their message came through loud and clear. No matter how bad it was living with constant pain, there were many who had it ten times worse and then some.

CHAPTER TWENTY-ONE

The pain became a driving force within, pushing Grady into one battle after another with the workman's compensation insurance company. He had gone through his entire savings account from the oil rig days, money at one time he never thought he could spend. The last six months he had been unable to make his mortgage payments on the house in Williston. For a while he had rented it out, but the tenants stopped paying the rent, and on top of that, trashed the house. The foreclosure process was already in motion.

Ever since Billings, he'd lived life like a tightrope walker—fearless, undaunted. It hadn't mattered if he was greasing pulleys at the top of an oil rig one hundred sixty feet off the ground or welding steel beams thirty floors up; he had never been afraid of anything or anyone, not dependent on any person. But ever since he'd injured his back, things had spiraled downward in every aspect, leaving him broke and broken.

Grady could barely afford the rent, let alone eat out or see a movie. In August he sold his Kawasaki for six hundred in cash to cover the rent and groceries. Earlier in the week he sold his stereo to buy some groceries and get him through September.

In the evenings when he couldn't swim, he went for walks—the next best thing—usually late at night when it was cool. He liked it best right after a rain; the air smelled as if he were walking through a greenhouse. September in L.A. was still plenty warm, and he spent most days in a T-shirt and shorts.

Grady walked south on Cherry Avenue. Cars zipped by as he shuffled down the darkened street. He neared the corner streetlight and his angled shadow grew from short to long and back to short as he made his way down the block and fell under the glare of the next light. He passed the little flower shop at Market Street displaying a potpourri of flower arrangements. One large spray in the center with pink Oriental lilies, white chrysanthemums, yellow carnations, white gladiolus, and red aster looked like it was waiting for a funeral.

A yellow Suzuki Samurai, still with dealer plates, honked at an older model Cadillac Seville, then raced around it. Everyone was in a big rush to go nowhere. He hated walking with no place to go. No friends, no family nearby. He crossed Plymouth Street and his eyes affixed on the train trestle that crossed over Cherry Avenue just past Fifty-third Street.

He stared at the concrete bridge that held the tracks. *Maybe I'll just I climb up there and jump. End it right here and now. That'd be one surefire way to get rid of this pain.* He stood on the cracked sidewalk, letting the thought rest in his mind. *Why not, Grady? Do it and get it over with. Hell, even the flowers are ready.* He shuffled toward the trestle before the idea completely registered. He walked now with a purpose, a destination, unlike his usual late night wanderings, focused on the embankment to the railroad tracks.

He moved into the darkness behind the corner building and started up the earthen side in switchback fashion. It was steep and he winced in pain as his tennis shoe slipped over some loose stones. Near the top he cut through a patch of weeds to the gravel ledge, in constant driving, shooting pain. He stopped to catch his breath. No sight of a train. He stepped over the rail and followed the tracks a few yards until he stood directly over Cherry Avenue.

He walked to the edge of the trestle and looked down. A Jaguar heading south honked its horn and he wanted to scream, *Leave me alone! If I want to jump, I'll jump!* Seconds, then minutes, passed as he paced back and forth. He glanced to the pavement below, debating.

Who would even care that he was gone? Dad had Chandra now and he was happy in love with her, going to church all the time, the two of them praying and praising God day and night. It would be the hardest on his mom, he knew that for sure. But shoot, he hadn't lived at home since the week he'd turned eighteen, so nothing would change for her.

At one time he thought he and Sarah'd had a chance to be husband and wife, start a family. But she'd ditched out on him when he couldn't be the fun guy anymore. What kind of love was that, to walk away when he really needed her? He had a rotten life half the time anyway; why not end it here and now?

He stared at the blackened railroad ties spaced evenly as they disappeared into the night like a long, dark tunnel. He looked over the edge again. *Go ahead, chicken, and do it. You've never been afraid of anything in your life. Do it and get it over with.*

He figured the trestle had a fifteen-foot clearance, and then another five feet in depth; that would make twenty. Was twenty feet enough? *With your luck, man, you'll mess this up and end up a quad like those guys in therapy.* He wiped his eyes, choking back the tears. What was the point of going on? He swallowed hard, fighting the emotions that raged within his mind. Finally, he burst into sobs. *What a loser you are. You're so bad off, you can't even commit suicide right.*

* * *

There were ups and downs, better days and worse days, but the pain never went away for long. A couple times he thought he was out of the woods, only to have it flare up again. Motivated daily by the images of the men in wheelchairs, he swam every morning to strengthen his abdomen and core muscles, a necessity no matter which route doctors chose next. So far none of the treatments or therapy solved the problem. As soon as he completed the six-week pain management therapy, he went back to the workman's compensation doctor begging for one last option—spine fusion surgery.

"Fusion surgery isn't the answer, Grady. It doesn't have a good success rate; you just need more therapy."

Grady stood and told him in a not-so-polite manner he could take his damn therapy and shove it. He'd had enough, period. For once, his complaining had made a difference. The doctor gave in and authorized the surgery. He wasted no time, scheduling it for the following Wednesday.

He punched the familiar Montana area code into the phone and a wave of homesickness swept over him. "Hey, Mom." He tried his best to sound normal, cheerful even.

"Grady . . ."

He missed her voice, how she articulated his name, *Grady,* with a soft cadence that stemmed from the heart. He lay back on his mattress—the long chord stretched across his chest—and shut his eyes. He wondered how to tell her the news without adding to her own problems. Her husband had run out on her and left her with a pile of debts. She was fighting to work herself out of that mess, holding down two jobs.

243

"Are you doing okay?" she asked.

"I'm going in Wednesday to have my spine fused. I'm finally gonna have the surgery."

"Surgery!" she gasped. "When did that get decided?"

"Just this week."

"But—"

"It's a good thing, Mom. It's what I need. I can't . . . I can't deal with this pain any longer. I've been begging for this for two and a half years. I'm gonna go get it done."

"Who's going to be there with you?" Her voice turned to a whisper and Grady heard the catch in her throat.

"Mom, it's okay."

She was crying now, fifteen hundred miles away in her little house in Beach. He didn't want to make her cry. Just like when he was nine years old and she saw his face sliced wide open. It was the first time he'd seen her cry, *really* cry. He'd felt bad for making her cry so hard that day.

"Just a minute," she said. He heard her move the phone away so she could blow her nose. "There, that's better. Can your dad and Chandra come and stay with you?"

"I'd rather go it alone than have them crammed in this little apartment with me."

"But you can't go through this alone, Grady; it's not right," she said, crying again.

"I'll be fine, I promise."

"Oh, Grady, I wish I could come."

"I know, Mom." He rolled onto his side, sharp pains shooting down his back.

"When Russ left . . . it's been hard." She took a deep breath. "I'm working twelve-hour days, but I'll get out of it; it'll just take time."

"You got enough to worry about without me adding to it."

"Maybe I could still come—"

"No." Grady said a little too quickly. He squeezed his
eyes shut, fighting back his own tears. He couldn't let her see
him like this. The bare apartment, his mattress and box spring on
the floor without a bed frame. No food in his apartment. All
busted up and barely able to function. It would be too much for
her. He cleared his throat, trying to find a strong voice. "I'll be
fine, really."

"How are you getting to the hospital?"

"I'll take a cab." He pressed the receiver against his ear,
wishing he could somehow ease her guilt.

"Grady, oh, Grady . . . I should be there with you . . ."
Her voice trailed off. The tone in her voice jolted him back in
time. Back to when he was nine years old, propped on the front
seat of their '59 Rambler station wagon, his face pressed into his
mother's chest, listening to her cry and pray the entire frantic
ride to the hospital from their little logging camp, down the
mountain road into Missoula.

"It's okay, Grady, we're gonna make it. Oh, Dear Jesus,
save him, *pleeease* save my little boy." He had felt her chest rise
and fall as she sucked in a deep breath. "Grady, you're gonna be
okay, you're gonna be okay. We're on the way; we'll be at the
hospital soon," she said, reassuring him. "Talk to me Grady, talk
to me. Say *something*." He never heard such desperation in her
voice before, even when Kurt had gotten lost the day after he
turned three years old.

"Did we . . . just cross the Blackfoot . . . right there?" he
asked, catching his breath between words, the towel stuck to his
lips.

"Yes, yes!" she cried, squeezing his shoulder.

"I heard the tires . . . it sounded different."

"See, Grady, you're gonna be fine, just keep talking, keep
talking . . ." Her voice trailed off into deep sobs.

Grady couldn't see anything; her hands held the wet
towel pressed across his face. When she first put it on back at the

house, it was cold with water. Now it was warm and sticky. He didn't try to move it though, he just leaned against her arms, his head resting against her bosom, a cushy pillow.

He knew they were off the gravel now and on Montana Route 200, the long curvy highway that wound down the mountain into Bonner where the mill was, and then into Missoula, the bigger city with a hospital. They lived in the Twin Creeks logging camp in the Potomoc Valley, and the highway into Missoula crossed the Blackfoot River ten times between home and town. He knew the road by heart because every Saturday they all went into town for groceries. Bored on the long ride, he and Melinda would count the bridges and make up games to make the time go faster.

The car lurched to the side and for a moment it felt like the Rambler wagon was on two wheels. "Frank! Be careful!" Carol tightened her grip on Grady's arms to keep him from sliding.

"Don't worry!" he said. "I got it."

The car swerved hard to the right. Both he and his mother slid several inches on the seat as his dad made the corner and pressed down on the gas again. Grady figured that was the big S-curve. He heard his dad's foot hit the clutch and the engine rev as he switched gears, changing speeds every few minutes. Grady braced his feet against the floorboards as the car sped up for a few seconds, then slowed for a curve.

"Don't pass yet!" Carol shouted in Grady's ear.

"I see him . . ."

"Frank, *wait!*"

"Where the hell's a highway patrol when you need one, damn it anyway!" His dad pounded a fist on the steering wheel and downshifted again.

"Oh, dear God," Carol said softly.

The engine revved again and Grady felt the car jerk to the left and gain speed. "Get over!" Frank said, honking the horn.

Carol took a deep breath and held it for several seconds. "Oh, thank God," she whispered as the car swerved back to the right. The tires slipped off the pavement, hitting the shoulder, and then jerked back onto the roadway.

"Idiot!" Frank shouted.

"He doesn't know," Carol whispered, "what happened."

"He's goin' slower'n snot, taking up the whole damn road!"

Carol caressed Grady's arm, kissing his neckline. "Jesus, oh, Jesus, please save my boy, save by boy," she whispered in Grady's ear. Then her tone turned firmer, "Grady, say something, talk to me."

"I can tell . . . we're on the . . . straightaway now."

"That's good, that's my boy."

Carol released her grip for a second, then pulled him in close again. "We're gonna make it. Mother Mary—"

"Hold onto him!" Frank shouted as the car hit a bump and went airborne for a second.

Carol gasped. "*Frank!* Watch out!" she said as the car swerved again.

"Damn it, Carol!" He slammed a hand on the seat. "I drive logging trucks down this road three times a day, every blasted day. If I can get a full load of logs down the mountain without going off the side, I can get this car down. For crying out loud, I'll get him there, I promise!"

"I know, I know! It's just every time his heart beats, Frank, the blood . . . it just keeps coming. I can't stop it."

"Hold the towel and keep him talking. Grady, can you hear me?"

Grady swallowed, tasting blood. "Yeah, Dad."

"That's my boy," Carol said. "That's my sweet boy." She paused a moment and her voice seemed louder.

"Grady . . . Grady? Did you hear me? What time is the surgery on Wednesday?"

"Huh?" Grady felt the receiver pressed against his ear.

"I said, what time is the surgery scheduled?"

"Oh . . ." Grady opened his eyes, surprised to see the bare walls in his bedroom. His thoughts just then—the old Rambler, the frantic ride—were so vivid, so real. "Um, eight a.m."

"Who is going to take care of you when you get out?" She paused, waiting. "Grady, are you okay?"

He rubbed his temples, trying to clear his thoughts. "Um, yeah. Workman's comp set it up so a nurse will come in once a day for the first week or so. She can change the dressing and cook for me. I'm sure I'll be fine."

"I'll call you as soon as you get home."

He wiped his eyes. "Just like you do every time I get a little banged up," he said, his voice barely a whisper.

"I promise, Grady. I love you."

"I know, Mom. I love you too." He hung up and rolled onto his side, thinking of that day in the Rambler. That was when he learned the true meaning of a mother's love, when she had held him, letting his blood soak her clothes. He could still remember when they arrived at St. Patrick Hospital. His dad had screeched to a stop at the emergency room door and helped him out of the car. The towel still covered Grady's face, his eyes closed.

His dad scooped him up and carried him toward the doors. "We need some help here," Frank's voice bellowed.

"Help!" Carol called. "Help my boy!"

All of sudden he heard a number of unfamiliar voices excitedly shouting out orders. The next thing he knew someone picked him up and laid him on some kind of a strange bed on wheels. Cold fingers peeled the towel off his face and Grady blinked, wincing, nearly blinded by the bright lights.

He heard a gasp and a woman's voice, "Oh, my God . . ."

"What in heaven's name happened to him?" a man asked, his voice was low and serious. He had thick arms and a white jacketlike shirt on.

"Chainsaw . . ." his dad said, clasping his hands.

"Holy Mother Mary . . ."

"It was an accident. Damn it, hurry!" Frank said, his breaths hurried. "He's already lost a lot of blood. I got him here as fast as I could. We were . . . way up, cutting wood on Gold Creek Road, up past Twin Creeks." He bent over and put his face in his hands.

Frenzied voices continued, "Get his vitals!"

"Start an IV!"

"Grab a scissors, cut off his shirt!"

"Ma'am, he's gonna need surgery right away. Will you give us permission to perform the surgery?"

"Yes, my God, yes," Carol said. "Do what you have to do!"

Two nurses in white dresses and white nylons skirted past him, grabbing cloths and metal instruments. Their crisp white hats looked kinda like the sailor hat his uncle wore in his Navy photo. Someone poked a needle into his right arm and Grady saw a plastic bag hooked to a skinny metal pole with watery stuff dripping into a plastic hose hooked up to his arm.

"Clean him up and get the O.R. set up, now!"

"Call Dr. Ferrell!" called one of the nurses. She was real pretty and her hair was poofed up high on her head. He wondered how come her little white hat didn't fall off.

"Already did," another voice responded. "He's on the way. Said he'd be in here in four."

"Four minutes might be too long—I can see his sinuses!"

"We gotta stop the bleeding!"

"Ma'am, what's his name?" asked a nurse who looked sorta like his Grandma Hoffman.

Carol cleared her throat. "It's Graden . . . but we call him

Grady."

"Hey, Grady, what a nice name," the grandma nurse said, patting his arm. "How are you doing? We're going to get you all fixed up, okay? Our best doctor is on his way. His name is Dr. Ferrell."

"Okay, let's get him in the O.R.—stat!" a deep voice shouted.

Grady felt the bed on wheels moving again. "Ma'am, ma'am, you have to let go." His mother's hands still clutched his left arm, holding onto him with a death grip.

Multiple sets of hands, some wearing plastic gloves, guided him down the shiny hallway. He stared at the ceiling, all white, lights so bright it hurt his eyes. "Ma'am," the grandma nurse stressed a little harder now, "I'm sorry but you have to let go of him now." The bed stopped at a double doorway. "You can't come in here."

Grady watched as she pried his mother's fingers from his arm. "I'm sorry, ma'am."

No! Mom, please stay with me.

He thought he'd said it, but it didn't seem like anyone heard him. He looked up at his mom. Terror filled her eyes, which were puffy and red like he never saw before, her face white as a sheet. Or maybe it just looked white because her blouse was soaked in dark red blood. He lifted his arm, reaching back for her hand.

Stay, Mom! I need my Mom!

CHAPTER TWENTY-TWO

Grady woke up in more pain than he ever felt before, more than he thought imaginable. "*Aaaaaaaaaaah!*" He gasped for breath and screamed again, "Aaaaah!" Flat on his back, excruciating pains shot through his body. He tried to lunge forward and three nurses rushed to his bedside, coaxing him back.

"Relax, Mr. Kramer," the blonde one said, her cotton scrub covered in smiling kittens in a dozen different colors. "You're going to tear up what the doctor just repaired. Lay back now, that's it . . . there you go." She took the drip bag in her hands, reading the marks scribbled on the side. "Let's up the morphine."

Grady grimaced, fighting the urge to scream again as the nurses switched the drip bag. Each second seemed like an hour of prolonged pain. Within a minute or two he felt his body relaxing, the pain diminishing. Still breathing hard, he squeezed his eyes shut. Had he done the right thing? Or was this Strike Three? Either way, it was too late. He drifted off . . .

He was awake later in the day when the spine surgeon came in to check on him. Grady's throat was dry and it was hard to talk. "Wha . . . what'd you use on me, Doc, a chainsaw?" He tried to swallow and pointed to the cup of ice chips on the bed tray.

The doctor handed him the cup. "It's a tough one, I know. But it went well, Grady. We harvested twenty-two pieces of bone about the size of a match stick from your left hip bone. We inserted those into thumblike cages in your spine. Now it just takes time to promote growth between the vertebrae."

"What . . . the hell . . . is harvesting?"

"Think back to when you were in woodworking class. You had the gouge tool for a lathe? We use the same tool, only smaller, and we put that against your hip and use a mallet to chisel off pieces of bones from your hip."

"No wonder . . . my entire hip is on fire," Grady said through clenched teeth.

"Don't worry, the body wants to heal itself. You can't hop out of bed today, but these sweet nurses will have you up and around tomorrow morning."

"I can . . . hardly wait," Grady whispered. He sucked on the ice, letting the cool water slide down his throat.

* * *

A tube inserted in his lower back drained the fluid into a plastic bladder beside the bed. As usual, the nurses had nothing but good news and he was beginning to hate the sight of their bright neon kittens and flowers covering their casual uniforms.

"They cut the muscle off your hip to harvest the bone, Mr. Kramer, so the muscle has to reattach," one said in too cheery a tone the following day. "Let's see if you can take a step."

Grady stood next to the bed, his hands gripping the walker in front of him. He took a shuffled step with his right leg. As soon as tried to step with the left leg, incredible pain shot up his entire left side. "Aaah!" He gripped the handles of the walker. Tiny black dots blurred his vision and beads of sweat spread across his forehead.

"That's okay, we'll take it slow," the nurse said. "Try it again."

It took every ounce of strength to make it down the hall. He returned to his room and collapsed in his bed. "So . . . when can I get the hell outta here?"

"As soon as you can walk down a flight of stairs and back up—using only a cane."

"Not a problem," he said.

Three days after the surgery, Grady took a cab home from the hospital. It took a good fifteen minutes to climb the stairs to his apartment. As soon as he got inside, he swallowed another hydrocodone and passed out on the mattress.

His mom called right away, as promised, but he couldn't talk long. An in-home nurse came the next morning to change the dressing and clean the incision. She went through his therapy exercises with him and then left. The next day, as soon as she left, he took one look at the empty refrigerator and knew he had to get some groceries. Climbing up was one thing, but going down hurt like hell. With nerves of steel, he started down the single flight of stairs with the cane. He gritted his teeth, arms shaking, as he went down one careful step at a time. Bullheaded determination had gotten him through a lot of things in life and he needed every ounce of it to get down the full flight. It wasn't captured on TV and watched by millions, but reaching the bottom step was his Kirk Gibson moment. He hobbled to the corner dairy, shuffling along with his cane, unable to pick up his left leg. It took forty-five minutes to walk the block and a half, but he made it.

When he got back to his apartment, he put the carton of milk and sandwich meat in the fridge. He gripped the cane and stared into the whiteness of the bare refrigerator. The stark, bare shelves seemed to echo the emptiness in his life. Too weak to make a sandwich, Grady left the bread on the counter and shuffled to his bed, ready for another Vicodin. He needed to rest before he could muster up the strength to eat.

Chandra called, but talking with her always put him on edge. Every single conversation turned back to Jesus, to the point where he wanted to stuff a sock in her mouth. He could've used a ride to the grocery store or someone to cook a few meals a hell of a lot more than her holy-roller prayers.

He lay on his right side, careful not to bump the dressing on his back. His clothing of choice now was cut-off sweats with a drawstring or bibs, nothing tight at the waist. Staring at his sparsely covered walls, he let his thoughts drift. He wondered how Melinda was doing with her three little girls. He knew she was a good mom. Dean and Kurt had called, but Grady hadn't felt good enough to talk very long. Besides, he wasn't the best at conversation these days. He hadn't worked in two and a half years, hadn't felt like a normal man for that long. He missed the camaraderie with the other guys at work. Oil rigs or ironworkers, either place he'd always managed to get along with most everyone and build some good friendships through the years. In L.A. he loved it whenever a group of guys got together and went to the Angels games. His all-time favorite was watching Wayne Gretzky and the Kings. Man, could that guy skate and shoot the puck! Those were some good times, taking Terry's Lincoln Continental down to Inglewood to watch Gretzky play hockey.

He wondered how come the good times never lasted very long. There had been some good times on the oil rigs, and then they went bust. Oil had fallen from forty-six dollars a barrel down to seventeen in a flash. He'd had some good times in high school, dances, hanging out on the slab, and then Naomi dumped him. Before that, the good times had always been interrupted by his dad's drinking. Not even Christmas Day had been spared. When he was a real little kid, he loved going fishing with his dad, especially when they lived in the logging camp near Missoula in the heart of the Rocky Mountains. His dad knew all the back roads from driving logging trucks, all the best fishing spots, the crystal clear mountain streams. Man, those were some of the best fishing times he'd ever had.

Twin Creeks logging camp was nothing more than a collection of small trailers and wood frame houses tucked in the smaller Potomoc Valley that fit within the larger Blackfoot Valley, a pristine mountain valley. He could still picture their little trailer house with a small wooden deck by the door. His mom had wanted to start a vegetable garden, but the ground at that elevation was too rocky. She asked his dad to build her a little spot with logs where they could bring up some topsoil from the meadow and grow tomatoes and cucumbers.

One morning his dad borrowed the neighbor's chainsaw and took both Grady and Kurt. "C'mon boys, we're gonna head up to one of the trash piles and cut some logs to build a garden for your ma."

His dad followed nearby Gold Creek Road, one of the old logging roads, up the forested mountainside a couple miles from their camp. "There's the pile we can cut from," he said, pointing to a collection of dried brush and logs. The area, once covered in tamarack and Douglas fir, had already been thinned by loggers. "You boys stand back a ways, and after I get it cut, you can move it out of the way before I cut the next one, okay?"

"Sure, Dad," Grady said. He stepped from a log to a stump, working his way across the pile of logs.

"How long we gonna be here?" Kurt asked, poking a crooked stick into the dirt.

Frank pulled a nice thick pine log from the pile and propped one end on another log. "Till we get the job done, young man. Now stand back."

Already bored, Kurt saw a ground squirrel and took off after it with his stick. Grady walked around a few large branches and stood next to his dad. Frank set the saw on the ground and pulled the chord three, four, five times. "C'mon, you son of a blasted thing," he said between pulls. He closed the choke and pulled the chord again. The motor started up and he pushed the throttle; the chain spun around the blade as the motor revved. "It's about time," Frank said. He turned the saw toward the log and positioned the blade on the top. In a matter of seconds the saw sliced through the thick trunk top to bottom, a flurry of shavings spitting out on both sides of the motor. As soon as his dad let off the throttle, the motor lowered to an idle. "There's one," he said, kicking it away with his boot. "Pretty slick, huh?"

"Good one, Dad," Grady said. It fascinated him to watch the sharp blade cut through a whole tree trunk in mere seconds.

"Give it another push," he said.

Grady put both palms on the log and gave it a thrust. It rolled down the hillside a few feet until it hit a stump. "All right, here we go again." His dad rested the blade on the next log, propped up by broken branches. The blade skipped as he hit the throttle, leaving a notch in the bark. He pressed it into the log, cutting all the way through in seconds, shavings flying in all directions. Grady pushed the log aside and it got caught in some brush. "That's okay," his dad said. "We'll get it in a minute."

Grady stood straight across from his dad, watching him trim off the small branches from the next log. His dad steered the blade into the tree trunk, shavings landing on Grady's tennis shoes. He heard the motor grind and whine harder.

"Damn it," Frank said, focused on the saw. "Now it's wedged in there." Grady moved in closer to get a better view. His dad pried the blade out of the log, the sharp teeth on the chain still spinning as he hit the throttle and then repositioned it at the bottom. "I'll have to finish the cut, bottom to top," he said to Grady.

As soon the tip of the blade touched the log, it buckled. The saw shot straight up like a bullet. It struck Grady in the center of his nose and knocked his head back, running straight up his face between his eyes to the top of his head. The hit was hard, like someone had smacked him in the face with a baseball bat. He looked up, not sure what just happened.

"Oh, my God!" Frank screamed. He reached for the saw, still running, and killed the motor, then threw it a good thirty feet. Grady heard a loud *clang!* as it hit the back end of the pickup.

Grady froze, afraid to breathe. By the look in his dad's eyes, he was in trouble, *big* trouble. He tasted blood on his lips and blinked, trying to see through the strings of flesh that hung over his eyes.

Frank whipped out his red handkerchief and held it against Grady's face. "Kuuuurt!" he yelled at the top of his voice. "Kuuuurt! Get over here! Right now!"

Grady's heart pounded in fear of what his dad would say or do next. He could feel the blood dripping off his lips, down his chin. He waited, scared to move a muscle.

Grady heard Kurt's footsteps run up to them. "What's wrong, Dad? Aghh . . . what happened to Grady?"

"Get in the truck right now! You gotta hold this on his face and don't let go, no matter what. You hear me?"

Kurt made a gagging sound and said something Grady couldn't understand.

"Get in the truck. Now!" his dad shouted.

Frank carried Grady to the pickup and sat him next to Kurt. "Keep him sitting up," he said to Kurt. "Don't let him lay down, you hear me?"

Grady leaned into Kurt. His head hurt and he wanted to lie down, but he didn't dare. He didn't want to get in more trouble than he already was. The door slammed shut and he heard his father run around the truck. Within seconds, the pickup engine revved and jerked forward, and the tires spun, trying to gain traction in the dirt.

"Hold that tight," his dad said to Kurt. "And whatever you do, don't let go."

"But, Dad—"

"Just hold it, I said!"

Blindfolded, Grady didn't know what to think. How bad was it? It had all happened so fast. He was sure he'd get punished as soon as his mom got him fixed him up. He could already hear his dad, *That'll teach you for not listening to me, you good for nothin' little shit! Don't you have a brain in that head of yours?* The pickup bounced as the front left tire hit a deep hole. His dad downshifted and pressed on the gas; gravel and rocks clinked against the wheel well underneath.

"You okay?" Frank asked.

Grady heard him hit the clutch and shift again, the back end fishtailing in the gravel. "Uh-huh," he said under the handkerchief. He tried to act like it wasn't that bad, hoping to thwart the severity of punishment.

"Hang on, we're almost home." Grady sat up against Kurt, listening to his dad work the gears. It seemed like forever, and then again it seemed like only a few minutes; he couldn't tell for sure. His dad laid on the horn and Grady thought he'd turned into the road for the logging camp. Sure enough, the truck slid to a sharp halt. "Wait right there," he said and came around to the other side of the truck. He picked up Grady in his arms. "Okay, get out," he said to Kurt, his voice rushed. "Go tell your ma Grady's been cut. Run!"

Grady heard Kurt's footsteps take off in a mad dash as Frank carried him across the small yard. He didn't dare cry—that would only make things worse. The last time he got whipped, Grady didn't cry once—at least not in front of his dad. Grady heard the screen door open and through a tiny opening he could see his mother standing on the wooden porch, holding some Band-Aids. Her face turned pure white and the Band-Aids fell from her hands, fluttering to the ground like feathers.

"Oh, my God!" she screamed. "What happened? Frank, *what happened to him?*" Her voice turned to more of a shriek, a frantic wail that he'd never heard before.

"The blade . . . it got wedged. And before I knew it, the damn thing flew up and hit him," Frank said, adjusting Grady in his arms, "right in the face," he finished in a hoarse whisper.

"Oh, my God! My God!" Carol's screams turned more frenzied. "Get him in the bathroom, go! Quick!"

Frank carried him down the narrow hallway to the small bathroom. He sat on the toilet, holding Grady on his lap. Grady heard the faucet turn on and felt his mom's hands gently peel the handkerchief away from his face. He looked in the medicine cabinet mirror above the sink. Big dark eyes stared back at him, but it didn't look like his own face. It reminded him of the slaughtered pig he'd seen once on his uncle's farm. Blood dripped from every part, side to side, top to bottom. His nose was as wide as his cheeks; strings of flesh hung down on both sides, gnarled and twisted in bloody shredded strands. Every time his heart beat, more blood gushed out.

"He's gonna die!" Carol cried in a long wail.

"Get a cold rag," shouted Frank. "You gotta stop the bleeding!"

Melinda stood in the doorway whimpering, Kurt beside her, watching the horrific scene unfold. His mom sobbed uncontrollably, shoulders heaving, as she soaked the towel in cold water. "Frank, we'll never stop it. He's bleeding too bad." She froze in place, hands affixed to her own face, mumbling under her breath. Grady watched in the mirror as his mom collapsed. Was he really going to die?

Frank grabbed her by the shoulders. "Damn it, Carol, I need your help if he's gonna make it!" She nodded, still wailing, shaking. "If we're gonna save him, we gotta go—now!"

"Okay, okay," she said, gasping between sobs.

"Wring out the towel and put it on his face."

She let out another frantic wail as she picked up the towel and wrung out the water.

Frank rinsed the blood off his hands and turned around. "Melinda, grab the baby and take Kurt. Go next door to Franchuck's and wait until we get home. Tell 'em Grady got hurt," he said, sucking in a deep breath, "and it's bad."

His orders were followed by several minutes of commotion. Dean started crying for his mama. Melinda tried her best to soothe him. "It's okay, little buddy. C'mon, we're gonna go play. Kurt, c'mon."

"We're taking the wagon," Frank said to Carol. "Get in first and I'll prop him up against you."

"Okay, okay," Carol said between sobs.

Grady heard a kitchen drawer open and slam shut, then a chair slide across the linoleum. "Where's the keys? *Where's the keys!?*"

"Right there! By the radio!"

Blindfolded once again, Frank carried him out to the car. Grady could only hear sounds around him as his father started up the car and raced out of the logging camp, the back end fishtailing as rocks hit against the fenders.

Grady thought about it every so often, how his ol' man had raced down the mountain road that day road to get him to the hospital. He half wondered who his dad had been more afraid for—himself or Grady. Altogether, after four and a half hours of surgery, he ended up with 115 stitches—85 on his forehead and 35 in his nose. Dr. Ferrell, fresh from a stint in a Vietnam trauma unit, had the expertise needed to sew his face together with the least amount of scarring. He had cut off the shredded skin on both sides from the center of his eyebrow and up. Then he took a piece of stainless steel wire and placed it on Grady's skull. The doctor stretched the flesh underneath and sewed it to the wire, stretching the other skin as much as possible. He used tape and two split shots from his tackle box to hold it in place. For six weeks Grady had one split shot on the bridge of his nose and one at the top of his head. The two silver bolts made him feel like Frankenstein's monster.

He couldn't go back to school during those six weeks, in case he accidentally ripped the bolts out of his forehead at recess. Miss Sundstrom, his teacher, sent assignments home so he could keep up with his schoolwork. His first day back, his face was still a deep dark purple and swollen. Miss Sundstrom told the class what happened, so they wouldn't be traumatized when he came in, but it hadn't made a difference. By the looks on their faces, he could tell they were in shock. His best friend—a kid named Lee Hinman—came right up to him and started talking like everything was okay, while the others had stared in horrified silence.

Despite his dad's lifelong reputation, Grady was sure he hadn't been drinking that day on the mountain. He clearly remembered they left home too early in the morning and he hadn't seen any bottles in the truck. Of course, the way his dad told it he hadn't done anything wrong. It was Grady's fault for standing in the wrong spot. It wasn't long after that that his dad quit his job driving logging trucks to work the weigh station and they moved to Wibaux.

Every so often, though, when he stopped to think about the accident, he couldn't help but wonder about the whole thing. His face had been split wide open with a chainsaw—sharp, jagged teeth that could cut through a solid log in seconds, yet the blade walked straight up the middle of his face and skull without penetrating the bone. What were the odds of that?

CHAPTER TWENTY-THREE

By December, Grady started to believe he had a chance to be normal again. The chronic pain had all but disappeared, and he was careful not to twist or bend in the wrong way. He still swam every morning at the community pool to keep his back muscles strong. He accepted the fact he could no longer work in a physically demanding job and started a computer-aided drafting course at the nearby Orange campus of MTI College. Through it all he managed to hang onto his apartment and pickup.

Maybe it was the thought of Christmas coming, but something was calling him home. *Home,* as in Montana. He hadn't been back to Wibaux in ages. The more he thought about it, the more the idea took hold. The travel agent called back with a bargain basement ticket price if he waited until after Christmas, so he scraped together the money and flew to Billings on December twenty-eighth.

Carol, Melinda, and her girls picked him up at the airport and drove him back to Beach.

"Oh, it's so good to have you home, Grady. I mean that," Carol said from her favorite rocking chair. Her green eyes sparkled just the way he remembered. Grady thought she looked younger than many women her age, slim and fit, wearing the latest fashion. She colored her hair now, covering the gray with a brownish blonde. It suited her though—fixed in short, stylish curls. She'd bought a little house in Beach and fixed it up real nice. A table-sized Christmas tree took up the coffee table, covered in twinkling lights and church bazaar ornaments. Her chair was positioned in front of the living room bay window to keep an eye on the squirrels and birds in the big feeders; the snow was peppered with birdseed all around. "Better entertainment than that thing," she said, pointing to the television. "Are ya hungry? I can rustle you up some leftover roast and potatoes real quick."

Grady rubbed his stomach. "That'd be great. I'm starved." Carol hopped up from her chair and he followed her into the kitchen.

"This is the best Christmas present, you know," she said, tying an apron around her slender waist. "Having my kids and grandkids home around the holidays. How 'bout Melinda's littlest one—ain't she somethin'?" His mom broke out in laughter. "She's the stinker of the three, let me tell you. She told her mama she didn't want to go along to Billings, so Melinda had to promise a stop at McDonald's before she'd get in the car. She loves the play area, crawling up them tubes and sliding down. Course, Melinda prêt-near has to crawl up after her when it's time to go!" Carol pushed up the sleeves on her sweater, exposing a tissue tucked under her watchband. "So whacha got planned?"

Grady grinned at his mother's lifelong habit of keeping a tissue close at hand. "Not much really."

Carol took out a green Tupperware container from the fridge and pulled back the lid. "Don't forget, the Shamrock is having their big doings on New Year's Eve."

"They still do that?"

"Of course! How could the folks 'round here bring in the New Year without that? That's tradition!" She smiled her same sweet smile and took out a plate and an amber glass from one of the aqua cupboard doors.

"Shoot, maybe I'll run down there," Grady said, rubbing his beard. "See who's around that I still know."

"Have you kept in touch with Tom Lorentz, or Jake Wensman, Wes Scheinburg, Kevin Thompson—any of those boys from high school?" She took out a carton of milk and poured a full glass.

"Yeah, me and Tom have talked, mended our fences about the house. Just one of those things; no one's fault really."

"He always asks about you."

"I kind of lost touch with the others after I moved to California, especially after I got hurt."

"Lands sake, I know you've had a hard time of it, that's for sure," she said, wiping her hands on the apron. "You look kinda thin, aren't ya?"

"I lost some weight and muscle tone after the surgery. Thanks," he said as she handed him the glass of milk. "I'll get it back though; I'm not worried."

"I just made some pumpkin bread. How 'bout a piece of your mom's famous pumpkin bread?"

"Mmmm, yes, ma'am," he said, loving the smell of his mother's baking.

Carol sliced two thick pieces of the bread and lathered them with butter. "Here, you can start on this while I get the meat and potatoes warmed up. The roast is from Ralph Swenson's ranch. Oooh, he's got good meats, real tender. Do you know Ralph?"

Grady shook his head. "Don't think so."

He sat in the warmth of his mom's kitchen. Maybe it was his imagination, but in the midst of his mother's love he could almost feel his body healing, the bones in his back mending. It didn't matter that it wasn't the same house he'd grown up in. He was *home.*

* * *

New Year's Eve night, Grady showered and put on a yellow flannel shirt—a Christmas present from his mom. Since the surgery, he couldn't stand anything too tight on his waistline, so he wore suspenders instead of a belt, green ones this time, for Christmas. He combed his dark hair, cut short now, and smoothed the clipped whiskers of his beard. He splashed on a dab of Cool Water cologne and walked out to the living room. "Guess I'll run over to Wibaux and head down to the Shamrock."

"Okay, then," Carol said from her rocking chair, an open magazine lying on her lap. The beige drapes were pulled across the darkened window. "Keys are in the car. I already pulled it out of the garage for you."

"Mom, you didn't have to do that."

"Shoveled the sidewalk for you too." She laid the magazine on a basket overflowing in copies of *Woman's Day* and *Ladies Home Journal.*

"*Mom,* I'm supposed to do that for you."

"Got bored with my magazine," she said with a giggle.

"I said I'd do it when I got out of the shower."

"Aw, I don't mind," she said, shooing him toward the door. "You go on now and have a good time."

"Thanks." Grady slipped on his jacket.

Carol jumped to her feet and followed him to the door. "I wanna hear all about it in the morning. Maybe you'll see some of your old friends."

Grady bent down and kissed her on the cheek. "See you later."

Cold air rushed in as Carol held the door open. She stood in the doorway watching Grady back out of the driveway, waving as he turned the corner. The night turned cold and a winter storm watch was in effect. He took the interstate from Beach to Wibaux, the seven-mile stretch he'd driven countless times back in high school. It was so odd—after living in Los Angeles where driving somewhere, anywhere, could be a virtual traffic nightmare—to return to the simplicity of life in Wibaux.

Main Street didn't look anything like he remembered; many of the storefronts downtown were empty and dark, several were boarded up. Helvick's Grocery had closed up long ago, so had the Gambles store. Beckel's Drugstore was an antique shop now—go figure. Small towns didn't have much to hold them together these days. It was harder than ever to make a living farming or ranching. Many of the kids in his generation left the rural areas in search of good paying jobs in bigger towns and cities.

Winds whipped the snow around, swirling it in magical patterns around the streetlights in front of the Shamrock and Stockman bars next door to each other. Snow-covered pickup trucks outnumbered the cars at least six to one. A variety of king cabs, single cabs, and extended cabs were parked at an angle in a long row on both sides of the street. Some ranchers in these parts were worth millions, and their brand-new duallies with fancy cargo boxes and chrome wheels stuck out among the beat up F150s—the kind that had over 300,000 miles on mostly gravel roads. Several more pickups were parked down the street in front of the Silver Dollar. Funny, even though many of the stores had closed up, the bars were open and thriving.

The annoying twang of Alan Jackson or George Strait spilled onto the sidewalk as the door opened and a young couple deep in conversation exited the Shamrock. Grady stepped inside and did a quick survey. Sure enough, the ceiling was still covered in metal horse bits and branding symbols. The massive head of a Texas Longhorn hung proudly over the center of the bar where it always had. The room was awash in pearl-snap cowboy shirts with trimmed yolks, Carhartts, and faded Levis; the girls in fringed sweaters and stonewashed blue jeans.

Grady inched his way toward the bar, recognizing a few familiar faces through the smoky haze. Wall-sized framed prints of cowboys and Montana scenery in sepia hung on several walls. Big glass displays were mounted on three of the walls with antique rifles, spurs, horseshoes, and other cowboy memorabilia. There was no mistakin' it, he was back in ranchin' country.

"Graa-dy!" he heard someone yell above the noise. "Hey, Kramer, down here!"

He looked down the row of cowboy hats and spotted Tom Lorentz at the far end of the bar waving him over. Grady pushed his way through the crowd.

"Hey! How are ya, man?" Tom said above the noise. The sleeves on his heavyweight flannel shirt were pushed up to his elbows, and he gripped Grady's hand in a solid handshake.

"Not bad, not bad," Grady said. "It's good to be home." The bartender looked familiar but he couldn't remember his name. "Shot of Jack Daniels, please."

"Coming right up," the sixtyish man said. A tattoo on his right arm stretched from his wrist to his bicep as he wiped the counter with a bar rag.

"How long ya been in town?" Tom asked, slightly thicker in the midsection and thinner in the hair department than during their roughnecking days.

"Flew into Billings a few days ago. Mom and Melinda picked me up. Had a late Christmas with most of the family."

"How is your mom? I always liked her chocolate chip cookies after 4-H in ninth grade, remember that?"

Grady laughed. He hadn't thought about that in years.

"Here you go." The bartender set the shot glass in front of Grady. "Buck-fifty."

Grady put two dollar bills on the century-old counter and turned back to Tom. "How's it going 'round here?" He took a glance around the room and downed his shot, his throat muscles tightening as the warm liquid slid down. "Man, they're bustin' at the seams in here tonight."

Young cowboys, skinny as a row of Montana fence posts, crowded the pool tables, cue stick in one hand, beer in the other. Most of them didn't look old enough to drink, even though the drinking age had upped to twenty-one. In the back section a D.J. played a mix of country and rock songs to a crowd of people already on the dance floor. Tables were set up with BBQ ribs in the far corner, wings, meatballs, a relish tray. For six bucks anyone could grab a plate and fill up, but he'd already eaten a big supper at his mom's.

"Did ya forget you're in Wibaux, man? Shit, there ain't nothin' happenin' in this lame town," Tom said above the music. "This is it, big New Years Eve and all."

"Hey, can I get a Pabst?" Grady asked, waving a couple dollars at the bartender.

"You betcha," he said, reaching into a cooler. He popped the cap off and set it on the bar. "There you go."

"You're better off out in L.A. than being stuck in Wibaux," Tom said. "Are you back workin' yet?"

"Not yet." Grady took a swig, holding the bottle by the neck. "Believe it or not, I'm back in school."

"Oh, yeah? What for?"

"Computer-aided drafting. Workman's comp set it up after my injury."

"Yeah, I heard about that. Not good."

"Two years of nothing but chronic pain." Grady shook his head. "I think the worst is over. I had my spine fused in October."

"Damn, that sounds serious."

He nodded. "It finally fixed the problem."

"You gonna stay in L.A.?"

"May as well. The odds are better out there for finding a job." Grady took another swallow. A loud *whoop* erupted from the dance floor and he turned to see who was having the most fun. Nothing in particular caught his eye until he noticed two girls on the other side of the dance floor. The taller one looked especially familiar; her dark hair was long in the back, and shorter and curled in the front.

"It's hard to find a decent job around here unless your ol' man owns the John Deere dealership or something." Tom leaned both elbows on the bar. "Some folks are driving all the way to Dickinson and Bismarck for work. No one used to—"

Grady tapped his shoulder, cutting him off. "Hey, is that Naomi Braden over there?"

Tom turned on his stool and studied the faces at the far table. "Yeah, that's her. She's living in Beach again." He swiveled back to face Grady. "Anyway, like I was saying—"

Grady left Tom hang in midsentence and plowed across the center of the dance floor like a road grader clearing a section road after a long messy winter. He walked up to Naomi, beer in hand, recognizing the other girl now as her sister. "Hello, Naomi," he said, feeling a wide grin spread across his face. "How are you?"

The look on Naomi's face was one of complete surprise. Her eyes lit up and she smiled. "Hi."

"Do you even remember me?"

Naomi laughed and moved a step closer. "Of course I do, although you look a lot different with short hair and a beard. How are you, Grady?" She glanced at her sister and laughed again. "Gosh, it's good to see you. It's been a long time."

He nodded, unable to stop the grin from spreading past his whiskered cheeks across the width of the room. "Yes, it has. Hi, Janice," he said, acknowledging her sister.

"Hey, Grady. How are you?" Janice said.

"Good," he said, nodding. "Doing good."

"What are you doing in Wibaux?" Naomi asked.

"Came home for a late Christmas," Grady said. The D.J. switched from country to an up-tempo rock song and he held out his hand to Naomi. "Do you want to dance?"

"Sure," she said, taking his hand.

Grady put his beer on the table. "Follow me." He worked his way through the crowded dance floor. Simply holding Naomi's hand sent shivers up the full length of his arm. How amazing was that—her hand still fit his *perfectly.* Joan Jett's "I Love Rock 'n' Roll" boomed through the speakers, making it hard to talk, so they danced to the beat, exchanging quick glances and surprised smiles through the song. She hadn't changed; her eyes were still vivid blue, her hair shiny brown the way he remembered, although it was shorter and curlier in the front. And now that he had a chance to look at her close up, he thought she was much prettier, more womanlike than teenage girl, quite possibly *beautiful.*

The song ended and Grady tried to think of a reason to stall. He couldn't let her go already. "Out of breath there," he said.

"Yeah," Naomi said in agreement. The dance floor slowly emptied as the D.J. made one last pitch for the six-dollar buffet of fried food. The lights dimmed and distinctive beginning piano notes started for the next song.

Grady looked into Naomi's eyes, took her hand, and without hesitation asked, "One more?"

She lifted her face toward him, nodding. "Sure."

He recognized the song now. "The Dance" by Garth Brooks. *Absolutely apropos.* Grady pulled her in close for the

271

slow song, wrapping both arms around her waist. He thought he'd died and went to heaven as her arms slid around his neck. The softness of her hair against his cheek sent shivers down his spine as Garth's deep voice accompanied by the melodious piano and guitar reverberated across the dance floor.

> *Looking back, on the memory of*
> *The dance we shared, 'neath the stars above*
> *For a moment, all the world was right*
> *How could I have known, that you'd ever say good-bye*

Garth's emotive voice enunciating the words suddenly had a far greater impact on him than ever before. The violin picked up the melody . . .

> *And now, I'm glad I didn't know*
> *The way it all would end, the way it all would go*
> *Our lives are better left to chance, I could have missed*
> *the pain*
> *But I'd'a had to miss the dance*

The words were so timely and perfect. *Our lives are better left to chance.* As the guitar and violin transitioned to the next verse, Grady could only wonder: what kind of chance was this? To run into Naomi out of the blue after all this time? Better yet, to hold her in his arms and *dance* with her, swaying ever so gently to the music? He too could have missed the pain, but there's no way he would have *ever* missed this dance with her. No way.

"This is too funny," he said, feeling her body moving in rhythm with his.

"What is?" She looked up at him, her blue eyes penetrating his innermost thoughts.

He bent down a little closer. "Remember when we first met, at the Wibaux dancehall, back in what, tenth and eleventh grade?"

"Of course, I do."

"And now . . . here we are at another dance."

She turned her face toward his, her cheeks slightly flushed. "That is pretty funny when you think about it."

"Kinda cool, though, isn't it?"

She nodded, relaxing in his arms. He relished the moment, not wanting it to end. He closed his eyes, listening to Garth sing the words as though they were meant for him and his beautiful Naomi.

Holding you, I held everything
For a moment, wasn't I a king
But if I'd only known,. how the king would fall
Hey, who's to say, you know I might have changed it all

And now, I'm glad I didn't know
The way it all would end, the way it all would go
Our lives are better left to chance, I could have missed the pain
But I'd'a had to miss the dance

Yes, my life, is better left to chance
I could have missed the pain, but I'd of had to miss the dance

He leaned down and whispered against her ear as the piano played out the last few notes. "How long has it been, anyway?"

"Mmm, right about fourteen years."

"Fourteen years is a long time," he said softly.

The song faded to an end . . . and with it that once-in-a-lifetime *perfect* moment in time. He inhaled deeply and walked Naomi back to her table. After a few minutes of social politeness with the others cloistered on both sides, he pulled her aside. "Say, um . . . can I call you tomorrow?" He watched her eyes for clues. Was it his hopefulness or did they indicate *yes* before he heard her speak.

"Yes, of course."

"Well, I didn't know . . ." he said, and the words caught in his throat like a clump of dry oats, "if you were single, or with someone."

Naomi laughed and squeezed his hand as she looked into his eyes. "I'm single, and I'd like to see you again tomorrow."

CHAPTER TWENTY-FOUR

Unbelievable! After fourteen years he had a date lined up with Naomi Braden. If he wasn't worried about blowing out another disc in his back, he would flip head over heels in cartwheels. With it being New Year's Day, nothing was open in Beach or Wibaux so they decided to drive over to Dickinson for dinner. It was a solid sixty miles one way, and Grady figured it would give them plenty of time to talk.

"You ran into Naomi Braden?" his mom asked that morning when he shared the good news. "Really?" Her eyes turned watery and she slapped her thighs. "You don't say!"

Grady laughed, nodding. "I swear, you can call her up if you like."

"Oooh, I don't have to, Graden Kramer; I can see it on your face," she said, clapping her hands. "Your eyes are beaming like a couple of shiny brown agates. Boy, howdy, ain't that somthin' after all these years! I always *knew* you two were right for each other, didn't I?" She nearly danced as she flipped the pieces of French toast for their breakfast.

"Yes, ma'am," Grady said, still absorbing his good fortune. He put out two place settings and the butter and syrup on the table.

"You know she was married once," Carol said, taking a peek at the bottom of the toast.

"Yeah, you told me that."

"It didn't last long and they got divorced. I don't remember what year that was though."

"It was a few years back."

"And then she had that baby and gave it up, I told you 'bout that too, didn't I?"

Grady smiled at his mother. "Yup, you always kept me up to speed with what was happening in her life."

"Just in case; you never know what might come of it," Carol said with a nod.

"Well, I didn't know if she had somebody else in her life now, but she said she didn't."

"There you go."

"Hold your horses now, it's just a date."

"Listen here, you two runnin' into each other like this, it's more than a date. It's fate," she said, pointing the spatula at him.

Grady replayed his mother's words as he pulled up in front of Naomi's house at eleven o'clock—a small white cottage on the corner of Second Avenue and Third Street. She told him she had lived there alone for the past several years. Well, almost alone—she had a cat named Spooky.

"I think it's done snowing now," Naomi said. Grady held the driver's door open as she slid into the front seat.

"It's kinda pretty." Grady climbed in beside her. "I haven't seen this much snow since I left Williston."

"Is that when you moved to California?"

"Yup."

"When was that?"

"Back in eighty-four, so I guess that makes six years. Wait, it's 1991 now, isn't it?"

"Yes it is; happy New Year," Naomi said.

"It sure is," Grady responded.

Grady drove the few blocks through Beach with Naomi tucked close beside him, just like back in high school. Skelly's Truck Stop, where he used to take her for burgers, was a Flying J Travel Plaza now, where his mom worked. He turned onto the interstate and headed east toward Dickinson. The roads were plowed and in decent driving condition considering how much snow had fallen overnight. The glistening layer of bright white snow covered the buttes and breaks that bordered both sides of the roadway on the periphery, like a bridal veil stretched mile after mile. Here and there, fence posts protruded the snowdrifts, up and down, up and down again, as the fence line followed the cragged ravines. The wintry white scenery lent a mystical elegance to the morning drive.

At Medora they passed the entrance to the Theodore Roosevelt National Park and the scenic North Dakota Badlands, a rustic and expansive site that covered over a hundred square miles with colorful hillsides and scoria-covered buttes, North Dakota's main tourism area. "Hey, maybe we should stop here on the way back," Naomi said. "It's always so pretty here."

"Sure." She could've just as well said let's forgo all others and run away to Canada, or let's hitchhike to Mexico and live on the beach, or backpack to Alaska and find an old shack in the bush. Right now, with Naomi at his side, anything she suggested sounded like the most wondrous idea he'd ever heard.

"How's everybody in the family doing?" Naomi asked.

"Melinda is doing great. Her three little girls are somethin' else, let me tell you. The littlest one stole my heart this week. Somethin' about little girls and dimples. Kurt's remarried and doing really good now. Dean is married and living in Minneapolis."

"And your mom?"

"Oh, she had a rough go of it after Russ moved out. She's doing better now, getting back on her feet. She hasn't had it easy through the years; I'll give her that. Yet, she never complains. She always has a smile and something positive to say. I respect her so much for that."

Naomi nodded. "Remember when we'd stop down to Beckel's and share a shake?"

"One tall glass and two straws, every time."

"So you do remember."

"Trust me, I remember," Grady said. "How's all your family doing?"

By the time Naomi filled him in on the updates for all nine of her sisters and brothers, they'd arrived in Dickinson. Grady took Third Avenue into town—the main drag—and drove past the Bonanza, Taco Johns, Pizza Hut, Happy Joes Pizza, and Country Kitchen. Each one had a large HAPPY NEW YEAR banner posted right above the CLOSED sign. "We're not having much luck," Grady said. He turned around in the parking lot of the Country Kitchen, the car idling.

"Maybe we should try the mall."

Grady drove north of the freeway to the Prairie Hills Mall. The giant Herbergers and JCPenney signs were both dark. "I dunno; I don't think it's open either."

"Drive around by the Showhall," Naomi suggested.

"Hey, it looks open," Grady said, pulling up to the marquee.

"Hmm, there's not much to pick from." She leaned forward to read the movie posters. "Well, how about *Kindergarten Cop* with Arnold Schwarzenegger? I haven't heard if it's any good or not."

"May as well," Grady said. "We're running out of options."

"It doesn't start for almost an hour."

"Let's go in and get our tickets anyway. Guess we can have a big bucket of popcorn. How's that for a fancy New Year's dinner!"

Naomi broke into giggles as they walked into the empty theater. "I think we have the pick of the whole place," she said, looking at the empty rows of chairs.

"Didn't you know? I rented the whole place, just for us. Hey, it echo-oo-oos. Hel-oooo!"

"You're still a nut," Naomi said with a laugh.

"I confess," Grady said. "How about right here, madame?"

"Some things never change," she said, taking a seat.

"Like Wibaux." Grady took off his jacket, shaking his head.

"*You've* changed, I'll have you know," Naomi said. "Last time I saw you, your hair touched your shoulders. Now look at you."

"Yeah, not only is it getting shorter, it's creepin' up in the front." He lifted his cap and rubbed his forehead. "That's why I grow it on my face."

Naomi laughed. "Yeah, so don't go talking about Wibaux."

"So many businesses are closed; the houses look more rundown. Back when we were kids, all the houses looked so neat and well kept up."

"I guess I haven't noticed. Probably because I haven't moved away like you did."

"Why did you stay?"

Naomi shrugged. "No where else to go, really. I like being close to family. I've got a good job at my uncle's store—

bought my little house, you know. Settled in." She took a sip of Coke. "What about Los Angeles—do you like it out there?"

"Oh, California's neat, you should see it. I mean, there's the mountains, the desert. But the ocean—that's the best part. It's only three miles from my apartment."

"Seriously?"

"Yeah, I live in Long Beach, so I can get down to the beach in no time—"

"Wait—" She rested a hand on his arm.

"What?"

"I just realized . . . you live in Long Beach and I live in Beach."

"Yeah, but your Beach doesn't have a coastline," he said with a laugh, and Naomi laughed with him. "Or we could say, I live on the Pacific Coastline and you're on the coast of Montana."

Naomi giggled and then looked up at him. "Oh, Grady, this is the best Christmas present ever."

"Yeah?" He felt his heartbeat quicken.

"To be here, like this, on date with you." She smiled and Grady thought the incision in his back would bust wide open. They talked until the lights dimmed, the long curtains parted, and the huge screen lit up in front of them and the dozen others who had filtered in for the matinee.

On the drive back to Beach, Grady took Naomi's suggestion and exited at Medora. "It's so pretty right now with the snow, isn't it?" she said.

He followed the Scenic Loop Drive into the Theodore Roosevelt National Park. The little visitor booth at the entrance was locked up tight for the winter. "Looks like the main road into the park is open."

"Good," she said, resting against his shoulder. "Let's drive through." Tufts of big sage clung to the base of the buttes as though cemented in by the roots. There weren't any other cars as Grady drove past a wooden sign marking a prairie dog town. "Hey, what do you suppose they do in the winter?" asked Naomi, pointing to the snow-covered mounds.

"Fly south, or maybe take a Greyhound."

"Funny. Look at the all holes in the ground; there's so many."

"It's a big town, bigger'n Wibaux even." He drove past the Skyline Vista and River Woodland Overlook, but at the next roadway the gates were closed. "Ooops, I guess we can't go any farther."

"Let's get out and walk around. Want to?" Naomi asked.

"Sure."

"Oh, look," Naomi said, zipping up her ski jacket. She walked across the snow-crusted field and motioned for Grady to follow her. "There's another prairie dog town down here." Some of their burrows were right up to the road's edge.

"This town looks bigger; it must be Beach."

They walked past clumps of yucca and skunkbush, kicking up snow along the way. All around them the land rose up in rugged buttes and sandstone formations. Newly fallen snow dressed the ground and cedar trees in the purest form of white, fresh from the heavens, like a shimmering garment befitting the newness of a brand-new year. Grady walked beside Naomi, her hand clasped in his, enjoying the moment.

At the end of the path, they reached an overlook to the river valley below. "Oh, look," she said out of breath, "it's so beautiful. I don't think I've ever stopped here in the winter. And look what we've missed." Color variations in the buttes—reds, rust, browns, and gray—showed through the snow, looking like giant-sized platters of sugarcoated gumdrops.

"Sometimes the best things are right in front of us, you know." Grady sucked in a breath of frosty air and released it slowly. "Oh, I am so happy right now," he said, his eyes gleaming. "I feel so good in here." He put an arm around Naomi and tapped his chest.

"You remember in Bambi?" Naomi asked, her eyes glistening in the cold, a smile forming at the curves of her mouth. "When Flower the Skunk sees the two birds in love and asks, 'What's the matter with them?' and I think Thumper says, 'Why are they acting that way?' And then the Owl says, 'Don't you know? They're twitterpated.' That's it Grady; that's how I feel." She giggled. "Is that silly?"

He looked into her eyes and shook his head. "No . . . not at all."

The broken and bent plateaus in the distance looked like an enchanted castle from centuries ago. As though burdened with a treasure too heavy to keep, low lying clouds opened their secret compartments, releasing sparkling snowflakes that dropped from the sky like diamonds. "Oh Grady," Naomi said, wrapping an arm around his waist. "Look, it's like a snow globe, isn't it?"

He reached both arms around her and held her tightly; their ski jackets *swished* against each other as they watched the snow fall on each other. "Mmmm, it is," he said in a whisper. He bent down and kissed Naomi. To his delight he felt her kissing him back. Deep inside, his emotions surged. The spark that had been dormant for fourteen long years reignited in a tender, passion-filled kiss under the falling snow.

* * *

The remainder of his time in Beach flew by faster than a coal train coming down Beaver Hill at full speed. He and Naomi spent three amazing days together. Being in Wibaux and Beach, they couldn't do anything spectacular, so they simply enjoyed each other's company. One day they ate at Mary's Place, a little diner in Beach. Naomi had broccoli cheese soup and he had a grilled ham and cheese with grilled onions. They played pinochle with Naomi's family one evening and then went to his mom's for dessert with all of his family. It was as if their time together was too good to be true, surreal almost. After everything he'd gone through in the last couple of years, he hardly knew how to handle this much goodness packed into three days.

Naomi fixed supper for them on their last night together, and he helped her clean up the kitchen. He leaned against the counter, drying the last blue dinner plate as an unwelcome awkwardness seeped into her cozy kitchen and hovered above them like a dark thunderstorm, threatening to erupt in a massive downpour and wash away what had just begun. Would they keep in touch? Or was it a quick romantic rendezvous—a flashback to what they once had as teenagers, and then gone again forever.

"This is it," he said, his voice hoarse and raspy.

Naomi nodded, running her fingers along the edge of the counter. Her blue sweater brought out the blue in her eyes. "It's been so great, Grady. I wish you didn't have to go."

"Tell me about it." He tried to read her thoughts.

"California is so far away."

"Yeah." It was like they both knew what the other was thinking but neither one wanted to say it out loud. If it didn't work when they were three hundred miles apart, how would it ever work when they were fifteen hundred miles apart? His life was in California; hers was in Beach. He cleared his throat. "I want to try. These past three days have been the best thing ever, Naomi. Please, trust me when I say I want it to work."

She nodded, tucking a lock of long dark hair behind her ear. "I do too."

Tears formed in his eyes and he took her in her arms. "I don't want to say good-bye," he said. She leaned her head into his chest and took his hand as he fought back the tears. "*Te amo.*"

"I love you too."

CHAPTER TWENTY-FIVE

Grady could hardly stay in his seat for the flight back to
L.A., and for once it had nothing to do with his back. This time it
was his heart. With each beat he thought of Naomi and their
unbelievable time together. He replayed every conversation over
in his head, reliving each tiny detail. They'd kept things light and
fun and enjoyed their time together for what it was. No fixed
plans for the future, although they promised to write and see
where it could lead from there. The hope in that simple promise
pulsated through his veins with every heartbeat as the giant tires
under the DC9 skidded to a stop at LAX.

Grady was halfway through the drafting program at MTI
and at the top of his Algebra class, which surprised him to no
end. He never thought of himself as being good in math, but he
even passed up some of the other students who had started the
course months before him. In the electronics class they were
running instrument tests, and he was starting to grasp what all the
calculations meant. If he could scrape by another few months, he

would graduate in May and could get a job with a steady paycheck once again.

Seven a.m. sharp every Saturday morning like clockwork, Grady drove the four miles down palm tree–lined Long Beach Boulevard to the Long Beach Community Hospital. "Morning, Judy," he said, walking into the neonatal intensive-care nursery.

"Hey, Grady," the long-time nurse replied. "We've got a brand-new one for you this morning. The little guy was born last night around midnight. He's not as delicate as some we've had lately. Just shy of four pounds." Judy yawned and covered her mouth; her eyes looked tired, watery. "Sorry, I worked a double. Anyway, mom had a difficult delivery and they're watching her around clock. There's no dad in the picture. I think mom's sister was with her through the night."

"Sure thing." Grady had on his white slacks and a striped white golf shirt that he wore on his shifts. "Let me go sign in and scrub up." He poked his head into Steve's office. "Morning."

Steve glanced up from his small metal desk. "Hey, Grady." He looked like a man on a mission with folders and notepaper spread all over, his office space more cramped than ever. "Got some new apps to go over."

"I hope you give them as hard of a time as you gave me," Grady said, pointing his finger.

"C'mon, now, I went easy on you."

"You made me feel like a criminal seeking a pardon from the president, for crying out loud. Man oh man, you gotta lighten up in your old age."

"Who you calling old? I still know *people*." Steve winked and picked up the schedule spreadsheet. "Say, thanks for covering for Annette Thursday night."

"No problem," Grady said. "Hey, did you get rocked to sleep last night? There were some pretty strong winds in the bay, I heard." Steve and his girlfriend lived on a sailboat in the marina.

"Slept like a baby, I'll have you know. Carrie didn't like it none too well," he said with a laugh. He reached in his shirt pocket and counted out four meal tickets. "Here's a couple extra," he said, handing them to Grady. "I appreciate that you're always willing to cover when we need it. Listen, a guy your size needs something in his stomach besides a pack of wimpy Asian noodles. You can't live off that five nights a week."

Steve must have found out his supper most nights consisted of ramen noodles, the cheapest thing he could find at Ralphs that filled him up. "Thanks," Grady said, tucking them in his pants pocket.

"When you ever gonna get a woman in your life?"

"I'm working on that."

Steve stuck a sheet in the tabletop copier. "Whoa, tell me more."

"I ran into an old girlfriend when I was home for Christmas." Grady was unable to wipe the smile from his face as he told the story.

"You don't say."

"She still lives in Beach."

"North Dakota?"

"Good memory," Grady said. "We've been writing, calling when we can. She's coming out for a visit in July."

"By the look on your face, I'd say you're pretty darn excited about that."

"Won't argue with you there."

Steve slapped Grady on the shoulder. "When she gets here, call me up. We'll have you down to the marina one night for a drink and some appetizers."

Grady went through the swinging doors to the large stainless steel basin and pressed the bar with his knee to turn on the water. He picked up a brush and scrubbed his hands and arms, fingertips to elbows for three full minutes. He rinsed off and dried with a sterilized towel. Then he unfolded a sterilized gown and tied it over his clothes. He went through the first set of doors for the gurneys and then the automatic doors into the ICU that held the most fragile newborns from southern California and beyond.

Judy looked up from an isolet. "All set?"

"Yup," Grady said. Judy gave him the recap and picked up the tiny infant. "Oooo, he's a sweet one, this one," she said, handing him to Grady. "His name is Kyle. I thought he'd be a good one for you."

At less than four pounds, baby boy Kyle was bigger than many of the premies at Long Beach. As a level-one regional neonatal intensive care, the facility handled the most critical babies flown in from all over Nevada, Arizona, and all of California—some weighing less than a pound. Others might be big six-pounders with bad bilirubin or respiratory issues. Some stayed six to twelve weeks, depending on their situation.

Grady looked into the tiny rounded face of pinkish red skin, eyes closed tight, lips curled slightly. A picture of pure innocence lay in his arms, emitting a sense of newness, hope. The baby's cheeks and nose were delicate, the tiny nostrils flaring slightly as he breathed. Like many preemies, his skin was so wrinkled it looked like there was too much skin and not enough body. Grady laid him on the changing table and unwrapped the receiving blanket, blue veins showing through the baby's translucent skin. Grady had his own special way to wrap his babies. First, he folded the bottom up, then the right side, and the left, wrapping it nice and snug around the miniature body.

He cradled Kyle against the crook in his neck, the infant's feet barely reaching Grady's heart. Grady always picked the rocker farthest from the bright lights of the isolets, in a darkened corner. He sat down and pushed gently with his feet to keep the rocker gliding back and forth in slow, smooth motions. Within a few minutes he could feel the little guy burrow into his chest a little further. Kyle offered up a little gasp and then settled back to a sound sleep, breathing softly against his neck.

"Hey there, little Kyle," he said, talking in a soft whisper. "You're almost one day old already. What do you think about that?" It always amazed people when he shared how a baby only weighing five hundred grams could perceive a different person holding him. He learned early on how to tell if a baby was stressed. He'd been a cuddler long enough to know that "his" babies knew him, knew his touch. Sometimes he got calls in the middle of the night, asking him to come down to the nursery because no one else could calm "his" baby. And other times he'd pick up another cuddler's baby only to have it cry and cry no matter what he tried.

This morning, though, little Kyle connected with Grady. He hadn't fussed once, his breaths coming evenly against Grady's chest. "It's okay, little buddy," Grady said barely above a whisper. Gently, he patted the baby's back, rocking slowly. "I bet your mama is doing better today and she'll be back to hold you before you know it."

Grady shut his eyes, loving the scent of the delicate newborn, a breath of brand-new life pressed against his chin, unaffected by the passage of time and the world around him. *God, if you decide to bless me with a son or a daughter, I promise I will never raise a hand to my children. I will never beat them or whip them or do any of the cruel things my father did to me, I swear this above all else, God.* And he wouldn't. He knew it with every fiber inside him. He would *never* abuse his kids.

He remembered once, way back, when he was only three years old, four at the most. They were living in the old Kramer farm site then, without running water, so his mom had to haul water from the well about twenty yards from the house for Saturday night baths. She'd heat it on the wood stove and pour it into a galvanized washtub and they'd all get scrubbed up nice and clean, first Melinda, then Grady. Afterward, his dad popped popcorn on the stove and propped him on his lap to watch Lawrence Welk and Gunsmoke on their little black-and-white television. Grady felt like a prince, sitting on the king's lap, special, loved. He breathed in the fresh scent of Lux soap on his dad's neck, munching popcorn, all of them laughing when his dad mimicked Lawrence Welk's accent. "Do it again," Melinda would say, and he'd do it again.

The very next Saturday during his bath, he told his dad he had to go to the bathroom and his dad told him he had to wait. He said he couldn't, but his dad told him he had to. When he stood up to dry off, his dad reached in the tub to grab the bar of soap and found something else. He pulled him out of the washtub and, over his knee, dripping wet, pounded his backside with his calloused hand. It was like his dad was out of control and couldn't stop. His mom kept screaming, "Frank, stop! He's just a kid! Stop!" But he didn't. He kept hitting and hitting. He had gotten beat badly that night.

The contrast of his dad's temperament from one Saturday night to the next had played on his mind throughout the years. Hard as he tried sometimes, he couldn't erase those painful memories. The ugliest ones surfaced when he least expected them. Was he so bad a kid that he hadn't deserved a better dad?

Kyle gasped, his little body stiffening for a moment as he took a big breath, then relaxing again. Grady started humming under his breath.

> *Amazing Grace, how sweet the sound,*
> *That saved a wretch like me.*
> *I once was lost, but now I'm found,*
> *Was blind, but now I see.*
> *T'was grace that taught my heart to fear,*
> *And grace, my fears relieved.*

How precious did that grace appear,
The hour I first believed.

Words Grady thought he'd forgotten long ago suddenly fell from his lips as Kyle's tiny heart beat against his own.

* * *

Ranked one of the highest in his class, Grady aced his certification test, which put him at the top of the placement list. Within days, Bolt Electric hired him—an electrical company that served industrial and commercial customers all across Los Angeles and Orange Counties. Although the company was only eleven years old, Grady heard it already had an excellent reputation and signed on as an electromechanical drafter.

As the detailer, he drafted installation layouts and power connections for large machine shops, plastic or wood recycling plants, and other industrial or commercial businesses. He loved being back at work, using his brain now instead of his back. For the first time in three years he felt productive again.

As promised, Naomi bought a plane ticket to Los Angeles. This time they would get a whole week together, far from the prying eyes of their families or town gossips. Grady drew up a list of places he wanted to take her. For sure the Santa Monica Pier, the Japanese Gardens at Cal State, the Mount Palomar Observatory, the USC Rose Garden, the Rancho La Brea tar pits near downtown L.A. He also wanted to show her some of the skyscrapers he'd worked on: the Taco Bell tower, Fox Plaza tower, and the First Interstate Bank Building, formerly known as The Library Tower. Finding something to do in L.A. was the opposite of their situation in Beach on New Year's Day. She could stay a whole year and they wouldn't run out of things to do.

Money was still tight, so he planned things that didn't cost a fortune. It killed him to think he used to make more money on his lunch hour as an ironworker than he did all day now. His average wage had dropped from twenty-five bucks an hour to a piddly nine bucks. He was thirty-three years old and starting a brand-new career.

* * *

Grady signed the rental agreement at Hermosa Cyclery and paid the fee. "Remember now," he said, "this is a *two*-person bike. You gotta help." He wheeled the tandem bike across the street to the bike path.

"Wait up a sec," Naomi said, glancing around. "I want to look at the ocean. Oh, my goodness, this is so cool!" California's famous beachside bike path offered amazing views of the ocean the entire twenty miles. "It's so beautiful. Oh, it's so exciting to be here! I can smell the salt in the air." She turned to Grady, lifting her white-framed sunglasses above her eyes. She had on a sleeveless pink shirt and stonewashed jean shorts. "I *do* like your beach better than mine!" She slipped her sunglasses back down and looked toward the ocean again. "Look how wide the beach is . . . oh, Grady, this is wonderful. I'm so glad we came down here. Can you tell it's my first time seeing the ocean?"

He loved watching her excitement and enthusiasm, thrilled to be the one sharing the experience with her. "You gonna keep yakking away back there, or are you ready to ride?" They planned to spend the whole day on the bike path, riding up to the Santa Monica pier and back.

"I can't help it!" Naomi grabbed the handlebars on the back half and climbed onto her seat. "Okay, I'm ready. You can pedal now."

"Excuse me?" he said, turning around to face Naomi. Grady adjusted his cap to keep the sun out of his eyes and climbed onto his seat.

"What?"

"*We* can pedal now," he said, pointing to her legs. "Are you ready back there?"

She laughed again and adjusted her tennis shoes on the pedals. "Okay, I'm ready." Naomi gave his shoulders a squeeze with one hand and tickled the back of his neck. "You have to lead though. I don't know my way around here."

Grady loved the feel of her fingers on his skin. He laughed and pressed down on the pedals, first the left, then the right, using his leg strength to gain momentum. He had on denim shorts and a Washington Redskins T-shirt. His arms and legs were a deep bronze from all his time in the sun, darker than ever before. The beach and bike path were busy with walkers, rollerbladers, bikers, and the usual array of sunseekers. The path was split into a two-way bike side and a two-way pedestrian and rollerblade side with painted indicators to direct each type of traffic.

"Look over there," Naomi said, pointing. A dozen or so men and women with California-perfect beach bodies played a game of sand volleyball. "Oh, that looks like fun."

"Uh-huh," he said, out of breath. "One of us is busy working here."

Grady looked up just as a bikinied rollerblader with a four-legged, long-haired mop on a leash came right at them. He quickly turned the front handlebars in order to miss the terrier and nearly went off the edge. He overcorrected and the bike leaned to the left.

"Careful up there; we crossed the center line, Grady."

"Yeah, I might get arrested and you'll be on your own."

"On your left!" a man's voice shouted as a ten-speed bicycle sped past them, the rider in bright yellow and black spandex.

"Whoa!" Naomi said. "He about scared me to death."

The breeze coming off the ocean felt good as Grady worked the pedals in a steady rhythm. Near the Manhattan Beach Pier, sections of colorful condos stood out, stacked like children's building blocks. "Stop sign coming up," he said. They slowed to a stop for the cross path that led down to the beach.

"How far we going, Captain?"

"It depends how fast we ride—or should I say, how slow we ride?"

Naomi rubbed the muscles in his back for a quick minute. "You're doing great so far."

"I think I'm being had here," he said, starting to pedal again. Up around Dockweiller Beach the crowds thinned out and they rode without interference, pretty purple flowers lining the hillside on the right. To their left the waves pounded the beach constantly; the white tops curved and rolled up the sand until they disappeared.

"I see a few surfers out there," Naomi said.

"Yeah, this is one of the good spots."

"I love the sun . . . and the blue sky. Look how the ocean just goes forever. Oh, Grady, is it this perfect every day?"

He hesitated. *Only when I'm with you.* "Yeah, this is pretty typical for the summer."

"When are we stopping?"

"About eight more miles. We'll take a walk on the Santa Monica Pier."

"Oh, cool. Guess I better start pedaling back here!"

"That'd be nice!"

They spent a good hour on the pier watching the surfers ride the waves. Fishermen and walkers filled the lengthy wooden pier; behind them white hotels and condos spread along the coastline into the far distance in each direction. Even though Grady was in good shape, the thirty-mile loop back to Hermosa in the heat of the day had given him more of a workout than he'd anticipated.

"It's still perfect out," Naomi said. The sun was low on the horizon, a giant orange sphere hovering above the water and lighting up the sky as though the other side of the world was on fire. A nice breeze came off the ocean, rustling the banner over a fish market nearby. Seagulls squawked in the background, and gray pelicans dove for fish as the waves pounding in rhythm: *whoooosh, whoooosh, whoosh.*

"I've got an idea." Grady lifted his cap and rubbed his forehead. "There's a nice little seafood place in Redondo Beach. We can sit outside, have dinner, and watch the sun go down."

Naomi squeezed his arm and reached up on tippy toes to give him a quick kiss. "Sounds like the perfect end to a perfect day."

Grady found an open spot on the patio at Captain Kidd's. They sat down at one of the red wooden picnic tables adorned with Coca-Cola umbrellas. A college-age gal in shorts and a tank top pushed through the screen door. "Can I get you something to drink? Beer? Wine? Fresh-squeezed lemonade?"

"Oooh, lemonade sounds good," Naomi said. "I'm really thirsty."

"Make that two." He looked at Naomi as she watched a juggler performing for a small crowd on the beach. Each time he looked at her he felt there was something about her that stood out, something he couldn't quite put his finger on. He supposed it was her persona, her character, the way she viewed things in life.

It was like they had only been apart days, not years. Their conversations were relaxed, comfortable. And when they came together, alone, in private, they did so with love and passion. He loved holding her close, not rushed. They took time to get to know each other tenderly and intimately. It was like nothing he'd experienced before.

"Grady?" Naomi lifted her face, studying him. Her nose was red, sunburned from their day at the beach. "You okay?"

He took her hand and kissed it. "Mmm, couldn't be better."

* * *

"Did you get the popcorn?" Naomi called from the kitchen.

"Yup, it's in that paper bag. I already took the cooler down and put it in the truck."

"So, what's left?"

"Just the Papasan." He stood with both hands on his hips. "Think you can help me get this baby down the stairs?"

"I'm used to moving furniture at the store." Naomi worked in her uncle's home interior store that sold furniture, wallpaper, paint, carpets, flooring—a little bit of everything.

"Okay, you take the cushion and I'll grab the chair." He picked it up and tipped it sideways to get it through the apartment door. "Can you lock the door?"

"Got it," Naomi said. They made their way down the second-level walkway to the stairs.

Grady looked through the wicker frame to see where to step. "I'll go down first. That way if I fall, I won't roll right over you."

"Be careful!"

They made it down without a problem, and Grady put the Papasan in the back of the pickup. He pushed the cooler into the corner and drove to Togo's to pick up a couple sandwiches. They drove to Signal Hill, an area in Los Angeles where oil had been discovered around the turn of the century. At one time the entire hill had been covered in derricks and old-style rigs. Both were long gone, and now it was just another California hillside that developers mapped out for future neighborhoods.

Grady followed the curved street up the hillside to the top. There were several other cars there already, and he parked the truck so it faced up the hill, with the rear end facing toward the bay. A few people were already in lawn chairs a littler farther up the hill on the grass. Others gathered down below in a small park.

From their choice spot they could see Long Beach and Seal Beach along the ocean's edge. Palm and coconut trees lined the boulevards and roads along the harbor with tall white skyscrapers and hotels hugging a narrow strip near the beach and marina. The Queen Mary was docked there, dwarfing the sailboats, cabin cruisers, and yachts that circled the harbor for the Fourth of July festivities. Grady figured that rather than get caught in the craziness along the beach, they could sit in the back of his pickup on the hill and have the perfect viewing spot for the fireworks.

"Wow, what a view," Naomi said, surveying the picturesque seascape below.

"It's only five o'clock," he said, looking at his watch. "Fireworks won't start till ten. I guess we're a little early."

"I don't mind," she said, shrugging her shoulders. "Think about it—how often do I get to see a view like this? This is so great, Grady."

He helped Naomi climb into the truck bed. He squished the cushion back into the framework of the Papasan and they sat in it, side by side. He pulled the cooler within reach and handed Naomi her sandwich and a Coke. From the back end of the pickup they had an unobstructed view of San Pedro Bay and Fisherman's Village below, and watched the crowd congregating on the grassy area in front of the Queen Mary for the festivities.

"Pretty cozy, don't ya think?" he said.

Naomi nodded. "Definitely."

A couple walked past them toting a blanket and cooler. "Hey, right on, man; that's an awesome idea!" the guy said with a nod of approval.

"Thanks," Grady said, reaching an arm around Naomi. "I think so too."

So far, each day of Naomi's visit had been perfect in every sense and today was no different. The temps were in the comfortable eighties each day—not too hot, not too windy. To Grady, every single day had been amazing, and from what he could tell, Naomi felt the same. They'd even ventured all the way down into Mexico one day and got lost. Grady'd had to rent a hotel room because they ran out of time to get back across the border. The spontaneity of their overnight excursion to Tijuana had only added to the overall sense that they belonged together.

"Tomorrow's Friday already," Naomi said. "Only one more day. I don't want to go back. This has been a great week, Grady. Everything we did was so refreshing, so *fun*. I loved flying a kite at Seal Beach, the Japanese Gardens, *everything.* "

"I agree one hundred percent."

She put her Coke on the truck rail and turned her face to Grady. "Where do we go from here?"

"I think you know how I feel," Grady said. "I love being with you. You've made me so happy this week. Honestly, I haven't felt this good inside since . . . well, since ever."

"It's just so hard, being so far apart."

Grady grew silent. Those words were an echo of what she'd said fourteen years earlier. "Yeah, I know." For a moment he couldn't breathe. He didn't want to go through that again. He didn't want to get his hopes up only to have them crushed. He couldn't survive that twice.

"Don't you wish you could look into a glass ball sometimes?" Naomi asked.

"Hmmm, it all depends," Grady said. *Not if it's good-bye.*

"I mean, I wish I had my life all figured out."

"I don't think we ever have it all figured out. We just have to take one day at a time and see what works best."

"I love being together like this, Grady, but my house, my job—all that is in Beach. I pretty much gave up on finding a husband. I'm thirty-two, you know."

"Last time I checked they still allow people this age to get married."

Naomi laughed. "You know what I mean. After the divorce, I dated some, but I always knew after a few dates it wasn't *right*."

Grady nodded. "Yeah, I have a pretty good idea."

"The hardest was giving up Angela. Gosh, she's nine years old now. I think about her, you know."

"Do you wish . . ." He paused.

"I planned right from the start that I would give her up for adoption. I mean, I knew Mike and I shouldn't have gotten married. He wasn't what I wanted in a husband, but I'd gotten pregnant and decided I should handle it the right way. Our whole family was dealing with my dad's drinking issues too. We broke up early in the pregnancy. It was hard, but I didn't hide it. I was working at the store back then too. You know how it's a small town; there aren't any secrets. Most people were nice about it, knew the story and reason."

"Was Mike okay with the adoption?"

"Oh, yeah. He didn't want to stick around and raise a baby. And it was best that way."

"Then I met Brad shortly after that and we started dating. I was only twenty-three and still hurting, you know, from giving up the baby. I didn't realize it at the time, until later."

Grady bent his head and kissed Naomi's temple. "I know that all too well," he said softly. "Things from when I was kid will come to the surface when I least expect it."

She squeezed his arm and rested her head on his shoulder. "I know you had it rough, Grady. Everyone in town knew your dad was hard on you kids."

Grady slowly nodded, staring at the panoramic scene spread out before them like a giant movie screen.

"Brad and I married too quickly and, just like that, he got really rough a couple times. The violence scared me," she said, pausing to wipe a tear from her cheek. "And that was it. I wanted out. I've been on my own ever since—seven years."

"You did the right thing," Grady said reassuringly. "There was only one time I came close to getting married. Her name was Sarah. Everything was great in the beginning and we were pretty serious with each other."

"What happened?" she asked.

"That's when I hurt my back and couldn't do all the things we used to do. Didn't have as much money to go on dates, and I'll admit it—a man in constant pain does not make the best company."

"I'm sure you couldn't help it." She ran her fingers on his arm again. "I guess we've both been through some difficult things. We're bound to, after fourteen years." She took a sip of Coke. "I'd gotten to a point where I was okay being single. You know, live my life and let it go at that. Enjoy my nieces and nephews, work hard, just like everybody else . . . and not wish for something I couldn't have."

"You mean a husband and kids?"

"Yeah. I was okay; I'd accepted it."

"And now?"

She leaned her head back against the cushion. "That was before New Years, before I ran into you again. Now I feel like maybe that's something you and I could have."

Grady felt his heartbeat quicken. "I've been in no hurry to get married. But now I can say I can't think of anything I'd like more." He saw tears forming in Naomi's eyes. "What's the matter?"

"Are you sure, about me?" she said softly. "I mean, I've had a baby and I've been married and divorced. Would you even want me after all that?"

"*Yes,* I'm sure," he said with conviction. Grady sat up straight and turned to look her directly in the eyes. "Naomi, you are the one person I've always loved. *Yes*, I want you."

She nodded, wiping away the tears.

"Listen here, there's a lot of dumb men in Beach— that's all I can say. Letting you slip through their fingers."

Naomi gave a soft laugh. "You would say that."

"Of course I would, because it's true. I can't believe you're still single." He leaned back and wrapped an arm around her again. She rested her head against his and they sat in the quiet evening, dusk nearing, the sun slipping lower in the sky until it bathed the ocean in a shimmering golden glow. They talked until the sky darkened to midnight blue and the first rocket of red, white, and blue colors lit the sky in a spectacular display. Somewhere in the distance Ray Charles's version of "America, the Beautiful" echoed across the hillside.

PART V

CHAPTER TWENTY-SIX

Minneapolis, Minnesota, 1998

Kari's cries echoed through the bedroom walls. "Mommy! Mommy!"

Grady rolled onto his back. "I can get her," he mumbled in a deep moan.

Naomi's hand touched his chest. "Mmm, that's okay. It's only three-thirty; I'll go."

"She wasn't feeling good last night when I put her to bed."

In minutes the crying subsided, followed by every parent's godsend: silence. Grady pulled Naomi up against him; his body curled around hers in a crescent moon, legs intertwined. "I've got fifteen minutes before my alarm goes off. What are the chances for a little romance?" He kissed the soft spot on the back of her neck.

"Mmm," she said sleepily, "probably about as good as getting that brand-new van."

"We can be quick." He ran a hand along Naomi's thigh until Kari's cries resumed across the hall.

"Not quick enough, I'm afraid." She lifted his arm and crawled out of bed.

"A man can dream, can't he?"

"About the van or the other?" She turned on the lamp and slipped on a fuzzy lavender robe.

By 4:27 a.m. Grady was on the freeway for his twenty-mile commute to Roxel Manufacturing. He punched the button to WCCO-AM to catch the weather, but the only talk on the pre-morning drive time was on the sickening scandal with President Clinton and Monica Lewinsky, getting more disgusting by the day.

Grady's life experiences with farm machinery, oil rigs, and hoisting equipment had paid off in his new job. Roxel was an OEM, Original Equipment Manufacturer, developing coordinate measuring machines for businesses around the globe. According to the bosses, Grady brought a fresh perspective to Roxel's machine design and production methods and they were impressed when he helped solve complex design issues with simple solutions he'd used before.

After Naomi's initial visit to California, they had made sure their relationship worked. Lots of letters, cards, and long distance phone calls had led to her moving to Long Beach. She got a job at the K-Mart across the street and they settled in until the Rodney King riots erupted in April 1992. It frightened them to look out their apartment window and see the neighborhood liquor store burn to the ground. Helicopters circled overhead with bright spotlights looking for looters; gunshots erupted at random hours day and night, followed by sirens. Other times there was only silence . . . and that was equally eerie. K-Mart brought in truckloads of straw bales to barricade their parking lot and hired armed guards to man it throughout the riots, so it wouldn't get looted.

In the aftermath Grady and Naomi decided L.A. was no place to raise a family. They drove back to North Dakota and got married at Saint John's Catholic Church in Beach on May 15, 1992, with family and a few close friends. Grady hunted for job prospects while they were home, but couldn't come up with anything. Dean sent him a copy of the Minneapolis Star Tribune and Grady scoured the want ads. He applied with Roxel Manufacturing, got hired within three weeks, and had been with them ever since. Naomi transferred with K-Mart to a store only two miles from their house.

Justin was born in June 1993 and it was then that Grady knew what life was all about. Holding his own son in his arms made him think back to all the newborns he'd held in the neonatal ICU. Taking Naomi as his wife had made him feel whole, but when Justin was born, he realized what he'd been missing all those years—a *family*.

Grady started woodworking as a hobby, and when Naomi got pregnant the second time, he decided to make a cradle for the baby. As usual, he put it off till the end of her pregnancy. As Naomi's due date approached, he worked on it feverishly every evening. He finished it one night around ten o'clock and, sure enough, Naomi's water broke about four o'clock the next morning and they were off to the hospital. Kari was born at six a.m., and the cradle was waiting at home, two and a half years after Justin had come into the world.

* * *

Overseas trips to Roxel's headquarters in Stuttgart, Germany, had become routine. The last trip involved a solid week of twelve- to fourteen-hour days. At the end of it Grady was mentally drained and ready to get back to their three-bedroom rambler and a normal schedule. During the long flight home he and the other engineer, Ronny Sturm, had a dozen hours to talk about everything under the sun, including their common interest in fishing. Much to his surprise, three weeks later Ronny invited Grady on a fishing excursion to Montana. A large fishing outfitter had donated the three-day fishing package for four to a silent auction fundraiser and Ronny's friend had gotten the winning bid. When one of the guys backed out at the last minute, Ronny had offered the open spot to Grady, all expenses paid. Grady was all the more thrilled to discover their destination was the beautiful Bitterroot River near Missoula, not far from where he'd lived as a kid.

Nygren Outfitters served as the host camp with cabins and an on-site lodge for meals. He'd never experienced such an elite style of fishing with top-of-the-line Bass Pro gear and accommodations, all prearranged and ready to go. The three Minnesotans had never fished the icy streams of the Bitterroot and Sapphire mountain ranges before and soaked up their guide's every word. Grady didn't need someone telling him how or where to throw a line, but he enjoyed the chatter: slow mornings, brookies hard to come by, nymph rigs, worms, blue wings and olive hatches, river running at 906 cubic feet per second.

The Bitterroot River was an angler's treasure, flowing with cutthroat and brown rainbow in the riffles and deep pools of the crystal-clear water. The rushing water tumbled over the rocks and stones in musical rhythms, like a never-ending song. As though painted one stroke at a time, the picturesque backdrop to their time on the river was breathtaking. Sweeping forests of deep green, white-tipped mountain peaks cut against the rich blue sky, trickling waterfalls mixed with intoxicating evergreens. Each time Grady dipped his hands into the rushing stream to pluck a wiggling trout from his line, he felt like a kid on the Blackfoot again.

He was half-tempted to take a drive up Highway 200 through Bonner to see if the old logging camp was still there. Back in their day, the Bonner lumber mill and Bonner bar had buzzed with the men who worked hard and drank even harder, a bruised and rough brotherhood of sorts who had something to prove and nothing to lose. Grady and his siblings spent nearly every Saturday in the car with their mom in front of the Bonner bar, waiting for his dad to come out so they could go into town and buy groceries. Funny, it seemed for every good childhood memory there were a dozen bad ones to dispel it.

Still, three days of fishing in the Bitterroot refreshed his spirit more than any Sunday morning mass ever had. The men packed their catch on ice for the trip home, admittedly envious of their hosts' lives on the river. They took the rental car back to Missoula and arrived in town a couple of hours early. "We've got some time before our flight. May as well hit the bar," Ronny said, scouting the streets. "Hey, there's one called the Busted Nut. We gotta check that out!"

Acting on impulse, Grady checked his watch. "Listen guys, why don't I drop you off? There's someone in town I'd like to go say hello to. Be back in an hour." Grady made his way downtown to St. Patrick's Hospital, now a sprawling complex of medical buildings that had quadrupled in size since he was there last. It hardly resembled the white building from his childhood memory.

Grady approached the information desk. "By chance does Dr. Ferrell still work here?"

"As a matter of fact, he just announced his retirement," the woman said.

Grady felt his shoulders slump. "Shoot, I was hoping to say hello."

"Oh, he's still here," she said, reaching for the phone. "He's got another few months to go. It won't be the same around here without him though. Are you a patient?"

Grady explained his connection to Dr. Ferrell and followed the assigned volunteer through a maze of hallways and elevators to a series of small offices on the surgical floor. "Right through here," the woman said, ushering Grady through the doorway.

An older gentleman stood and extended his hand. His white doctor's coat hung loosely over his crisp white shirt and blue tie. "My goodness, what a surprise! I couldn't believe it when my assistant told me who was on the way up."

Grady shook his hand, trying to remember the doctor's face from 1967; he couldn't place him as a younger man, in his memory. "I was in the area on a fishing trip, just wanted to stop and say hello." Dr. Ferrell was smaller in stature than Grady remembered. Somehow he'd always envisioned the man who saved him as larger than life. Instead, he was shorter than Grady with thinning gray hair and deep permanent wrinkles engraved around his smile.

"I'm so glad you did. Sit down," he said. "Wait, let me get a look at your face." He stepped toward Grady, his cheeks ruddy with loose skin sagging under his chin.

"Don't have to pull my bangs back to show it anymore," Grady said with a laugh, rubbing his bare head. "I usually wear a cap, so it's kinda white up there too."

"Let's see how my work fared all these years." Dr. Ferrell put a hand on Grady's shoulder and studied his face and forehead close up. "In this doctor's humble opinion, I'd say it looks pretty good," he said, and offered a smile.

"Yeah, I think so too." Grady felt the doctor's soft fingers trace the long scar.

"Healed up pretty smooth, considering what we had to work with," he said, shaking his head. Dr. Ferrell took the leather chair behind his desk and offered the one in front to Grady. "Last time I saw you, you weren't but nine years old, is that right?"

Grady nodded. "Long time ago."

"Which tells you how old I am, doesn't it?" he said with a laugh. "I'll never forget walking into the OR that morning, to see a young boy in your condition. The teeth on the chainsaw shredded your facial skin like I'd never seen before. Working on your face had a greater impact on me as a surgeon, even after everything I saw in 'Nam."

"It's probably long overdue, but I wanted to say thank you in person, Doctor."

Dr. Ferrell nodded in humility. "That's mighty kind of you, Son. Are you still in Montana?"

"Oh, no." Grady leaned on the chair arm, admiring the framed certificates that covered the walls. "Been from Montana to North Dakota to California, and now Minneapolis."

"Is life treating you okay?" he asked, his eyes a silvery blue.

"Oh, yeah. Got a wife, two kids—even a minivan," Grady said with a laugh. "Live in the suburbs and do the commute."

"How about your folks?"

"Mom's in North Dakota, right near the Montana border. And Dad's out in California, the desert area by the Salton Sea."

"You know," Dr. Ferrell said, looking thoughtful. "I may have stitched your face back together, but your dad is the one who really saved your life that day." He leaned back, rocking slowly, his hands clasped in a prayer-like fold.

Grady's eyebrows pushed together and he leaned forward. "What do you mean?"

"It's because of him you even survived. First," he said, pointing his right forefinger, "he knew enough to keep your head above your heart to minimize the loss of blood. Keeping you upright after the accident automatically slowed the blood loss. If he'd let you lay down, you'd have never made it to the hospital, not from that far away. I mean you were clear up by Potomac; we're talking close to an hour. That's a long drive down the mountain, especially back in 1967 before they straightened out some of those curves and turns. He must've worked magic with the gas pedal and brakes, getting you down that mountain in time. That alone is a miracle in an old car like he had."

Grady was silent; he'd never considered that before.

"Before I started the surgery I went out to talk to your folks. I've never seen a man more sorry for something in my life before. The look on his face said it all. I can't tell you how many times he said to me, 'I'm sorry, I'm so sorry.' It was tough to watch him beat himself up for what he'd done. I knew the surgery would take all day, so I told your folks to go home. They were both covered in blood and I thought it would be best for them to get cleaned up. When they came back first thing the next morning, your dad sat by your bed, holding your hand."

Grady bit back the smartass comment on the tip of his tongue. "That a fact?"

"You were in and out of consciousness that whole next day following the surgery."

"I couldn't wait to get out of here; I remember that."

"I don't blame you one bit. We were pretty tough on you."

He listened to Dr. Ferrell talk about his follow-up care until an intern with an urgent question interrupted their visit. Grady rejoined the guys at the Busted Nut, and Ronny's friend ordered him a shot of Jack Daniels. When he and Naomi had married, they'd pretty much given up alcohol, not wanting to inflict the dysfunction of their fathers onto their own children. In May they hit the six-year mark as husband and wife, although sometimes he felt like they were like two ships passing in the night. He worked days and she worked evenings so they didn't have to pay for daycare. Lately they'd hardly taken time for each other.

He swirled the honey-colored liquid, watching it coat the sides. It had been a long time since he tasted Jack's riches of the earth. Grady downed it in one swallow and fingered the empty glass, pondering his visit with Dr. Ferrell. What the good doctor didn't know, of course, was his ol' man's reputation. After the accident, every time family or neighbors came over his dad would holler, "Grady, come here! Uncle Ed wants to see your scar," like he was some kind of circus freak. His dad would crank his head sideways, push back his hair, and point to the spot where the split shot and wire were sewn to his head, as though his dad had bragging rights. Never mind that he *caused* the whole bloody mess. That didn't seem to faze him. Just have another drink and laugh about it.

Grady remembered having a sleepover at Lee Hinman's—his best friend in third grade. His folks were ranchers, so it was a big deal to get invited to a real ranch. Lee's mom had been so nice to him, gently asking questions about his ordeal. She fixed a makeshift bed for the boys in the front porch for their overnight adventure. He sensed—but didn't understand back then—neighbors' whispers about the little kids in the Kramer house.

Regardless, the good doctor's hands'd had a healing touch. The scar was far less visible now and some people didn't even notice it right away. Too bad there wasn't a physician that could heal the other wounds inflicted by his father. Crushing, hurtful words spoken long ago that had seared his soul, burned and blackened like the tree trunks that covered a Montana mountainside after a devastating forest fire, branded him for a lifetime, stripped him of identity and self-worth.

Then again, maybe the old doctor's memory had faded through the years. Otherwise, the way he told it, his father should have had the guts just once to tell Grady he was sorry.

CHAPTER TWENTY-SEVEN

Grady had to admit autumn in Minnesota was beautiful. Houses in their neighborhood were nestled under canopies of tall leafy trees, their branches extended outward in a protective arboreal covering. The two big maple trees in their front yard were always the first on the street to turn color, their tops already a deep shade of reddish bronze, as though they knew a secret the ash and oak trees didn't. The kids enjoyed plenty of warm fall days on the swing set and in the sandbox he'd built for them in the backyard.

A welcome evening breeze filtered through the patio screen as Naomi washed spaghetti sauce from Kari's face and hands. Grady carried his plate and silverware to the sink. "I better get out to the garage."

"Tonight? I thought maybe we could do something with the four of us since I don't have to work." Naomi's hair was pulled back into a ponytail. She had on a pair of khaki shorts and a white T-shirt, her blue eyes awaiting his answer.

"I promised Bill I'd have another set of packaging boxes finished by next Friday." When his boss had found out Grady did woodworking, he asked Grady to build protective packaging for air bearings. He made a covered wooden box with foam inserts as a prototype, and his boss immediately requested sixty boxes. He'd supplied Roxel with packaging units on a regular basis ever since.

Grady put away the Parmesan cheese and wrapped up the leftover bread. "Do you want some help with the dishes?"

"No, go ahead. I've got it."

Grady retreated to the garage-turned-workshop. Upon moving to Minneapolis, Grady had kept his allegiance with the American League and followed the Minnesota Twins. Anaheim, his old team, had just been to Minnesota, and the teams had split a two-game series. Grady turned on the Twins baseball game with the White Sox and fired up the table saw. He'd already been to Knox Lumber and picked up five-by-five-foot sheets of Baltic birch plywood. He pulled the pencil from his ear to scribble down the measurements for this order: 7 ¾" x 8 ¾" x 7". He took the first sheet of three-quarter inch plywood and pushed it through, shavings flying off both sides. The loud *screech* drowned out the Twins–White Sox play-by-play as each piece *zinged* through the spinning blade.

Grady spent a good hour cutting the first set of pieces. Thirsty and hot, he went in the house in search of a cold drink.

"Is that you?" Naomi called from the living room.

"Just getting a drink," he said, grabbing the pitcher of ice tea from the fridge.

Naomi came around the corner and smiled. "The kids and I are going to walk up to Wendy's for a shake. Why don't you come with us?"

"I told you, I've gotta get that order done."

"It's only Tuesday."

"This order alone will take at least two weeks." Grady chugged the glass of tea and wiped his mouth. "You don't get it, do you? I can't come home and sit on my duff like some guys can. These side orders from Roxel are important—they keep us afloat. I can't just blow it off."

Naomi held her breath for a moment. "I know that, Grady," she said, her voice barely above a whisper. "You don't have to get all tight-jawed about it. It's just . . . lately we've hardly seen each other."

"Well, when you figure out how else to pay all the bills, let me know. In the meantime I'll be in the shop." He slid the patio door open and walked back to the garage, irritated by her comments. Of course he'd rather go for a walk with Naomi and the kids. What dad wouldn't? But it was up to him to support the family. The kids always needed stuff. Shoes, jackets, cereal, milk, trips to the doctor. He'd spent hours under the hood of his old pickup this summer to keep it running rather than buy a different one. And this was the thanks he got.

Grady resumed cutting boards, the saw drowning out his agitated thoughts. He organized the pieces into piles: top, bottom, and sides. Now he needed to cut the finger joints at each end to make slots and grooves to fit the pieces together. Grady got out the stacking saw blade with the half-inch groove and picked up the first piece, turning it over in his hand. "Wait a minute," he said in a growl. He grabbed the tape measure and his pencil.

"Damn it!" he yelled at the top of his lungs, smashing the piece into the workbench. "*Grrrr!!*" Grady picked up the stack of plywood and threw the pieces against the wall. He'd cut all the sections a quarter inch too short. "You stupid piece of shit! Now look what you've done—you wasted all that wood, all that blasted time, all that money! You're nothing but a stupid, no-good, piece a shit loser! Don't have a brain in your head!*"

Grady kicked the box of scraps out of his way and picked up the hammer. With one swift move he slammed it into the corner beam, again and again, yelling at himself for the costly mistake.

"Grady! What's wrong?" Naomi stood in the doorway with a look of alarm, hand to her chest. "I can hear you all the way in the house."

"I cut all the damn pieces too short," he yelled at her. "There—are you happy? I wasted my whole evening out here and you were right!"

"Grady, stop this . . . please."

"Leave me alone!" He picked up the hammer and slammed it into the bench. When he stopped, Naomi was gone.

Grady stayed in the garage until Naomi got back from the walk. The kids were in their rooms, getting ready for bed. Calmed down and ready to apologize, he followed Naomi into the bathroom. He sat silent on the toilet while she washed her face and dabbed her cheeks with a dry towel, going about her nightly routine. Grady cleared his throat, absentmindedly spinning the toilet paper roll. "I'm sorry about tonight," he said with a long pause. "I don't know why I go off like that."

She leaned her back against the ceramic counter and faced him. A sadness showed in her eyes, her pale skin smooth and beautiful even without makeup. "Grady, you can't do this. It scares the kids." She folded her arms, tears forming. "It scares *me*."

"I don't *want* to do it, Naomi; it just happens," he said, feeling his defenses rising to the surface. "And before I know it, I'm out of control." He stood up and gently caressed her arms.

She leaned into him, resting her head on his shoulder. "You need to open up and talk to me. Grady, I love you, you know that." She tilted her head and wiped her eyes. "You don't need to keep everything bottled up inside until you explode. Talk to me, *please*."

313

Grady held her tight, brushing her hair with his fingers. "I know, babe."

* * *

Roxel sent Grady to work with a vendor in Ontario, California, on a joint venture for developing new shrouds made from plastic instead of fiberglass. For once things went according to plan and the project wrapped up a day early. He knew he couldn't fit in the long drive to Salton City to see his dad and Chandra, but in the obligatory phone call he found out they were house sitting for friends in Hemet, less than an hour away.

Grady pulled up to the yellow one-story in a nice neighborhood of look-alike houses separated by barely a few feet, a single palm tree in each yard. An overhang created a porch in front, trimmed with geometric metal fencing painted white. Chandra opened the screen door as he walked up the sidewalk, the front yard a mix of rock and dried grass. "Grady! It's so good to see you again."

"Hi, Chandra," he said, giving her a hug. "How are you?"

She had on a pair of orange slacks and a yellow checkered blouse that nearly blinded him. "I'm good, doing good." She smiled and ushered him inside. "C'mon in; let's get out of the heat." She laughed and shut the metal screen door behind him. "You know how it is out here; the heat never changes."

Grady walked into the living room and rolled his carry-on next to the couch. The interior looked like it had been completely refurbished with new carpeting and fresh paint, all in soft pastel colors. "Hey, Dad," he said, reaching a hand toward him.

"Grady, it's good—" Frank coughed, covering his mouth. He coughed hard several more times and then regained his composure. "Sorry about that. I . . . need to catch my breath. It's good to see you again. We sure miss having you in California."

"I miss the ocean but not these darn freeways."

"Sit down," Chandra said. "Can I get you some ice tea or water?"

"Water's fine," Grady said, taking a deeper look at his father. He seemed different—his skin color, his eyes, something. "You doing okay, Dad?"

Before Frank could answer, he flew into a coughing fit that lasted nearly a minute, and then lowered himself onto a chair at the kitchen table.

"Here's your water, Grady," Chandra said. Her hair was a darker shade of red now and her eyes held the same fiery spirit. "Have a chair."

"Oh, I've been sitting in the car for an hour. Actually, it feels good to stand," Grady said, rubbing his back.

"Say, how is your back, since that last surgery you had?" she asked.

"The spine fusion? That was the best thing I ever did, honestly. Saved my life."

"Oooh, praise Jesus, isn't that good," Chandra said in a patronizing tone. "Let's see some pictures of the kids. Did you bring any?"

"Yeah, sure." Grady put down his glass of water and sat next to his dad. "I've got some new ones from K-Mart to show you. I think Naomi brings the kids in every time they have a photographer in the store." He opened his wallet and took out their most recent pictures. "Here's Justin; he turned five in June."

"Oh, my stars!" said Chandra, standing behind Frank, her hands on his shoulders. "What a handsome little fella."

"Looks just like his dad, I'd say," Frank said.

How many times had he heard people say that about him? He studied his father a little closer. Since he'd quit drinking, it didn't seem like such a negative comment anymore. "And here's little Kari; she just turned two and a half, last week in fact."

Chandra took the picture from his hands and sucked in a deep breath. "She's a princess, an absolute princess," she said with great flair and enthusiasm. "Look, Frank, isn't she?"

Frank leaned in closer. "Oh, look at that smile. That could melt a heart now, couldn't it?"

"Now I know how kids get spoiled," Grady said with a wide grin, pointing. "She's got a dimple in her right cheek."

"Oh, I see it," Chandra said.

"She looks up at me with those brown eyes and I melt, right there on the spot."

"She's pretty sweet, that one," Frank said.

"Justin's the one who will give me gray hairs; that kid can get under my skin in a hurry. He's our strong-willed child."

"You're looking good, Grady," Frank said. "What they got you doing in L.A.?"

"We're developing new shrouds out of plastic instead of fiberglass. Our vendor out here makes the molds for us. I had to design and develop a new set of shrouds."

"Sounds pretty interesting."

"Yeah, it's been a good fit with Roxel."

"Isn't that something," Chandra said. "Jesus is wonderful, isn't he?"

Chandra's single-minded viewpoint caused the hair on the back of his neck to stand straight up, like always. *Let it go . . .*

Frank nodded and coughed again. He pulled a handkerchief out of his pants pocket and held it to his mouth. This time the coughing episode lasted several minutes.

Grady put a hand on his back. "Dad, what's wrong?"

Frank regained his composure and glanced at Chandra, then his eyes shot downward. "Oh, the doctors say I have cancer, but we know it's not," he said, shooing his hands as if to dismiss the severity.

"Cancer!" Stunned, Grady looked at his dad and then at Chandra. "What do you mean, you know it's not?"

Frank remained silent. "This is from Satan, it's not cancer—" Chandra started.

Grady cut her off. "Dad, the doctors know if it's cancer or not. What do you mean, it's from Satan?"

"The doctors are just labeling it as cancer," Chandra said in a pompous tone. She took Frank's arm and rubbed it gently, moving between Grady and Frank. "But we know for a fact it's from Satan. We're just gonna pray it right out of him; that's what we're gonna do, aren't we?" She looked into Frank's eyes and he gave her a quick smile.

"We'll deal with it," Frank said, catching Grady's worried expression.

"Dad . . ." Grady looked him directly in the eye. He saw a tiredness he'd never seen before. "What is it? What kind of cancer?"

"They said it's in the lungs."

Grady thought of all the times his dad had lit up a Winston. He didn't quit until after he and Chandra were married—obviously not soon enough. "Dad, you need talk to the doctors and see what they can do for you."

"We've already done that," Chandra said, directing Frank to move to the couch. "We've been to the doctor, we've seen the specialists, and this is our conclusion. We've decided we're gonna take this to the Lord and let Almighty God deal with this directly. That's all we can do at this point."

Grady followed his dad into the living room. "What'd the doctors say?"

Frank looked pained as he eased onto the cushions, avoiding eye contact with Grady. "The doctors don't know what they're talking about," Chandra said, answering for him. "Our faith is strong enough to see this through; you'll see."

Why hadn't they been told? None of the kids had any clue their dad was sick. "This is *cancer,* Chandra. You can't treat it like a common cold," Grady said, the anger rising.

Chandra stood her ground. "I saw the X-ray, sure. The doctor, the nurse—they both said it was cancer, but I said nope. They wanted to admit him, but I refused. I said, 'I'm taking him home, where he belongs.' They made me sign the papers and I was happy to do it," she said proudly. She held her head high in a signal of victory.

"What papers?"

"That I'm responsible for his health and wellbeing. Otherwise they wanted to admit him."

"Who?"

"The doctors out in Coachella."

"Out by Salton City; that's where we've been doctoring," Frank said.

"Prayer works just as much as doctoring," Chandra said, continuing her explanation on Grady's behalf. "We've seen it before—prayer works! I told the doctor in Coachella," she said, finger pointed at Grady, "we're gonna be back here a year from now and you're gonna eat your words!"

Dumbfounded, Grady could only stare blankly at the peach walls closing in around him. There was no question his dad had changed after he'd met Chandra. As soon as he gave up the booze, he lost his edge, as though he lacked the courage to be confrontational, and let her direct things. Throughout Chandra's entire dramatic explanation, his dad hadn't argued or disagreed with her once.

"Here, come over here." Chandra reached for the thick Bible near her purse and patted the seat cushion next to her. "I'll give you a list of the verses that we are standing on." She opened it to the New Testament and flipped several pages with notes scribbled in ink. "Right here, 2 Corinthians 12:7 says, 'And lest I should be exalted above measure by the abundance of the revelations, a thorn in the flesh was given to me, a messenger of Satan to buffet me, less I be exalted above measure.' That's how Satan works," she said for Grady's benefit and turned a few more pages. "But we're gonna claim Christ's power and his divine healing. Look what it says in James 5:16: 'Confess your trespasses to one another and pray for one another, that you may be healed.' "

Chandra's tone turned firmer as she pressed a bright fuchsia fingernail on the page. "'The effective, fervent prayer of a righteous man avails much.'" She looked up at Grady, her eyes fixed on his. "Do you see what I'm saying? The Bible says that your dad will be healed. Acts 14:9: 'This man heard Paul speaking. Paul, observing him intently and seeing that he had faith to be healed.' Faith to be healed, Grady. That's what your dad and I believe, what our church believes. Matthew 4:24: 'Then His fame went throughout all Syria; and they brought to Him all sick people who were afflicted with various diseases and torments, and those who were demon-possessed, epileptics, and paralytics; and He healed them.' Luke 4:23: 'He said to them, "You will surely say this proverb to Me, 'Physician, heal yourself!'"'"

Chandra flipped more pages. "There it is, in red letters. This is what we're standing on, isn't it, Frank?" She took a notebook and pen from her purse. "I can go on, Grady. I'll even write down the whole list for you. Luke 8:40–48, Luke 9:37–42, Matthew 4:23, Isaiah 58:8, Psalm 103:3."

Grady's head swirled, at a loss how to react. He and Naomi attended a Catholic church back home, but he didn't know Scripture well enough to contradict what Chandra was saying. It was one thing to discover his dad had lung cancer, but to find out they weren't going to have it treated medically—that was a whole different ballgame.

* * *

Grady returned to Minneapolis, upset beyond words. "I can't believe it!" he said to Naomi as he opened his suitcase on the bed. "They've given up on doctors and medicine completely. It's like that's not even an option."

"Grady, I don't get it. Why would they do that?"

"I don't know. Don't get me wrong—I know she believes in Jesus and has a stronger faith than I've ever seen, but I feel she's misguided in it somehow. She knows the Bible front to back and back again, but it's like she twists the verses to make her case." Grady tossed his dirty underwear and socks in the hamper.

"What does your dad say?"

"It's the strangest thing—he won't say anything contrary to her. I've never seen him so compliant, almost childlike." He sunk onto the side of their bed. "Am I wrong? Doesn't God give us doctors and medicine too? I mean, where would I be without a surgeon's hands?" He shook his head and gritted his teeth. "I think she's killing him."

Naomi sat down next to him and wrapped an arm around his back. "I'm so sorry . . ."

Grady nodded, fighting back a surge of anger. "When Chandra was out of earshot I asked Dad, 'Are you really believing this? Do you believe this is not cancer, just something you can pray away?' And he said, 'Oh, I think we're in it too deep to back out now.' Like he didn't buy into everything she said, but he was going along with it." Grady buried his face against Naomi, his voice barely a whisper, "I can't believe he's going to die and they're not going to do anything about it."

CHAPTER TWENTY-EIGHT

Living in Minnesota meant Grady and Naomi and the
kids could make the drive back to Beach and Wibaux much
easier than when they were in California. They tried to make it
home once in the summer and during the holidays. Grady called
out to California at least once a month to keep tabs on his dad.
Chandra hadn't changed her ways one iota. They were fighting
the cancer with prayer and nothing else.

By September 1999, when his dad passed the one-year
mark, Grady held out hope that maybe things weren't as bad as
he thought. Justin started first grade at the elementary school a
few blocks from their house. Naomi worked it out with her
supervisor to stay part-time so she could start her shift after
Justin got home from school and Grady got home from work.
They settled in and got to know a few people in their
neighborhood, even visited a few other churches.

Every fall Grady found he really missed hunting and was
thrilled when a couple of guys from work invited him to go deer

hunting. They drove four hours to the woods in northern Minnesota—a wide expanse of forests and lakes the locals simply called "up north." Well before dawn the men each climbed into deer stands that had been built up in the trees. They sat in the weird little stands for hours not making a sound, waiting for a deer to walk past. Grady was bored out of his mind. Where he'd come from, that wasn't *hunting*.

The world survived the Y2K scare on December 31, 1999, and rolled into the new millennium without so much as a hiccup. Thankfully, another brutal winter was over, and as the end of April neared, daylight hours in the Upper Midwest lengthened considerably. Neighbors came out of hibernation and once again stood at the mailbox or along backyard fences, catching up on all that had transpired through the long winter. Kids were out on bikes—including Justin, who loved riding on the street in front of their house.

Grady had just made another trip to Stuttgart and was still suffering from a bad case of jetlag. "Are you gonna finish your potatoes and carrots?" he asked Kari with a yawn.

She pushed the plate back and made a face. "I don't like it."

"There's nothing wrong with it, Kari."

"I ate it all, Dad," Justin said.

"I know. See that, Kari? Justin ate it."

"Did Mom make cookies today?" Justin asked.

"Check the cookie jar," Grady said. "And just take two."

Justin pulled the ceramic bunny-shaped cookie jar to the edge of the counter and reached in. "Can I have three?"

"What'd I say, Justin? Two is enough for now."

"Mom always lets me." He put three cookies under his T-shirt and pushed the jar back.

"Well, I'm not Mom. Now, put one back, Justin."

"No!" He ran around the table on the far side and down the steps to the family room.

"Good grief," Grady said. "I've got one kid who won't eat enough and one that won't stop." He scraped Kari's plate into the garbage. At least he wouldn't make her sit at the table all night long the way he had to when he was a kid. The world would have come to an end before his dad would relent and let any of the kids get by without cleaning their plate.

Kari slipped down from the booster seat and lay on the floor next to their black and white cat, her dark hair spilling across the carpet. "Look, Daddy! Bubbles is licking my fingers."

"That's nice." Grady washed the dishes and cleaned off the counter. He carried Kari downstairs, where Justin played with a set of Legos. "Where's Kari's coloring books?"

"Right there," Justin said, pointing to the bookshelf.

"Good." He took down the pail of Crayons and two coloring books and gave them to Kari. "You can color for a while, okay?"

"Uh-huh," she said, nodding. "Can Bubbles color with me?"

"Yes, Bubbles can color with you."

"Dad, do you want to help me? I'm building a hospital for these army guys right here. They had the hugest battle ever and they need a hospital." Justin had an array of army figures and building blocks spread across the floor. "The bad guys won this time, but the army guys are gonna get fixed up and come back and beat 'em. Do you wanna help? You could be an army guy with me." Justin slid over, brushing away the cookie crumbs stuck to his arm.

"Not tonight. I've got some work in the garage."

"You *always* work in the dumb ol' garage."

"Just the way it is. Now keep an eye on your sister, okay?"

He picked up an army helicopter. "*Barooommmmm!* Oh, no, he's gonna crash! *Ker-pow!*"

"Justin? Keep an eye on her, okay?'

"Sure, Dad."

Grady was in the middle of repairing an oak dining table for Dean and his wife. Plus, he had another large order of packaging containers to make for Roxel. He took a quick survey of his projects and decided the boxes had priority over the table.

Grady found a classic rock station on the radio and organized the sheets of oak plywood for the next set of boxes. He started up the saws and cut the first dozen bottom pieces.

The garage door opened and Kari ran inside, tears tumbling down her cheeks. "Daddy!" she said between sobs. "Justin's being mean to me."

Grady took off his safety goggles and picked her up. "It's okay. Daddy will talk to him." He carried her through the patio door down to the family room. "What's going on, Justin?" he asked in a serious voice.

"Nothing."

"Look at me when I'm talking to you, young man."

Justin pasted a fake smile to his face. "I didn't do nothing."

"Justin William Kramer, I'm not in the mood for this."

"She pushed . . . she . . . um . . . Bubbles ran away because she pushed her and knocked over my whole wall I built."

"You're the big brother, remember?" Grady brushed the tears from Kari's face and gave her a kiss. "And you be careful around Justin's blocks. All better, okay?"

She nodded, wiping her nose on her sleeve, and sat down by the Crayon bucket. "Now, be nice to each other." Grady went back to the garage. It was only seven o'clock. If the kids behaved and he could get in a couple good hours of work, maybe he'd get caught up for once. He'd taken Kari fishing with him one evening, and she'd been fascinated with the whole concept, more so than Justin.

He cut up the first sheet of plywood when the door opened again. "Daadddy!" Kari cried in the doorway. "He hit me!" A red mark appeared on her cheek where her small index finger pointed.

"Doggone it anyhow!" He shut the saws down and scooped her into his arms. With Kari crying in his ear, he carried her to the patio door and grabbed the handle. "It's okay, sweetie. Calm down." The door didn't budge. He looked down and saw the dowel insert in place that blocked the door from sliding open. He stepped to the back door and tried the handle. Locked. Grady went back to the patio and pounded his fist on the glass doors. "Justin! Open this door right now."

Justin stood behind the table, a smirk spreading from ear to ear. A muffled version of "na-na-na-na-na-naaa!" filtered through the glass as he jumped on tippy toes.

"Justin, open it now! I mean it!"

With a look of victory, Justin shook his head. "Huh-uh!" he said loud enough for Grady to hear.

"That's it!" Grady put Kari down and ran to the angel statue in the flower bed that lined the garage. He tipped it back and reached into the bottom until his fingers found the extra house key. He unlocked the door and Kari followed him inside, still crying.

The instant the door opened, Justin took off toward his bedroom. Grady caught Justin as he tried to shut the bedroom door. Grady pushed the door open and grabbed Justin, pulling him into the hallway. Grady picked him up by the shirt and knocked him into the wall. "You think you're tough?" he screamed at top of his lungs, holding Justin at eye level. "Huh? Do you?" He shook him into the wall again. "Do you think you're tough? I've eaten sandwiches bigger'n you! You hear me?!"

Burning with anger, Grady looked into Justin's brown eyes and saw *fear* staring back. Time stood still. *Oh, my God . . .*

I've become my own dad. He froze, sickened by his actions. Hands shaking, he let Justin down. Grady slid to the floor and buried his face in his hands.

Justin ran downstairs and hid while Grady tried to regain his composure. He was sweating, shaking; his stomach turned inside out. "Is Justin still in trouble, Daddy?" Kari asked in innocence.

"Come here, sweetie," he said. "Justin was naughty, but it's okay." Still shaking, Grady took Kari out to the garage with him. There was no way he could focus on work and instead shut everything off and turned out the lights. "How about some popcorn?"

"Yeah!" Kari exclaimed. Grady popped a large bowlful and took it downstairs. Justin was playing with the Legos again, fashioning a new fortress for his soldiers.

"Justin," he said. "Daddy's sorry. Come here, bud. It's okay."

Justin wiped his eyes and got up from the floor. "How about we watch a movie together?" Justin nodded. "But you gotta learn, Son, when Daddy tells you to do something, you need to obey, okay?"

"Okay," he said softly.

"I promise, Justin, Daddy will never do that again." Tears began to flow from Justin's eyes and Grady gave in to his own tears. They cried and Grady held him tightly, trying his best to reassure Justin he would never hurt him. Within a few minutes, Justin relaxed and Kari tickled him to make him smile. Grady put in a Disney DVD and they munched popcorn, Kari tucked in on one side of him, Justin on the other.

Grady was oblivious to the movie. Instead, he replayed the frightening event over and over. It scared him to no end. He knew he'd have to tell Naomi. He leaned his head back against the couch and shut his eyes. He so desperately needed her calming spirit. Right now he felt lower than ever before.

All this time he'd sworn that he would never be like his father and look what he'd done. He'd been in such a rage that he came within a split second of beating the living daylights out of his six-year-old son.

God help him.

CHAPTER TWENTY-NINE

By mid-May their backyard was a shimmery green—grass, trees, and shrubbery, everything the color of fresh-picked pea pods. "Don't forget we have the elementary spring concert tomorrow night," Naomi said. She stood by the kitchen counter looking at the large wall calendar that hung next to the end cupboard.

"Oh, that's right," Grady said. He was making a curio cabinet for Naomi's mom and wanted to get it done before their annual trip in August to Beach and Wibaux.

"Well, you better get out there tonight then, 'cause you can't miss the concert."

"I know, I know." He puffed out his chest and tucked his shirt into his jeans. "Procrastination is a strength, not a weakness."

"Yeah, right," Naomi said. "See how far that gets you in life."

The wall phone right behind Naomi's head rang. She jumped and pressed a hand to her chest while Grady laughed at her surprised expression. "I swear it does that every time I look at the calendar," she said before picking up the receiver. "Hello? Oh, hi, Chandra. Yes, he's right here." Naomi passed the phone to Grady.

"Hello?"

"Grady? It's Chandra . . ."

"Yeah? How's Dad?"

"I have someone here that wants to talk to you—"

"Who?" he asked, interrupting her.

"Just listen to me." Her voice sounded stressed and on edge. "What she's gonna tell you is not true, but she's insisting that it is true. I don't want you to believe her side of it, okay? You need to listen to me, not her."

Grady rubbed his temple, trying to make sense of Chandra's ramblings. "What's going on, Chandra?"

"Hello, my name is Lynn Rodriguez," a woman said. "I'm the hospice nurse taking care of your father."

"Can you please tell me what's going on out there?"

"Your father is a very sick man. If you want to see him alive again, I'd suggest you be out here in less than seventy-two hours."

Grady didn't remember much else from either the nurse or Chandra. He hung up the phone and lowered himself into a chair at the dining room table.

"What she'd say?" Naomi rested her hands on his shoulders and gently rubbed them. Grady fought back the tears and cleared his throat. "She said if I want to see him alive, I should come now."

She gave him a hug and sat down, folding her hands around his. "Go, Grady," Naomi said, squeezing his hands. "You need to do this."

Grady flew into LAX and rented a car. He couldn't afford the airfare for the whole family, so he came alone. Grady's boss gave him the rest of the week off, which gave him four days to make the trip to Salton City and back. Dean and Kurt couldn't leave until next week at the earliest. Melinda and Gary lived in Glendive and were still deciding when to go. They all had jobs and families of their own, details to work out.

When Kari was a baby, the four of them had flown out to California for a little vacation. They did some sightseeing in L.A. and then visited his dad and Chandra. That was the last time he'd made the drive through the desert to Salton City. Frank and Chandra had bought a 1960s-style rambler, the typical dining/kitchen/living room combo, painted in the lighter colors of desert homes with a breezeway to the garage and awnings over the windows.

The town was still bare; most lots sat empty, marred by windblown debris that had caught in the tumbleweeds. As Grady turned the corner to their street, he saw several cars parked in front—no doubt the faithful flock from their holy-roller church. Grady shifted into Park and shut off the car, staring absent-mindedly at the desert landscape that surrounded their house, a mix of crushed rock, cactus plants, and one large Palo Verde tree for shade. He didn't want to go inside and face it all—Chandra especially. A part of him was angry with her. There were many instances where people were beating cancer, surviving many years after diagnoses. Prayer alone hadn't given his dad a fighting chance.

Grady grabbed his duffle bag from the backseat and rapped his knuckles on the metal screen door, engulfed by the stifling hot desert air. A tall, gray-haired man he didn't know invited him inside. "Hello there," he said in a deep voice. "I can tell from looking at you that you must be Frank's son." He offered a broad smile and shook Grady's hand. "Welcome."

"Grady Kramer." He stepped inside, the coolness a welcome relief.

"Pete Wilson," the man said. "Glad you made it. C'mon inside. Your dad's in the bedroom right now resting. Chandra's in there with him."

Grady entered the bedroom, unprepared for what he saw. His father was pale, his eyes off-color, yellowish. His breathing was labored, and he was hooked up to oxygen. It was obvious he was retaining fluid; his cheeks were flushed and puffy, evidence the kidneys and liver were already shutting down. "Hey, Dad," Grady said, taking his hand.

"Grady . . . I'm so glad you made it." His voice was raspy and weak.

Grady nodded in response. Without chemo and radiation treatments, the disease had ravaged his body. He sat next to him for an hour watching him rest, hardly knowing what to say. Soon someone knocked on the open door.

"Supper's ready, Grady."

Ladies from the church had brought over a plate of sandwiches, Jell-O salad, and chocolate-cherry cake. Grady went through the motions, eating dinner, making small talk with their church friends as a steady stream of people came and went. Around eleven he went in the spare bedroom and closed the door, trying to keep his emotions in check.

It was hard to see his dad completely dependent, a man who lived life strong, a fighter . . . someone Grady used to fear because of the strength he had over him. To see him reduced to the point where he needed help to sit up in bed or use the bathroom boggled his mind.

First thing the next morning Chandra proudly pointed out how people from their church were on a schedule of three-hour shifts in order to keep constant prayer going for Frank's healing. One by one they came to the house. Some prayed in the bedroom with his dad; others went to another part of the house to pray alone. Grady wanted to shout, "You guys aren't focusing here— he needs a doctor, not another misguided prayer!"

Each time someone walked past him, they'd say, "Today's gonna be the day! Frank's gonna get up outta that bed and make dinner for us." Other times he'd hear, "This could be the day Frank goes home and sees Jesus. Either way we'll be celebrating."

Grady found it a complete contradiction—if he died they'd celebrate, and if he lived they'd celebrate. Why all the fuss then? Why not just go home and let it happen. One minute Grady considered them a bunch of kooks, and the next instant he found himself admiring their deep faith. Their dedication was an incredible demonstration of how much they loved and respected his father, Frank Kramer.

"Your dad is one of the finest men I know," one man said.

"He's brought so many people to Christ," another one said. "He's a deacon, you know."

"Before he got sick, he spent nearly every day at the church. Fixing things, always helping other people."

A pretty woman in her forties rushed to join in. "Oh, you should have been there the Sunday Frank gave his testimony. Pete, do you remember that?"

"Of course I do. Who could forget that—it was powerful."

Grady didn't even try to hide the puzzled look affixed to his face. He couldn't help it. It was all so foreign. He could hear his dad coughing in the bedroom as they praised and exalted his every waking moment. By the sounds of their accolades, his dad must be venerable for sainthood. Oops, his dad wasn't Catholic anymore; he was Baptist. Where did that put him in the grand scheme of things?

Grady wanted to stand up and shout at them, *Boy, he's sure got the wool pulled over your eyes. You don't know the*

Frank Kramer I know. He's an alcoholic, adulterer, a man who used to beat his kids! That's the Frank Kramer I know—the REAL Frank Kramer!

Instead, he escaped through the patio door onto the breezeway, desperate to be alone. The whole situation was more than he could take. He sat on the end of a lounge chair and dropped his head into his hands. Flashbacks of the beatings, the constant put-downs, kneeling on those damn seeds played out in his mind like a long, sad movie that nobody wanted to see.

Grady rose to his feet and sucked in a deep breath. He wished he had someone to talk to. He made a quick call to Naomi, but there was no privacy in which to confide his frustrated thoughts.

After supper Frank pointed to the breezeway and asked Grady to join him. "Want to sit out there for a spell?"

"Sure, Dad." Pete, Chandra, and Grady helped him into a chair on the patio.

Chandra kissed his cheek and turned to go back inside. "You boys probably need to talk."

Grady waited until the glass door slid shut. He scooted his chair closer and leaned forward. "Dad, you look bad . . . really bad."

"Yeah, maybe we let this go a little far." Frank struggled for each breath, his face red, his eyes tired. "I'm doing okay though."

"But, Dad, I talked to the hospice nurse today. She doesn't think you're gonna last too long. She says you're dying."

"Well, that's her opinion," he said calmly. "We're holding out hope and praying for a miracle." He raised a shaky hand to wave toward the house. "These people are coming here every single day, praying for a miracle. It's gonna happen, Grady. I'm gonna be whole again." The way his dad spoke the words, it was as though he actually believed them.

"But why didn't you see a doctor? Why aren't you getting medical help?"

"We don't need it. God's the Almighty Healer . . . and if it's His will, He'll heal me."

Grady's anger and frustration burst forth in tears. "I just can't stand to see you like this," he said, his voice raspy.

Frank nodded and laid a hand on top of Grady's shoulder. "Grady, listen to me. I'm at peace now." His fingers squeezed Grady's shoulder and he paused, waiting for Grady to meet his gaze. "I need to ask you something."

Grady lifted his head. "Okay."

"When you were kids, growing up . . . I was hard on you." He stopped to cough and then caught his breath. "Looking back now, I realize how bad I was."

Grady listened, wondering where on earth his dad was going with this. This wasn't exactly news to Grady; he knew firsthand how hard the ol' man was on his kids. *Why don't you go out and tell those other people, Dad? I already know all about it.*

Frank rested a hand on Grady's arm. "I shoulda been put in prison for the way I treated you kids, the way I beat you up. You gotta believe me on this, Grady, that it wasn't the real me; that was the alcoholism in me." He took a deep breath, fighting back his own tears.

Grady contemplated his dad's comments. Was he blaming the alcoholism and not himself? Was that his excuse after all this time?

"Grady, I'm so sorry . . . I've been on my knees before God and I've asked him for forgiveness. I know he's forgiven me. And if I could I would get on my knees right now and ask for your forgiveness, I would. I am so sorry . . ."

It took a moment for the words to sink in. *I am sorry.* He couldn't believe he heard it come from his father's own mouth. Then he saw the look of sorrow etched in his father's eyes.

Frank wheezed and spoke again. "Grady, will you please forgive me? For all the sins I committed against you?"

Grady started to speak and then stopped. All the pain, the jar of wheat seeds, the razor strap. Even the chainsaw. Pain like that didn't go away overnight. Never in a million years had he expected to hear his father ask for forgiveness. And if he had asked, Grady was sure he'd have said no. But now, at this moment, he felt completely different—and he didn't know why. Something told him it was more than a dying man's wish, that his father had been dealing with this issue for a long while.

"Can you, Grady? Can you ever forgive me?"

Grady got out of his chair and knelt beside him, putting both arms around him. The shame and embarrassment of his father's reputation, the cruel punishments as a kid—all of it was like a gnarling vicious monster that he'd carried on his back as far back as he could remember, the weight unbearable at times.

Something stirred deep within. Yes, he could forgive him. But he couldn't forget.

"Yes, Dad . . . I forgive you."

"Oh, Grady, thank you," Frank said with a long sigh. "I love you, Grady, you know that. And I still pray for your mom. I still love her; I've always loved your mom and still do. I think, I hope she can forgive me too."

Grady grabbed the box of tissues and blew his nose. He sat down in his chair and looked up at the evening sky. "What now?"

"Well, I'm planning on either walking out of here healed or going to heaven. Either way it can glorify God."

They sat in silence for several moments. Grady pulled his chair next to his dad's and Frank rested his hands on top of Grady's. He stared at his father's hands, the skin pale and waxy. A dark purple bruise creased the backs of his hands and his fingers were puffy. Hands that had once caused so much pain now gently patted his. Grady hung his head, trying to take it all in.

Chandra slid the glass door open. "Frank, it's time for your nebulator treatment. Lynn is here."

Grady helped his dad back inside for his daily respiratory therapy. As soon as the nurse finished, he followed her outside to her car. "I need to know, straight up. How long do you expect him to live? I have a sister and two brothers back home and I need to let them know."

She put her bag on the front seat of her Toyota. "His organs are starting to shut down. You need to call them and tell them that if they want to see him while he's still coherent to be here within forty-eight hours."

Grady called Melinda and asked her to call the boys, passing on the nurse's prognosis. He would leave it up to each of them to decide what to do. Grady's flight home was already set for the next morning, which meant he had to leave before dawn. Emotionally drained, he sat down with his dad and Chandra for the start of the nightly news while a few people from church gathered in the kitchen, making coffee and praying. "Dad, I have to leave by four o'clock in order to catch my flight. I don't want to wake you up that early, so I'm gonna say my good-byes now."

Frank nodded, his face swollen and flushed. "It's okay, Grady. I love you."

Grady bent down and gave him a hug. "I love you too. Good-bye." He held him for a long moment and then let go.

Grady retreated to his room and changed into a cotton t-shirt and shorts. As soon as his head hit the pillow, his mind spun into fast-forward. He tossed and turned for a good hour, the conflicting images and turmoil rising like the ocean's tides through his tired mind. How could his dad have changed so drastically? Everything Grady witnessed these last two days contradicted his entire life. And why did they let his dad's condition deteriorate this far without medical intervention? The totality of it all taunted him. And yet whenever Grady looked into their eyes, both Frank and Chandra had such peace.

"Let it go and get some sleep!" Grady said, punching the pillow. Hard as he tried, he couldn't relax; his neck was tense and his temples throbbed. He threw the sheet off and walked out to the living room. Frank and Chandra were still watching TV, the volume down low.

Grady stood in the middle of the room. "I'm ready."

"Oh, no hon," Chandra said. "You go back to bed, it's not even close to four o'clock yet."

"No, I'm not ready to leave," Grady said, his voice catching. "I want what you have. I want the peace and faith I see in you." He took a deep breath. "I want Jesus in my life."

Chandra reached out a hand. "Come here," she said as Frank motioned him over. Grady knelt beside the recliner and Frank grabbed his hand and squeezed it. "I'll show you the way Grady. What I have is free. Just say this prayer with me," Frank began. "Confess you are a sinner; ask Jesus into your life; ask for forgiveness of your sins."

Grady repeated the phrases one by one. "Heavenly Father, I know that I'm a sinner and my sin separates me from You. I know You sent Your son Jesus Christ to pay the price for my sins. I want to ask forgiveness of my sin. Please help me repent of my sin." He paused. "I want to ask Jesus into my life as my Lord and Savior. Amen." The words slipped with ease from his tongue and settled in his heart. A thrust of energy, like a waterfall of charged particles, rushed through Grady with an overwhelming sense of assurance. God was real and His Holy Spirit was present. He knew that now in a powerful way. God was real and he was forgiven.

Grady retreated back to the bedroom, his bare feet slapping softly on the tile. A calmness came over him as he laid down and within seconds he was sound asleep.

By a quarter to four he was on the road, the silhouette of the rugged mountain ridges cutting a jagged edge against the celestial backdrop of the desert sky. He wouldn't be able to come back for the funeral, but that didn't seem to matter now. Grady opened the windows and breathed in the night air, thinking about the life-changing turn of events.

Just as he was leaving the house, Chandra said it was okay to say goodbye to Frank. He'd told him, "I'll see you again, Dad. If not on this earth, then in heaven."

Frank answered with, "I'll wait for you."

Chandra had walked him to the door. "Last night your dad told me that was the best day of his life." Grady had no words to respond.

A deep purple hue appeared on the horizon, sanctifying his thoughts in a brand-new way. His father had asked for forgiveness and he'd given it. He had asked God for forgiveness and received it.

The battle was over.

CHAPTER THIRTY

Grady drove west on Interstate I-94 across the barren North Dakota landscape toward Beach. The hot August sun beating down on the ranchlands on both sides reminded him of his long drives between oil rigs back in the eighties. He and the family were making the trip home to deliver the newly finished curio cabinet and visit both grandmas before the new school year started.

Carol had a new friend in her life—Ralph Swenson, a local rancher. They'd already met him several times and from what Grady could tell, he was one of the nicest, kindest men he'd ever known. A recent widower, he had a big spread of land north of Beach. He was mostly retired, lived in a nice house in town, and let his kids handle the ranching and cattle. He had a big RV and had taken Carol on several cross-country trips. Grady was thankful she had someone in her life who respected her. He enjoyed listening to their good-natured teasing, usually with an undeniable twinkling in their eyes.

As usual, the nine-hour drive from Minneapolis to Beach got long for the kids. He made an extra stop at Medora to let Kari and Justin run off some of their pent-up energy.

"You okay?" Naomi asked.

Grady watched Justin chasing Kari around a tree near the parking lot at the entrance to the Theodore Roosevelt National Park. "Yeah, why?"

"You seem a little distant."

He grabbed Naomi's hand and kissed it. "It's been a tough summer, that's all. C'mon kids, let's keep going." They piled into the car for the last leg of the long drive. Going home always brought back childhood memories and tangled thoughts of troubled times. Would it be any different this time?

Grady pulled up in front of his mom's house, still painted a vibrant aqua blue. Through the picture window he watched as she bolted out of her favorite chair toward the door.

"There's my little Kari," Carol said, rushing out to the car. "Come and give Gramma a hug." She scooped up Kari in her arms and gave her a big squeeze, cheek to cheek. "What a sweet thing you are!" Kari giggled as Carol put her down and turned to Justin. "Okay, big fella, you're next. Give your Gramma a big ol' bear hug." She wrapped her arms around Justin and he laughed. "My oh my, you're getting' to be a big sport, aren't ya?"

"Hey, Mom," Grady said, giving her a hug. "It's good to see you."

"Mmm, you too," she said. "Listen here, I've got supper all ready. Ralph will be over in a little bit. Come on in and relax; let these young'uns run off and play."

"That's for sure," Naomi said, reaching for a hug. "That drive gets longer each time."

"Oh, I like havin' you kids close enough to get home every now and then." Carol took Justin's hand and they followed her up the sidewalk. "Gramma might have a little surprise waiting for you."

"What is it, Gramma?" Justin asked, pulling on Carol's hand.

"Hold up there, young man," she said, sprinting with him up the front steps. Carol's green eyes danced as she busied herself in the kitchen. "I've got some top sirloin steak and potatoes, and fresh sweet corn. Got a dozen ears from Bruce Gedde's kids. They had a pickup full at the Flying J parking lot, fresh picked. Ralph brought the steak over; it's from what his kids butchered this year." She grabbed an apron from the stove handle and tied it around her slender waist.

"Sounds good, Mom," Grady said, rubbing his stomach. "Mmm, always smells good in your kitchen."

"How 'bout you put the plates and silverware out," she said, motioning to the cupboard.

The doorbell rang and Carol's face beamed. "Just in time," Grady heard Naomi say. Ralph came into the kitchen and greeted the family. He was a quiet man with mostly black hair mixed in with hints of gray, dressed in loose-fitting, soft blue jeans and a Western shirt. Carol grabbed a set of tongs and plucked the steaming ears of corn from the large kettle. Naomi gathered the kids and washed their hands before they all sat down to the table. Within minutes, Kari and Justin were done, begging to go play. Grady excused them and the four adults remained seated around the table.

"Ralph, you want your coffee yet?" Carol asked.

"You betcha," he said, pushing back his chair.

"Melinda and Gary and the kids said they'd drive over from Glendive on Saturday around three. I'll fix a roast for supper and she said she'd bring a pan of bars and cookies so I wouldn't have to make dessert."

"Good, I was hoping they'd make it," Grady said. "It'll be fun to see her girls again."

"You'll need to get over and see your folks, won't you, Naomi?" Carol asked.

"Yeah, I might walk over later with the kids. I need to stretch my legs a little."

"Say, Grady," Ralph said, "you feel like comin' out to the home place Saturday morning and help me thin out a few of them prairie dogs?"

"Seriously?"

"One of their towns is spreading clear into my pasture on the west end. They're expanding the city limits without a permit," he said with a wink. "Time to put a stop to it."

"Yeah, I'd love to."

"Did I tell you what this man did a couple weeks ago?" Carol asked, pointing a slender finger at Ralph.

"What?" Grady asked as Ralph's face gave into a wide grin.

"He likes taking that four-wheeler out, checking on newborn calves in the spring or checking fence lines. He's supposed to bring his cell phone in case somethin' were to happen. So all day long I try calling him and he doesn't answer. Then I start to worry, so I call up his daughter—"

"Then I got two of 'em worrying," Ralph whispered to Grady.

"You darn right!" Carol said, slapping her thigh. "Soon as I finished my shift at the Flying J I drive out to the ranch. Finally, around four o'clock, we hear the four-wheeler drive into the yard and he comes strollin' in like nobody's business." She laughed and shook her head.

Ralph tucked a toothpick in the corner of his mouth. "Maybe I don't necessarily *forget* to bring it." He winked at Naomi and smiled. "A man needs a little time without women always a frettin' and a worryin'," he said to Grady.

Grady helped his mom and Naomi clean up the kitchen. "You're kinda quiet tonight," Carol said, drying the last dish. "Everything okay?"

"Sure, mom." He took the serving bowl from her and put it in the cupboard. "Just tired."

Early the next morning Naomi took the kids over to her mom's house, only a few blocks away. With Naomi's large family, she and the kids gravitated to the bustling Braden house to visit with her siblings and their growing families. It bothered Grady some, but he did his best to include the kids with his mom and Ralph.

Ralph stopped over wearing a pair of faded overalls and a plaid, short-sleeved shirt. After three cups of Carol's coffee, he and Grady headed out in his new pickup, a sharp-looking truck in Chevrolet's newest edition of Dark Cherry Metallic and still carried that new vehicle smell. Ralph drove north and west of Beach about eight miles to his ranch. Grady was quiet, listening to Ralph's recap of the year's above-average rainfall and crop indicators as he followed the red ribbons of gravel that divided the rolling ranch lands.

The Swenson place was well kept and neat looking with a couple of small outbuildings, two large pole sheds, and the usual cattle pens on the far side. Ralph's daughter and her husband and family lived in the ranch house now. He drove through the farm yard and stopped behind the first pole shed. Grady hopped out and opened the gate north of the corrals, and Ralph turned down a two-lane trail that meandered through the pasture.

"I brought a .17 HMR Savage for you to use," Ralph said, nodding toward the rifle rack. "The magazine is full."

"That'll work."

"I've got my .22-250 Remington. Yeah, I had one ol' cow bust up her leg couple weeks back when she stepped in a hole. Had to put her down and get her butchered." Ralph parked the truck on the edge of a long draw that zigzagged south, trimmed with buffaloberry brush, wood's rose, shrubby cinquefoil, big sage, and spiny saltbrush. Grady and Ralph got out of the pickup and loaded the rifles.

"I'm not up for a lot of walking these days," Ralph said, pointing toward the rough terrain. "If it's all right with you, I'll wait here and see if I can pop off a couple from the ridge here." He wore his John Deere cap low to shield the bright morning sun.

"Sure thing," Grady said, pulling on his own cap and sunglasses.

"Take yer time."

Grady nodded and struck out toward the south, his boots leaving prints in the dry dusty ground. It felt good to be back in the wide open spaces where he'd grown up. It really *was* Big Sky County. The warm breeze warranted a perfect summer day as his eyes scanned the endless rolling terrain. Walking the rim of an earthen crevice, the air smelled of sage and grain and dirt. The variations of mustard golds, buttercup yellows, and sandcastle browns were a stark contrast to the green leafy trees and manicured yards that defined the suburban neighborhoods in Minneapolis.

He meandered across the rough ground, rifle in hand, watching for the pesky prairie dogs. Grady spotted a couple sitting on their haunches about a hundred yards out. Even from that distance he could hear their noisy *whistle-squeak* and bark. He squatted down behind a scrub cedar, watching the critters pop up and down like jack-in-the-boxes from their prairie potholes.

Grady chambered a round, resting his elbow on his knee and the forestock on his left hand. If he got any closer, they'd disappear into their tunnels. He lifted the rifle and drew a bead on one in the foreground. "Gotcha," he said under his breath. "A dead bang shot."

In an instant, he reverberated to an angry sixteen-year-old consumed with hate and justification, the rifle aimed on his dad's chest, watching him descend the gentle slope in long strides. He could clearly see his dad's shirt button through the iron sights on his Mauser, sense the moist gray skies overhead. Rage pulsated through his young body. He wanted so badly to make him pay. He deserved to die. Moreover, the man deserved to face the wrath of God and burn in hell after what he'd put his kids and wife through.

"Why did you have to be so mean?" Grady cried out. "Why couldn't you just love us? *Why!* I want to know why you couldn't love me the way I loved you!" He lowered the rifle and his head fell back in anguish. "*Why . . .*"

Suspended in time Grady fell to his knees and laid the gun on the ground. The years were like minutes, rewound to the moment of decision, s*queeze the trigger Grady, he deserves to die,* until he heard a voice contradict his own. *No . . .*

Grady lifted his head and felt the August heat bathe his face. He opened his eyes, stunned to see the prairie dogs and sun-drenched landscape. He broke out in a sweat, terrified at the vivid memory. He'd come so close to killing his father that day. What on earth had kept him from squeezing the trigger a hair farther? Whose voice had he heard? Grady shuddered, imagining having to live with that all these years. He'd have never had the chance to see his father change, to hear him ask for forgiveness. Isn't that what he'd wanted his whole life? To hear his father say he was sorry?

And to think that now, after all this time, he had. Grady'd had a few minutes alone with his mom the previous night, long enough to tell her what had happened back in May on his last visit with Frank. She'd cried and he'd held her. He thought about their tears, healing tears. Maybe something good could come from all the pain of the past.

Grady rose to his feet, no longer interested in the burrowing rodents nearby. Instead, he walked the rolling terrain, trying to wrap his mind around all that had transpired. Up the side of a shallow coulee, across a flat-topped plateau, down through another draw, and into a wide section of wheat, the tall stalks crunching beneath his boots. One more month and the giant combines in Ralph's pole sheds would be out day and night harvesting the valuable commodity. The wheat was chest high and the warm breeze sent a flowing ripple of waves across the pristine sea of gold. The silklike tips bent back and forth in slow motion rhythms, a musical *whish, whish, whish* all around him.

Grady turned in a circle, listening. It was as though the entire wheat field was lifting praises heavenward, and he had this innate sense that God was right there with him. In all this time, he'd never told a living soul about what happened that day, the day he nearly killed his dad. He couldn't even bring himself to tell Naomi, afraid she wouldn't love him if she knew.

He pulled off a handful of seeds, rolling them in the palm of his hand. Grady studied their granular texture, the same seeds his dad used to inflict pain and punishment. They no longer held the power they once had. These seeds would be harvested, planted, used for good. Taken from the earth; returned to the earth. Could he release the pain? Let go and start anew?

Naomi was right; he wasn't good at sharing his feelings. He had grown up in fear, always hiding his feelings. Could he learn to change? Or was it too late? He was forty-two years old. Yet, something in the soothing beauty of nature's song declared there was hope. He had, after all, witnessed God turn a heart of stone to one of flesh and bring a man like Frank Kramer to his knees in repentance. If he hadn't seen it himself, he doubted he could believe such a story. He brushed a tear from his cheek and pushed the seeds into his front jeans pocket.

By the time he worked his way back to the pickup, he found Ralph standing against the cab, leaning into a narrow piece of shade. "How'd it go on that side?" Ralph asked, wiping a trail of sweat from his sideburn.

Grady swallowed hard and adjusted the bill of his cap. "It's odd; I didn't take a shot." He felt the catch in his throat and shrugged. "Can't really explain it."

Ralph nodded, like a man up in years does, a man who made his living in the backbreaking business of ranching in a sometimes unforgiving land, a man who had buried both a wife and a daughter. His kindly eyes and weathered face communicated a wisdom gained through all that and more.

"Find what you were lookin' for?" Ralph asked.

Grady fingered the seeds in his pocket and sensed something eternally powerful within reach, timeless truths rooted and grounded deep beneath the hardened soil. His eyes swept the expansive wheat field.

"Yeah. I found peace."

Dear Reader,

After hearing Bernie's moving testimony on the mission trip, I knew in my heart it held a message worth sharing. Because of the sensitive nature to family members, we decided to turn his personal story into a novel. The truth is Bernie's life had every element of a great novel and my job was to simply capture the essence of his life over three decades.

Unbeknownst to me God was already at work, orchestrating events to ensure I got the details right…a humbling thought. One such instance occurred when I submitted Chapter One to a writing contest sponsored by the Bearlodge Writers in Sundance, Wyoming, and the Devils Tower National Monument. They too sensed something powerful in the opening scenes and I was honored to receive a one-week residency at the tower. On my way from Minneapolis to the Devils Tower I spent time with Bernie and his family in Wibaux, where I first saw the intriguing landscape of Eastern Montana. With that vivid imagery fresh in my mind, I spent the week weaving all I had seen into the manuscript.

Arriving back home I was ready to finalize the scene where Bernie's father has to drive down the mountain to get Bernie to the hospital. Questions lingered in my mind about distance and timing between the logging camp and Missoula. I called a reporter to inquire about the location of the logging camp and he referred me to a resort owner near Potomac, who then referred me to a local rancher named Bob Hall. "You can find him in the phone book," she said with a 'click.' Using the online White Pages I found a number and took a chance. It was the right Bob Hall but he was nearly 90 years old and had trouble understanding my questions. I explained I was writing a book about a chainsaw accident 30 years earlier and eventually ended the conversation without getting any answers.

Two nights later the phone rang. A man named Brad Hall asked if I had called his father. He went on to ask, "Are you writing a book about Bernie Mischel?" My heart stopped—I had never mentioned Bernie's name. "How do you know Bernie?" I asked. "He was my best friend in third grade. I remember when he got hurt," and went on to provide all the details I needed.

My writing journey has been a lesson in trust. When God assigns a task, it is my responsibility to respond in obedience. In turn He will equip me, often in distinct, profound ways. While writing *Seeds of Salton* I experienced God like never before, the very thing I had noted in my journal prior to the mission trip.

A number of heartfelt thanks go out to the 2006 Mexico Mission Trip team, our Trinity family, the Bearlodge Writers, the Devils Tower park staff, Brad Hall, my readers: Julie Saffrin, Dave Nygren, Roger Thompson, Char Friedges, Kay Kniefel, Judy Gustafson, Brian Miller, Sue Ambrowski, and Art Miller. Thank you to my editor, Susanne Lakin, who helped shape and polish the manuscript to its final draft, becoming one of the book's strongest supporters. As always, a special thank you to my husband John and our family for all their love and encouragement. And thank you to Bernie and his family, for trusting me to write his story in such a way that it will help others find peace.

To Him be all the praise,
Barbara Marshak

ABOUT THE AUTHOR

Barbara Marshak is the author of two nonfiction books, *Michigan and Rookie: Guardians of the Night* (2011), the remarkable story of a cop and his K9 partner, and *Hidden Heritage: The Story of Paul LaRoche* (2006), the inspiring biography of the Native American recording artist, Brulé. *Hidden Heritage* earned Finalist in the Biography category of the National Indie Excellence Awards (2007), and the USA Best Book Awards (2006). In 2008 Barbara won a writer's residency at the Devils Tower National Monument, co-sponsored by the Bearlodge Writers in Sundance, Wyoming, where she had the privilege to work on the manuscript for *Seeds of Salton*.

Barbara's writing portfolio includes over 150 published stories and articles. She is the creator of Sundance Imagery, a collection of framed photographs taken on research trips for her books. She is a regular presenter at writers' events and lives on a ranch in the beautiful Black Hills of South Dakota.